The forms and procedure in civil causes in the sheriff courts of Scotland : as regulated by 16 and 17 Vict. C. 80, commencing 1st Nov. 1853, and previous statutes and acts of sederunt / by David Johnston MacBrair and Robert Baird.

David Johnston MacBrair

The forms and procedure in civil causes in the sheriff courts of Scotland : as regulated by 16 and 17 Vict. C. 80, commencing 1st Nov. 1853, and previous statutes and acts of sederunt / by David Johnston MacBrair and Robert Baird.

MacBrair, David Johnston
collection ID ocm31787379
Reproduction from Harvard Law School Library
Edinburgh : T. & T. Clark, 1853.
viii, 129, 84 p. ; 25 cm.

The Making of Modern Law collection of legal archives constitutes a genuine revolution in historical legal research because it opens up a wealth of rare and previously inaccessible sources in legal, constitutional, administrative, political, cultural, intellectual, and social history. This unique collection consists of three extensive archives that provide insight into more than 300 years of American and British history. These collections include:

Legal Treatises, 1800-1926: over 20,000 legal treatises provide a comprehensive collection in legal history, business and economics, politics and government.

Trials, 1600-1926: nearly 10,000 titles reveal the drama of famous, infamous, and obscure courtroom cases in America and the British Empire across three centuries.

Primary Sources, 1620-1926: includes reports, statutes and regulations in American history, including early state codes, municipal ordinances, constitutional conventions and compilations, and law dictionaries.

These archives provide a unique research tool for tracking the development of our modern legal system and how it has affected our culture, government, business – nearly every aspect of our everyday life. For the first time, these high-quality digital scans of original works are available via print-on-demand, making them readily accessible to libraries, students, independent scholars, and readers of all ages.

The BiblioLife Network

This project was made possible in part by the BiblioLife Network (BLN), a project aimed at addressing some of the huge challenges facing book preservationists around the world. The BLN includes libraries, library networks, archives, subject matter experts, online communities and library service providers. We believe every book ever published should be available as a high-quality print reproduction; printed on-demand anywhere in the world. This insures the ongoing accessibility of the content and helps generate sustainable revenue for the libraries and organizations that work to preserve these important materials.

The following book is in the "public domain" and represents an authentic reproduction of the text as printed by the original publisher. While we have attempted to accurately maintain the integrity of the original work, there are sometimes problems with the original work or the micro-film from which the books were digitized. This can result in minor errors in reproduction. Possible imperfections include missing and blurred pages, poor pictures, markings and other reproduction issues beyond our control. Because this work is culturally important, we have made it available as part of our commitment to protecting, preserving, and promoting the world's literature.

GUIDE TO FOLD-OUTS MAPS and OVERSIZED IMAGES

The book you are reading was digitized from microfilm captured over the past thirty to forty years. Years after the creation of the original microfilm, the book was converted to digital files and made available in an online database.

In an online database, page images do not need to conform to the size restrictions found in a printed book. When converting these images back into a printed bound book, the page sizes are standardized in ways that maintain the detail of the original. For large images, such as fold-out maps, the original page image is split into two or more pages

Guidelines used to determine how to split the page image follows:

• Some images are split vertically; large images require vertical and horizontal splits.
• For horizontal splits, the content is split left to right.
• For vertical splits, the content is split from top to bottom.
• For both vertical and horizontal splits, the image is processed from top left to bottom right.

THE

FORMS AND PROCEDURE

IN CIVIL CAUSES

IN THE

SHERIFF COURTS OF SCOTLAND,

AS REGULATED BY 16 AND 17 VICT. C. 80,

COMMENCING 1st NOVEMBER 1853,

AND PREVIOUS STATUTES AND ACTS OF SEDERUNT.

BY

DAVID JOHNSTON MACBRAIR, ESQ. S.S.C.

AUTHOR OF "DIGEST OF DECISIONS IN THE COURT OF SESSION," ETC.
FROM NOVEMBER 1840 TO NOVEMBER 1850;

AND

ROBERT BAIRD, ESQ. A.M.

MEMBER OF THE FACULTY OF PROCURATORS, GLASGOW.

EDINBURGH:

T. & T. CLARK, LAW BOOKSELLERS.
GLASGOW · SMITH & SON LONDON BENNING & COMPANY,
AND STEVENS & NORTON.

MDCCCLIII

T&
M119112s

PRINTED BY STEVENSON AND COMPANY, 32 THISTLE STREET.

TO THE SHERIFFS OF SCOTLAND:

GENTLEMEN,

We beg, with the utmost respect, to dedicate to you this Volume. It is designed to afford facilities to our Professional Brethren in discharging their duties under the New Forms of Procedure. To you the Legislature has committed the sacred trust of administering Justice in the Courts to which this procedure applies, and with you that trust is abundantly safe.

We remain,

Your very obedient

And faithful Servants,

THE AUTHORS.

CONTENTS AND INDEX.

APPENDIX OF STATUTES.

PREFACE.

The Authors, in this brief Treatise, have endeavoured, in the short space that has intervened since the passing of the recent Sheriff Court Act, to analyse its provisions and throw together such observations as they believe would be useful to the Profession. This, it may well be conceived, has been done amid many interruptions incident to their professional avocations. Yet they trust that their labours will be found useful in guiding the Practitioner in the constantly recurring exigencies of business, and in supplying numerous forms adapted to the changes that have been introduced.

To have delayed the publication, even for a few months, till some of the difficult and important questions occurring under this, as under every Legislative measure, had received Judicial interpretation, would have greatly lightened their labours and lessened their feeling of responsibility as to what, in these pages, is matter of opinion; but they considered that the Volume would be much more useful and acceptable if given at once to the Profession.

They have only to add, that they have given much thought to the subject, and have availed themselves largely of the numerous opportunities that have been afforded them of hearing and comparing the opinions and views of Gentlemen of experience and ability in all branches of the Profession.

EDINBURGH,
29th October 1858.

THE FORMS AND PROCEDURE

IN THE

SHERIFF COURTS OF SCOTLAND.

CHAPTER I.
Of the Office of Sheriffs and Sheriff Substitutes.

In ancient times, extensive judicial powers, in both civil and criminal matters, were conferred by the Crown, as heritable rights, on certain of its vassals, within particular districts called Baronies, Sheriffdoms, Regalities, &c. But the Crown retained a concurrent or cumulative jurisdiction with these vassals, who were called *Comites*. As they frequently abused their rights, the Crown, in the exercise of its reserved jurisdiction, appointed Sheriffs for the ordinary administration of justice; hence the name *Vice-comites*, as supplying the place of the *Comites*, or feudal Lords.

By the Jurisdiction Act passed in 1748, all heritable jurisdictions, and also that of High Sheriffs or Stewards, were finally abolished, and provision was made for the appointment of a Sheriff-Depute as Judge-Ordinary of every shire; 20 Geo. II. c. 43. The addition, Depute, has been discontinued in all the late statutes, the appellation being Sheriff. The Sheriffs hold their commissions direct from the Crown, *ad vitam aut culpam*, in the same way as the Judges of the Supreme Court. Important and extensive as their jurisdiction and powers formerly were, these have been augmented by the recent statute.—See Chaps. II. and III. on Jurisdiction. They are selected from the Faculty of Advocates, and must be of at least three years' standing at the Bar, and in practice and attendance in the Supreme Courts; 1 and 2 Vict. c. 119. Only two of the Sheriffs are required to reside within their counties, viz. those of Edinburgh and Lanark.

There is at present a Sheriff for nearly every county; but by the Act recently passed, entitled " An Act to diminish the number of Sheriffs in Scotland, and to unite certain counties in Scotland, in so far as regards the jurisdiction of the Sheriff," it is provided, that certain counties, when vacancies occur in them, shall be united into one sheriffdom, and the functions of the Sheriff of the counties or county in which the vacancy shall occur, shall thereupon devolve on and be discharged by the Sheriff of such other counties or county so included therewith, and such Sheriff shall thereafter be, and be denominated the Sheriff of such united counties and sheriffdom, without the necessity of any new commission being issued in his favour, and shall have and exercise all the jurisdiction, powers, privileges, and authority competent to the Sheriffs of the said counties respectively ; 16 and 17 Vict. c 92, § 1.

The following are the counties to be thus united as respects the jurisdiction of the Sheriff :—

Counties to be united	Title of Sheriffdom	Title of Sheriff
The County of Banff and the Counties of Elgin and Nairn.	Banff, Elgin, & Nairn	The Sheriff of Banff, Elgin, and Nairn
The County of Dunbarton and the County of Bute.	Dunbarton and Bute	The Sheriff of Dunbarton and Bute.
The County of Haddington and the County of Berwick.	Haddington and Berwick	The Sheriff of Haddington and Berwick
The County of Linlithgow and the Counties of Clackmannan and Kinross	Linlithgow, Clackmannan, and Kinross.	The Sheriff of Linlithgow, Clackmannan, and Kinross.
The County of Mid-Lothian and the County of Peebles.	Mid-Lothian & Peebles	The Sheriff of Mid-Lothian and Peebles
The County of Roxburgh and the County of Selkirk	Roxburgh and Selkirk.	The Sheriff of Roxburgh and Selkirk
The County of Sutherland and the County of Caithness	Sutherland and Caithness	The Sheriff of Sutherland and Caithness.
The County of Wigton and the Stewartry of Kirkcudbright.	Wigton & Kirkcudbright.	The Sheriff of Wigton and Kirkcudbright

Whenever a vacancy occurs in any of these separate counties, the duties are to be discharged by the Sheriffs of the other county or counties so included therewith But in the case of Peebles, the union is only to take place when a vacancy shall occur in the sheriffship of Peebles.

It is also declared, that " excepting as regards the person by whom the office of Sheriff shall be held and discharged, nothing herein contained shall affect or alter in any way the rights, privileges, or liabilities of the said counties respectively." § 4

Sheriffs-Substitute.—Sheriffs-Substitute are appointed by the Sheriffs within their respective counties. They were formerly removable by the Sheriff at pleasure, and their appointment fell with his death or resignation ; but the Act 1 and 2 Vict. c. 119 provided that the Substitutes should continue to hold office notwithstanding the death, resignation, or removal of their principal. and that they should not be removable unless with the consent of the Lord President and Lord Justice-Clerk, expressed in writing.

The qualification for the office of substitute is being an advocate, a writer to the signet, a solicitor before the Supreme Courts, or a procurator before a Sheriff Court, of at least three years' standing The commission must have a certificate annexed to it, under the hand of the Lord President and Lord Justice-Clerk, bearing that he is duly qualified and capable of discharging the duties of the office; 6 Geo. IV. c. 23.

The following are the provisions of the recent Act with respect to the appointments and salaries of Sheriffs-Substitutes :—

Her Majesty may, on the joint recommendation of the Lord President, Lord Advocate, and Lord Justice-Clerk, expressly bearing that it is essentially necessary for the public service, grant authority to any Sheriff to appoint one or more additional Substitutes, but not exceeding two additional in each county. § 37.

The commissions already granted or to be granted by all Sheriffs to the Sheriffs-Substitute shall extend over the whole county. § 40.

The salaries of the Sheriffs-Substitute to range from L 500 to L.1000 a-year, as may be fixed by the Commissioners of the Treasury, and to be payable quarterly, § 37. The salaries of both Sheriffs and Substitutes to be in full of all fees and emoluments whatever. § 39.

The retiring allowances to the Sheriff's-Substitute, provided by 1 and 2 Vict., c. 119, may be granted, though the service may not have been continuous and may have been in different counties; but the periods of actual service taken together must extend to one or other of the periods in that Act. In computing the amount of the retiring allowance, the emoluments drawn on an average of the five preceding years shall be held to constitute the salary. § 38.

The Sheriff may appoint a temporary Substitute in the case of the absence or illness of the ordinary Substitute, and to him the provisions above stated, with respect to mode of appointment, removal, and salary, do not apply

The following is a list of the present Sheriffs and Sheriffs-Substitute of the whole counties of Scotland :—

COUNTIES.	SHERIFFS.	SHERIFF-SUBSTITUTES
ABERDEEN	Arch. Davidson	
Aberdeen	...	W. Watson.
Peterhead	...	James Skelton.
ARGYLE	E. F Maitland.	
Inverary	...	John Maclaurin.
Campbeltown	...	Jas. Gardiner.
Tobermory	..	Wm. Robertson.
AYR	Archibald Bell.	
Ayr	...	James Robison.
Kilmarnock	...	Thos Anderson.
BANFF	Alex. Currie.	John Pringle.
BERWICK	Robert Bell.	Alex Wood.
BUTE	Robert Hunter	A. C. Dick.
CAITHNESS	Robert Thomson.	Hamilton Russell
CLACKMANNAN	John Tait.	Will. Clark.
CROMARTY	Thos Mackenzie.	R. S. Taylor.
DUMBARTON	J. C. Colquhoun.	Wm. Steele
DUMFRIES	Mark Napier.	J. P. Trotter
EDINBURGH	John T. Gordon.	And. Jameson.
		Patrick Arkley.
ELGIN AND MORAY . . .	Ben. Rob. Bell.	Pat Cameron
FIFE	A Earle Monteith.	
Cupar	...	George Grant.
Dunfermline	. .	Chas. Shirreff.
FORFAR	James L'Amy.	
Forfar	. .	Chas. Dickson
Dundee	...	J. I. Henderson.
HADDINGTON	William Horne.	Robert Riddell.
INVERNESS	George Young.	
Inverness	...	W. H. Colquhoun.
Fort-William...... ..	...	Aw. Fraser.
Portree	...	Thos. Fraser
Lochmaddy	...	Chas Shaw.
KINCARDINE	John M. Bell	C. G. Robertson.
KINROSS	John Tait.	David Syme.
KIRKCUDBRIGHT	E. D. Sandford.	Wm. H. Dunbar
LANARK	Sir Archibald Alison, Bart.	
Glasgow	...	H. G. Bell.
		Geo. Skene.
Lanark	...	John Neil Dyce.
Hamilton	...	Jas. Veitch.
Airdrie	...	Arch. Smith
LINLITHGOW	John Cay	Francis Home.
NAIRN	Ben. Rob. Bell.	Alex. Falconar.
ORKNEY AND SHETLAND.	W. E. Aytoun	Jas. Robertson.
		Robt. Bell.
PEEBLES	George Napier.	Arthur Burnett.
PERTH	Jas. Craufurd.	
Perth	...	H. Barclay.
Dunblane	...	Andrew Cross
RENFREW	H J. Robertson.	
Paisley	...	R. R. Glasgow.
Greenock	...	Cl. Marshall.

COUNTIES.	SHERIFFS.	SHERIFF-SUBSTITUTES.
Ross	Thos. Mackenzie.	
Tain	..	R S Taylor.
Dingwall	...	Geo Cameron
Lewis	...	A L. M'Donald.
Roxburgh	W. O Rutherfurd.	
Jedburgh	...	John Craigie
Selkirk	George Dundas.	Francis Somerville.
Stirling................. .	Charles Baillie.	
Stirling	..	Sir John Hay, Bart.
Falkirk	...	Robert Robertson
Sutherland	Hugh Lumsden.	E Fraser.
Wigton	Adam Urquhart	Macduff Rhind.

CHAPTER II.

The Sheriffs' Small Debt Jurisdiction.

This most useful jurisdiction was first established in 1829 by 10 Geo. IV. c. 25, but that Act was repealed by 1 Vict c. 41, commencing 1st October 1837. This Act gave a summary jurisdiction in the following cases —

" All civil causes, and all prosecutions for statutory penalties, as well as all maritime, civil causes, and proceedings that may be competently brought before him (the Sheriff) wherein the debt, demand, or penalty in question shall not exceed the value of L 8, 6s. 8d. sterling, exclusive of expenses and fees of extract. 1 Vict. c. 41, § 2.

" Applications by landlords or others having right to the rents and hypothec for sequestration and sale of a tenant's effects, for recovery of rent, provided the rent or balance of rent claimed shall not exceed L.8, 6s 8d. Ib. § 5.

" Any person entitled to pursue an action of furthcoming, where the sum or demand sought to be recovered under the furthcoming shall not exceed the value of L 8. 6s. 8d., exclusive of expenses and fees of extract, who shall choose to have the same heard and determined according to the summary mode provided by this Act, shall proceed, &c. Ib. § 9.

" Where any person shall hold a fund or subject which shall not exceed the value of L.8, 6s. 8d. which shall be claimed by more than one party under arrestments or otherwise, it shall be competent to raise a Summons of Multiplepoinding in the Small Debt Court. Ib § 10.

" All actions of damages ' for compensation' for loss or injury by the act or acts of any unlawful, riotous, or tumultuous assembly in Scotland, or of any person engaged in or making part thereof, authorised to be brought by an act passed in the third year of the reign of His Majesty King George the Fourth, where the sum concluded for does not exceed L 8, 6s. 8d sterling; as also all actions for recovery of assessments, by virtue of an act passed in the ninth year of his said Majesty's reign, intituled, An Act for the Preservation of the Salmon Fisheries in Scotland, may be heard and determined in the summary way provided by this Act, and this, notwithstanding the amount of such assessments shall exceed L.8, 6s. 8d. sterling." *Ib.* § 22.

By the recent Statute the Small Debt jurisdiction is extended to cases of the nature above set forth, in which the debt, demand, or penalty in question, or the fund *in medio*, shall not exceed the value of L.12, exclusive of expenses and fees of extract, and to this effect the Small Debt Act, 1 Vict. c. 41, shall be read and construed as if the words L.12 were substituted for the words L 8, 6s. 8d , wherever these latter words occur in the Act 16 and 17 Vict. c 80.   § 26

Imprisonment for a debt not exceeding L.8, 6s 8d. was abolished after 9th September 1835 by 5 and 6 Will. IV c. 70.   Imprisonment on the Sheriff's small debt decree is competent where the sum exceeds L 8, 6s. 8d But where such decree has been put to execution by imprisonment, the party so imprisoned shall be entitled to bring it under review of the Sheriff, by way of suspension and liberation; such suspension and liberation to proceed in the form provided for summary petitions by the recent Act. § 26.

All civil causes competent before the Sheriff, though exceeding the value of L.12, may, of consent of parties, be tried in the summary way provided in the Small Debt Act.   § 23

In order to this, the parties may lodge in process a Minute, signed by themselves or by their procurators, setting forth their agreement that the cause should be so tried, " and the Sheriff shall thereupon hear, try, and de-" termine such action in such summary way ; and in such case, the whole " powers and provisions of the said first recited Act shall be held applicable " to said action ; provided always, that the parties or any of them shall be " entitled to appear and plead by a procurator of Court."   § 23.

In regard to landlords' sequestrations for rents under the Small Debt Act, the benefit of summary trial and determination provided by the Small Debt Act was, by the forms prescribed in the Schedules, limited to rents past due ; but it is now extended to all sequestrations applied for *currente termino*, or in security.   § 28.

The Sheriffs are once in the year to go on the Small Debt Circuit in use to be held by their Substitutes.   See Chap IV. *Terms and Sittings.*

CHAPTER III.

Sheriffs' Ordinary Jurisdiction.

We have shortly stated the jurisdiction of the Sheriff in Small Debt Cases, as established by the Statute 1 Vict. c. 41, and have now to treat of his civil jurisdiction in his ordinary Court. This is of a most extensive character; and it has been the policy of the Legislature in the course of late years greatly to extend it. Indeed, in many of the most important matters arising under local Statutes, &c the Sheriff's judgment is exclusive and without review. We shall first advert to the *exceptions* from the Sheriff's jurisdiction.

The **Court of Session** has a jurisdiction privative or exclusive of the Sheriff in the following cases :—

In all the Crown's actions (except those peculiar to Exchequer), or questions in which the Crown or Her Majesty's Advocate has an interest. Where inferior judges or magistrates are sued in their official capacity. Where the defender is abroad Where several defenders reside in different counties. The privilege of exemption from the Sheriff's jurisdiction, where the defender is a member of the College of Justice, is done away with by the recent Statute, § 48. But as a pursuer that privilege is undisturbed.

In all actions for proving the tenor or declaratory of the import of deeds and writings.

In all actions for reducing and cancelling decrees, deeds, and documents—reductions on the head of fraud, and fraudulent bankruptcy under 1696, c 5.

In all declarators of irritancy (with the exceptions after mentioned)—nullity or failure of a right—of failure in a contract—modification of penalties in a bond—exemption from customs and burdens—redemption—or to have a right of redemption declared forfeited.

In all actions for enforcing the transference of heritable property—adjudication (except two species of adjudication after mentioned, which seem also competent before the Sheriff), sequestration of land estates—divisions of commonty—cognition and sale at instance of apparent heir—and ranking and sale at instance of creditors—declarator of ward, non-entry, &c.—also in applications under the Entail Acts and various other Statutes.

In all actions of declarator of personal *status*—namely, declarators of marriage—freedom or putting to silence—legitimacy or bastardy—divorce—and separation *a mensa et thoro*.

In the appointment of factors—guardians for minors—and parties insane or *ab agendo*, also in actions of restitution at the instance of minors, and reduction on head of minority and lesion.   Actions for choosing of curators by minors are competent to the Sheriff.

In the review and suspension of inferior court decrees, except those after mentioned.

The Court of Session possesses what is termed the *Nobile officium*, including the redress of wrongs for which no express remedy exists—supplying a temporary vacancy caused by decease &c. of the incumbent, where urgency requires it.

The Court of Exchequer takes cognisance of questions affecting the revenue of the Crown, and all subjects and claims connected therewith, including questions affecting the salaries or fees of the servants and officers of the Crown.   Should any such point be depending in an action in the Sheriff Court, it may, by authority of the Court of Exchequer, be removed thither.

The Lord Lyon has the jurisdiction in matters of rank and precedency, and relative to bearing arms.   His judgments are reviewable by the Court of Session.

The Dean of Guild Courts (peculiar to Royal Burghs) regulate buildings within the Burgh or territory of the Court—their decisions being reviewable by the Court of Session.

Justices of the Peace, Kirk-Sessions, Parochial Boards, the **Poor Law Board, &c.** have certain jurisdictions and functions which need not be here particularly adverted to.

The Sheriff.—With the exceptions above mentioned, it may be generally stated that redress by ordinary action or petition lies with the Sheriff in all cases.   In some of these his jurisdiction is cumulative with that of the Court of Session and other Courts   In some it is privative in the first instance, and in others (by Statute) privative *in toto*, that is, subject to no review.

Personal Actions.—The Sheriff's jurisdiction extends to all personal actions founded on *contract* or obligation, such as sale, lease, hire, loan, pledge, deposit, mandate, or factory; cautionary obligations, bills and promissory-notes, copartnery, insurance, &c., &c.; or on *quasi contract*, or on delict for indemnification or reparation, or on *quasi* delict. In all such cases, whatever be the pecuniary amount involved, the Sheriff has jurisdiction.

If the sum concluded for does not exceed L 25, the Sheriff's jurisdiction is exclusive of that of the Court of Session, and his judgment is final.

The following actions may be particularly noticed.—

Aliment.—By the 1 Will IV., c. 69, § 32, actions of aliment may be instituted, heard, and determined in any Sheriff Court in Scotland.   But this seems not to comprehend actions of aliment by a wife against her husband, which must be founded on a separation *a mensa et thoro.* Such actions are competent only to the Court of Session, as coming in place of the Commissaries of Edinburgh.

Constitution.—Against the representatives of parties deceased, as charged to enter heirs to them.

Exhibition.—Actions of exhibition, either in order to obtain inspection of writings to answer some ulterior object, or at the instance of an heir-apparent *ad deliberandum* whether he will enter heir.

Forthcoming.—The action whereby an arrester seeks payment of the money or effects due or belonging to his debtor in the hands of a third party. This action is competent before the Sheriff, although the decree on which the arrestment proceeded was pronounced by the Court of Session or any other Court.

Multiplepoinding, or the action by which a fund or effects for which there are more claimants than one is brought into Court, for the purpose of the claims of competing parties being heard and determined.

Scandal.—The action of scandal is competent before the Sheriff. If there be a conclusion for a palinode, *i. e.* a judicial recantation by the defender, it must be brought before the Sheriff as *Commissary.*

Spuilzie and Vitious Intromission.—Actions of spuilzie are now nearly obsolete, being superseded by actions of damages. Spuilzie is defined to be the taking away or intermeddling with effects in the lawful possession of another, without consent or warrant of law, and the action usually concluded for violent profits.

Suspensions are, in the general case, peculiar to the Court of Session. But " where a charge shall be given on a decree of registration, proceeding on a bond, bill, contract, or other form of obligation, registered in the books of Council and Session, or Sheriff Court, or any other competent Court, or on letters of horning following on such decree for payment of a sum not exceeding L.25 of principal, exclusive of interest and expenses, a suspension is competent in the Sheriff Court; on caution being found for the amount charged for, with interest and expenses to be incurred, the Sheriff may sist execution, and try the case as in a summary action; 1 and 2 Vict. c. 119, § 19. Suspensions and liberations are also competent before the Sheriff in cases where a Small Debt decree for a sum exceeding L.8, 6s. 8d. shall have been put to execution by imprisonment. Recent Statute, § 26.

Transumpt.—The action of transumpt, which was for the purpose of having writs in which the pursuer had an interest produced, that copies might be taken, is competent before the Sheriff. This kind of action is now seldom resorted to.

Usury —Actions on the ground of usury under the 12th of Queen Anne, concluding for annulling the debt, and for penalties in terms of the Statute, were found competent before the Sheriff, and to be determined without a jury.

Heritable Property.—Actions and procedure connected with heritable property.

The Sheriff has jurisdiction in all actions relating to heritable property of a *possessory* nature, namely, to decide who is entitled to possess till the question of right shall be decided in the Supreme Court.

Adjudications are peculiar to the Court of Session. But the Sheriff has jurisdiction in adjudications, *contra hereditatem jacentem*, where the heir renounces the succession of his ancestor; and Erskine is of opinion that adjudications in implement are also competent before the Sheriff; 2 *Ersk.* 12, 53. In these cases the lands must be situated within the Sheriff's jurisdiction.

Collation —Actions of collation at the instance of heirs, are competent before the Sheriff; 3 Ersk. 9, 3.

Declarator of Irritancy.—Where a vassal in a subject not exceeding L 25 in yearly value runs in arrear of his feu-duty for two years, an action at the instance of the superior for payment—removing and irritancy is now competent; 16 and 17 Vict. c. 80, § 32; and the like remedy is given to a landlord against a tenant; *ib.*

Mails and Duties —The action of mails and duties which is raised either by a proprietor infeft, or by disponees, or adjudgers, for obtaining payment of the rents and profits of heritable subjects, is competent before the Sheriff, and he has power to determine the rights of parties with competing titles to payment of the rents sued for; 4 Ersk. i. 49 and 50.

March Fences, and straightening Marches, and dividing Runrig Lands.— An action by a proprietor of land to compel the neighbouring heritor to join with him in the expense of enclosing by a fence the march or boundary between them, is competent before the Sheriff. The action cannot be brought in the first instance before the Court of Session, but the judgment of the Sheriff is reviewable. So also actions for straightening the marches of contiguous proprietors, by adjudging such parts of the lands of each as projects into those of the other, and compensating the party who has got the portion least in value by an equivalent in money, are competent only before Sheriffs or other Judges-Ordinary, in the first instance. Act 1669, c. 17; also for dividing runrig lands.

Molestation.—The action of molestation, is that for continuing the occupant of an heritable subject in undisturbed possession thereof, till the point of right be determined.

Multures, (abstracted.)—The action of abstracted multures, which is one against tenants who abstract or withhold their corns from a mill to which a right of thirlage is attached, is competent before the Sheriff; 2 Ersk. 9, 32.]

Nuisance.—By 1 & 2 Vict. 119, § 15, it is enacted, "That the jurisdiction, power, and authority of Sheriffs of Scotland shall be, and the same are hereby extended to all actions or proceedings relative to questions of nuisance or damages, arising from the alleged undue exercise of the right of property, . . . and all parties against whom such actions or proceedings may be brought, shall be amenable to the jurisdiction of the Sheriff of the territory within which such property shall be situated."

Poinding of the Ground.—This action, which proceeds at the instance of a holder of a debt heritably secured, and is directed against goods or effects situated upon the lands, is competent before the Sheriff; 4 Ersk. 1, 11.

Removing.—By the A. S. 14th December 1756, a landlord might bring an action of removing to be called forty days before the term of Whitsunday, and this was competent only in the Sheriff Court. By the same A. S. an execution of a charge of horning obtained on the tack forty days before Whitsunday, was a sufficient warrant for the Sheriff to eject, also where a tenant had run one year's rent in arrear, or owed arrears of several years, which, taken together, amounted to one year's rent, or where he deserted the possession, leaving the farm unlaboured, at the usual period of labouring, the landlord might bring an action before the Sheriff, to have him ordained to find caution for the arrears and for the rents of the five following crops, or otherwise to have him ejected; and by the 1 & 2 Vict. 119, § 8, in cases of set for less than one year, and the rent not exceeding L.30 per annum, actions of removing may be prosecuted in a summary form before the Sheriff, whose judgment is not subject to review. Important provisions have been made by the recent statute connected with the subject of removing, for which see Chapter IX. *Removing.*

Sequestration.—(*Landlord's.*)—The petition of a landlord for sequestrating his tenant's effects in security or for payment of rent, is competent only before the Sheriff (or Magistrates in certain cases.) But the judgment may be reviewed by the Court of Session.

Servitude.—By 1 & 2 Vict. 119, c. 15, it is enacted that the jurisdiction, power, and authority of Sheriffs of Scotland shall be, and the same are hereby extended to all actions or proceedings relative to questions touching either the constitution or the exercise of real or predial servitudes, and all parties against whom such actions or proceedings may be brought, shall be amenable to the jurisdiction of the Sheriff of the territory within which such servitude shall be situated.

Thirlage, Commutation of.—Jurisdiction is conferred on the Sheriff, with a jury of heritors or tenants of L.30 yearly rent, to commute the servitude of thirlage affecting lands into an annual payment of grain or money, 39 Geo. III. c. 55. This may be done at the suit either of the proprietor of the lands astricted, or of the owner of the mill. The decree of the Sheriff, ascertaining the extent of the right of thirlage, is subject to advocation

Miscellaneous.—By many local statutes for the execution of Canals, Railways, and the like, and for determining questions as to the value or damage to property by the execution thereof, an exclusive jurisdiction is conferred on the Sheriff

Bankruptcy.—Actions and Procedure connected with Bankruptcy.

Cessio Bonorum—by which the person of an unfortunate debtor is, on his giving up his effects to his creditors protected against imprisonment for past debts—was formerly competent ι   the Court of Session, but is, by 6 and 7 Will. IV. c. 56, made con   ent in the Sheriff Court. The procedure will be given below, *voce Cessio Bonorum.*

Meditatio Fugæ Warran's.—The application by a creditor to have a debtor, as in *meditatio fugæ* from Scotland, ordained to find caution for his appearance on the suit of the applicant, must be made to the Sheriff or a Justice of Peace.

Mercantile Sequestration—Under the Bankrupt Statute, 2 and 3 Vict. c. 41 (amended by the recent statute, 16 and 17 Vict. c. 53), sequestration of the estates of bankrupts can be awarded only by the Court of Session. But the proceedings are remitted to the Sheriff of the county where the bankrupt resides, in whose Court the subsequent proceedings are conducted, some of them subject to the review of the Court of Session

Sale under Poinding—Poindings are reported to the Sheriff, and where there are competing creditors for the price of effects of a debtor sold under poinding, the preferences are settled by the Sheriff; 54 Geo. III. c 137, § 4, and 1 and 2 Vict. 114, § 23, et seq.

Admiralty Cases.

This jurisdiction was formerly in the High Court of Admiralty, and was by 1 Will. IV. c. 69, explained by 1 and 2 Vict. 119, § 21, transferred to the Sheriffs. " They shall, within their respective sheriffdoms, including the navigable rivers, ports, harbours, creeks, shores, and anchorage grounds in and adjoining such sheriffdoms, hold and exercise original jurisdiction in all maritime causes and proceedings, civil and criminal, including such as may apply to persons residing furth of Scotland, of the same nature as that heretofore held and exercised by the High Court of Admiralty." Admiralty cases, as defined by the Act 1681, c. 16, relate to questions of charter-parties, freights, salvages, wrecks, bottomries, policies of insurance, and in general all contracts concerning the lading or unlading of ships, or any other matter to be performed within the verge of the Admiral's jurisdiction, and all actions for delivery of goods sent on shipboard, or for recovering their value, or when the subject of the suit consists of goods transported by sea from one port to another.

Succession.—Cases connected with Succession.

Service of Heirs.—The service of heirs which used to proceed on brieves issued from Chancery, is, since the year 1847, effected in the case of general service by petition to the Sheriff of the County where the ancestor had his ordinary or principal domicile at the time of his death, and in special service, to the Sheriff of the County where the lands, if wholly in one County, are situated. In those cases of general service where the deceased had no domicile in Scotland at the time of his death, and of special service of lands lying in different Counties, the petition must, and in all other cases may, be presented to the Sheriff of Chancery; 10 and 11 Vict. c. 47. The forms of procedure in cases of service are given below, *voce Service of Heirs*

Brieves of terce, of perambulation, and of division among heirs-portioners, can only be directed to, and carried through by, the Sheriff or Judge Ordinary. So also brieves of idiotry and furiosity.

Confirmation of Executors—The power of granting confirmation used to be in the Commissaries, but is now in the Sheriffs; 2 Geo. IV. c. 97, and 1 Will. IV. c. 69. It comprehends the registering of settlements of deceased parties, and of inventories of their personal estates —judging in questions of competition for the office of executor, and granting confirmation in favour of executors—granting warrants for sealing the repositories of deceased parties, and for inventorying their effects. Where persons die furth of Scotland, having personal property in Scotland, the Sheriff of Edinburgh has the jurisdiction. The forms and procedure in confirmation are given below, *voce Confirmation*

Parliamentary and Burgh Representation.

Reform Act.—Sheriffs are, by the Reform Act, made judges of claims for the registration of electors within their respective Counties. There is an appeal to an Appeal Court, composed of the Sheriffs who attend the Circuit Courts of Justiciary within whose bounds the subject of the appellant's claim is situated; or if there are not three Sheriffs at such circuits, the circuit Judges appoint a member of the Bar of three years' standing to make the third; 2 and 3 Will. IV. c 65, and 5 and 6 Will. IV. c. 65.

Burgh Reform Act.—The judgments of the Chief Magistrate and Assessor of the Burgh admitting or rejecting any claimant for the right of electing town councillors, are subject to review by the Sheriffs composing the Appeal Court last mentioned, within whose bounds any Burgh not having a register of electors of members of parliament is situated; 3 and 4 Will. IV. c. 76.

Magistrates' Election Act.—In the election of Magistrates of Burghs (not Royal) which return or contribute to return members to parliament, where there is no Provost, or Chief or Senior Magistrate, the Sheriff is to preside and act as such; 3 and 4 Will. IV. c. 77, § 5.

Police.

The minutes of meetings of the inhabitants of Burghs, containing their resolutions as to adopting all or any of the provisions of the general Police Act, are appointed to be laid before the Sheriff of the bounds, who pronounces a deliverance, finding and declaring to what extent the powers and provisions of the Act have been adopted, which is recorded, *inter alia*, in the Sheriff Court Books; the Sheriff has also power to determine without appeal what subjects within the Burgh are or are not assessable under the Statute; also to try all offences specified in the Act 3 and 4 Will. IV. c. 156, and offences under the Police Improvement (Scotland) Act, 13 and 14 Vict. c. 33.

Miscellaneous.

By a variety of statutes, more particularly of recent date, jurisdiction is specially conferred on Sheriffs, and their judgments declared final and not subject to review by any superior Court.

Among these are the following.—Questions arising under the School-masters' Act, 43 Geo. III c. 54. The recovery of penalties under L 25 under the Hawk rs' Act, 55 Geo. III. c. 71. Questions arising under the Savings Bank Act, 59 Geo III. c 62. Penalties for breach of certificate under the Spirit Licenses Act 9 Geo IV c. 58. Jurisdiction is conferred on Sheriffs over all persons engaged in catching, curing, and dealing in herrings in all the lochs, bays, and arms of the sea, and in other matters connected with the herring fishery, 48 Geo. III. c. 110; 55 Geo. III. c. 94; and 14 and 15 Vict c. 26. Exclusive jurisdiction is committed to the Sheriffs and Justices of the Peace respectively, in questions under the General Turnpike Act; and their judgments are not subject to review in prosecutions for any expenses, toll-duty, penalty, forfeiture, or fine, 1 and 2 Will IV. c 43. Under the Companies' Clauses Consolidation Act, 8 Vict. c. 17, questions of damages, costs, or expenses, and the method of ascertaining the amount, or enforcing the payment thereof, where not otherwise provided, are to be ascertained and determined by the Sheriff or Justices, and summarily recovered before them By the Lands' Clauses Consolidation Act, 8 Vict. c. 19, questions of disputed compensation for lands taken are to be determined by the Sheriff, and penalties and forfeitures to be summarily recovered before him or two Justices. By the Railway Clauses Consolidation Act, 8 and 9 Vict. c. 33, the power of ordering approaches to and fences of highways crossing on the level, is committed to the Sheriff or Justices; also the ordering and repair of bridges, fences, approaches, gates, &c., and disputes as to works for the accommodation of the owners and occupiers of lands adjoining the railways, are to be settled by the Sheriff or Justices; also, where damages, charges, or expenses and penalties are by the Act directed to be paid, and the method of ascertaining the amount; or enforcing the payment thereof, is not provided for, such amount, in case of dispute, is to be ascertained and determined by the Sheriff, and the amount recovered by his warrant. By the Poor Law Act, 8 and 9 Vict. c. 83, the Sheriff has the power of determining disputes as to the validity of the election of any person as member of the Parochial Board; and all penalties or forfeitures imposed by the Act are to be recovered summarily before the Sheriff. By the Harbours, Docks, and Piers Act, 10 Vict. c. 27, disputes concerning the amount of any rates due, or the charges occasioned by any distress or arrestment, by virtue of the Act, are to be determined by the Sheriff.

Among the ministerial powers of Sheriffs may be enumerated the charge of *writs* issued from Exchequer in Crown processes—summoning Jurors—reporting on the Records within their counties—inspecting Jails and Madhouses, and striking annually the Fiars prices.

To the criminal jurisdiction of the Sheriff we do not advert in this work.

CHAPTER IV.

Terms and Sittings for the Small Debt Court.

In addition to the ordinary Small Debt Courts held by the Sheriffs or their Substitutes at the county town, they are appointed to hold Circuit Courts for the purposes of the Small Debt Act, at the places, and for the number of times within each place, not exceeding the number mentioned in Schedule (H.) as should be directed by warrant, and under Her Majesty's sign-manual at each Circuit, all the causes ready to be heard are to be disposed of. § 23. *

The warrant to be published in the London Gazette; § 23.

The places and times for such Circuit Courts may be changed or discontinued by the Sheriff, with the consent and approbation of one of the principal Secretaries of State. § 24.

The Schedule of places and times, with the changes which have taken place upon it, are now, or were very recently, as follows:—

---

* The sections cited at the end of the paragraphs in this Chapter are those of the Small Debt Act, 1 Vict. c. 41.

COUNTIES.	PLACES AT WHICH CIRCUITS ARE HELD	COUNTIES	PLACES AT WHICH CIRCUITS ARE HELD.
Aberdeen	Inverury .. .. Five Times. Tarland ...Five Times Turriff... ....Five Times. Huntly....... ...Five Times Old Deer... ..... Five Times. Fraserburgh ...Five Times.	Haddington...	North Berwick .. Four Times Dunbar .... Six Times Tranent .... Six Times.
Argyle	Oban . ...Four Times. Bowmore, Island of Islay...... } Four Times. Dunoon .... Four Times. Lochgilphead ... .Four Times.	Inverness......	Kingussie . ...Three Times. Fort Augustus . Three Times. Grantown . . . Three Times. Beauly . . .... .Three Times
Ayr	Beith ... . Four Times. Old Cumnock .. .Four Times. Girvan .. ..Three Times. Irvine .. . ... Six Times.	Kincardine	Laurencekirk ....Three Times Bervie.. .. ....Four Times. Durris ....Three Times.
Berwick	Lauder ... . .Three Times. Dunse .. ..Six Times. Coldstream ... .. Six Times. Ayton . . ... .Three Times.	Kirkcudbright	New Galloway . Three Times. Maxwelltown .. Four Times Castle Douglas ...Four Times. Creetown. . ...Three Times.
Berwick	Lauder ... . .Three Times. Dunse .. ..Six Times. Coldstream ... .. Six Times. Ayton . . ... .Three Times.	Lanark.........	Biggar ....Four Times. Douglas .. ....Three Times
Banff . ..	Buckie .... Three Times, Keith .. .. Six Times. Dufftown ... . Three Times. Tomintoul ... ..Two Times	Linlithgow	Bathgate ....Four Times. Queensferry. ... ...Three Times
Banff . ..	Buckie .... Three Times, Keith .. .. Six Times. Dufftown ... . Three Times. Tomintoul ... ..Two Times	Orkney	St Margaret's Hope Three Times. Stromness ... . Four Times.
Bute.............	Brodick in Arran Four Times. Milport .. ..Four Times.	Shetland	Burravoe.... ......Two Times
Caithness..	Thurso ... . Ten Times Lybster ...... .Ten Times	Perth	Crieff ... . Four Times Callander ....Four Times. Kincardine (Tullialan) } Four Times. Dunkeld .. . ... .Three Times Aberfeldy ... .Three Times. Blairgowrie ....Four Times. Coupar-Angus ..Four Times.
Dumbarton ...	Kirkintilloch . ... Four Times.	Perth	Crieff ... . Four Times Callander ....Four Times. Kincardine (Tullialan) } Four Times. Dunkeld .. . ... .Three Times Aberfeldy ... .Three Times. Blairgowrie ....Four Times. Coupar-Angus ..Four Times.
Dumbarton ...	Kirkintilloch . ... Four Times.	Renfrew	Pollokshaws ......Six Times.
Dumfries	Sanquhar. . .Three Times Annan .. ... .Three Times Langholm.... ....Three Times. Moffat ... Three Times Lockerbie ..... Three Times. Thornhill .... .Three Times.	Ross and Cromarty......	Ardgay. .. . .Two Times Kincardine ... Two Times. Jeantown ..... . Two Times. Fortrose ....Four Times. Invergordon ... .Four Times.
Edinburgh .	Dalkeith ... . TwelveTimes.	Roxburgh ..	Melrose ....Four Times Hawick ....Six Times. Kelso ....Six Times.
Elgin ....,	Rothes ... ...Three Times. Fochabers. . ...Three Times. Grantown . ...Three Times. Forres ....Six Times.	Selkirk..	Galashiels .... Four Times.
Fife	Auchtermuchty ...Four Times. Newburgh ....Four Times. St Andrews .. . . .Four Times. Colinsburgh ....Four Times. Kirkaldy . ...Six Times. Leven .... Four Times.	Stirling ...	Drymen .. ..Four Times. Lennoxtown of Campsie } Four Times. Balfron..,........Four Times.
Fife	Auchtermuchty ...Four Times. Newburgh ....Four Times. St Andrews .. . . .Four Times. Colinsburgh ....Four Times. Kirkaldy . ...Six Times. Leven .... Four Times.	Sutherland ...	Golspie . ...Four Times Lairg .. . . Three Times Tongue .... Three Times Helmsdale ....Three Times Scourie . ..Three Times Melvich .... Three Times.
Forfar	Brechin ...... Six Times. Montrose ... .Six Times. Arbroath . ..... Six Times. Kirriemuir ......Six Times	Wigton ..	Stranraer... ... ... .Six Times. Whithorn ......Four Times. Newton Stewart ...Four Times

, The Sheriff Clerk, either personally or by a Depute appointed by him, is to attend at and during the holding of such Circuit Courts, and perform the duties. § 25.

If such Depute-Clerk should not be resident in the place, he may appoint a proper person resident therein, or in its immediate vicinity, to issue the summonses or complaints which may be applied for and issued under the provisions of the Act, and the principal clerk is to give a notice in the following form, which is to be affixed on or near the doors of the church of the parish within which the Court is to be held ; and also, if he shall see cause, by advertisement in the newspaper or newspapers of the greatest reputed circulation in the neighbourhood. § 25.—The notice is as follows :—

Notice.

A.B. (*add designation*), residing   is the Depute Sheriff Clerk to whom application for summonses and every thing else necessary for the Sheriff circuit at this place, for small debt causes, must be made, or in case the Depute shall not be resident, say A.B. (*add designation and place of residence*) is the Depute Sheriff-Clerk who will officiate at   in the Sheriff's Small Debt Circuit Court, and C.D. (*add designation*) residing at   is the person who will issue summonses or complaints to be brought in such Court.

Date.

Place.

A notice must in like manner be given by the Sheriff-Clerk of the times at which such Courts shall be fixed to be held, in the following form :—

Notice.

The Sheriff will hold Circuit Courts for Small Debt Causes at on the   day of   at   of the clock, and on every (*fix the time periodically, or if not, new notice to be given.*) A.B. (*add designation and residence*) is the clerk for this place.

Date.

Place.

Three months before holding any of these Circuit Courts, the Sheriff shall, by a minute entered in the sederunt-book of his Court, and published in such manner as he may think proper, and of which a printed copy shall be publicly affixed at all times on the walls of every Sheriff Court Room within his sheriffdom, apportion the parishes or parts of the parishes which shall, for the purposes of this Act, be within the jurisdiction of any Small Debt Court to be held within his sheriffdom as aforesaid, and thereafter from time to time alter such apportionment as the circumstances may require, and such alteration shall be published as aforesaid, for at least three months, before the same shall take effect. § 26.

All causes shall be brought before the Ordinary Small Debt Court, or any Circuit Small Debt Court within the jurisdiction of which the defender shall reside, or to the jurisdiction of which he shall be amenable. § 26.

If there are more defenders than one in one cause of action amenable to the jurisdiction of different Courts, it is competent to the Sheriff, either upon summary application in writing made by or for the pursuer lodged with the Sheriff Clerk, or on verbal application in open Court, to order a summons or complaint to be issued, and the cause to be brought before his Ordinary Small Debt Court, or before any of his Circuit Small Debt Courts, as shall appear most convenient, and such summons or complaint shall be issued on the Sheriff writing and subscribing thereon the name of the Court before which it is to be heard.   § 26.

The Sheriff may also follow the same course, if from any other cause he shall be satisfied it is expedient for the ends of justice.   § 26.

The Sheriff may also, where the ends of justice and the convenience of the parties require it, adjourn and remove the farther hearing of, or procedure in, any cause from his Ordinary Small Debt Court to any of his Circuit Small Debt Courts, or from any of his Circuit Small Debt Courts to his Ordinary or any other Circuit Small Debt Court, or to any diet of his Ordinary Court, to be there dealt with according to the provisions of the Act, or to any other time or place specially appointed for the purpose.   § 27.

Such order of adjournment or removal shall be held due notice to the parties, unless farther notice shall be ordered.   § 27.

There is a special provision with respect to the upper district of Morayshire, allowing the Circuit Court for that district to be held at Granton in Inverness.   § 28.

CHAPTER V.

Terms and Sittings for the Ordinary Court.

There are to be three Sessions in the year (§ 43 *), namely—
From 15th January (or 1st ordinary Court day thereafter) to 15th March.
„   3d or 4th April to 31st July.
„   1st October (or 1st ordinary Court day) to 15th December.

Each Sheriff Court (except where a Sheriff-substitute does not reside)

---

* The sections cited at the end of the paragraphs in this chapter are those of the recent statute 16 and 17 Vict. c. 80.

shall sit for ordinary civil business, for such number of days weekly as shall be fixed by each Sheriff, by a regulation of Court to be approved of by the Lord President and Lord Justice-Clerk, and to be advertised at least once a year in a newspaper published in the county, failing which in some immediately adjoining county. § 42.

If at any time there be any arrear of business, it shall be the duty of the Sheriff to appoint additional Court days, whether in time of session or vacation, for the purpose of disposing thereof. § 43.

At least one Court day during each vacation for the dispatch of all ordinary civil business, including the calling of new causes, and receipt of papers due, shall be appointed by the Sheriff before the termination of each session. § 45.

All summary cases may proceed equally during vacation as during session. § 44

It shall be competent to the Sheriff (if he thinks fit) to pronounce interlocutors in time of vacation in all cases, whether summary or not. § 44.

Each Sheriff (Depute), excepting those of Mid-Lothian, Lanark, and Orkney, shall hold the following annual sittings in his county (unless prevented by indisposition or other unavoidable cause, of which due notice to be given). § 46.

Argyll. Banff Caithness Elgin and Nairn. Inverness. Ross and Cromarty. Sutherland.	Three such annual sittings at intervals of not less than six weeks, and to continue till the causes ready for trial or hearing at their commencement are disposed of.

All the other counties—four such annual sittings.

The places at which such sittings are to be held, are those where the ordinary Courts of the Sheriff-substitutes are held, and such other places within the county as the Sheriff, with approval of the Home Secretary, may appoint. But

In Argyll, Inverness, Ross,	at such places as the Sheriff, with approval of the Secretary of State, may appoint; provided the Sheriff shall hold one sitting at least twice a-year at each of the places where the ordinary Courts of the Substitute are held. § 46.

Each Sheriff shall once in the year go on the Small Debt Circuit in use to be held by the Sheriff-substitute, and shall on such occasions, in addition, to holding the Small Debt Court, dispatch as much of the ordinary business as may be ready for adjudication, or as time may permit.   § 46.

An annual return, within ten days after 12th November, is to be made by the Sheriff to the Home Secretary of the number and duration of such sittings, or cause of his absence.   § 46.

The county of Orkney and Zetland is exempted from these provisions, and the Sheriff's duties remain as fixed by 1 and 2 Vict. c. 119.   § 46.

Any Sheriff may pronounce and sign any interlocutor judgment, or decree, when furth of his sheriffdom.   § 47.

CHAPTER VI.

Procedure in the Small Debt Court.

The Act 1 Vict. c. 41, which commenced October 1, 1837, superseded the previous Small Debt Act, 10 Geo. IV. c. 55 (1829), and provided the existing machinery for causes not exceeding L 8, 6s. 8d., which is now extended in all cases not exceeding L 12.

The constitution of the jurisdiction and terms of sittings are given above.

It is not imperative on any person suing for the value of L.12 or under, to avail himself of the summary forms of the Small Debt Court. He may have his case tried by the ordinary forms in the Ordinary Court, and it cannot be removed to the Small Debt Court even by the Sheriff, without his consent. But if he do not pursue or give the consent where the debt was originally, or has come by partial payments, or otherwise, to be not above L.12, the expenses may be modified to those which would have been incurred by trial in the Small Debt Court. §§ 4 and 36.*

On the other hand, the pursuer in the Small Debt Court, " shall in all cases be held to have passed from and abandoned any remaining portion of any debt, demand, or penalty beyond the sum actually concluded for in any such cause or prosecution." § 2.

We shall exemplify the procedure according to the statutory forms in

---

* The sections quoted throughout this chapter are those of the Small Debt Act, 1 Vict. c. 41.

the case of a prosecution in the Small Debt Court for an account of goods furnished, noticing the points of incidental procedure in Chapter VIII.

Summons.

The following is the Statutory form of the

Summons or Complaint in a Civil Cause.

JOHN THOMSON GORDON, Esq , Advocate, Sheriff of the Shire of Edinburgh, To   Officers of Court, jointly and severally. Whereas it is humbly complained to me, by *A.B , Tailor and Clothier in Edinburgh;* THAT *C D., cabinet-maker, residing in Castle Street there,* Defender, is owing the Complainer the sum of *Ten Pounds Fifteen Shillings Sterling, being the amount of an account for goods sold by the Pursuer to the Defender, commencing the first day of January* 1852, *and ending the first day of February* 1853, which the said Defender refuses or delays to pay, and therefore the said Defender ought to be DECERNED and ORDAINED to make payment to the Complainer with Expenses, HEREFORE it is my Will, that, on sight hereof, ye lawfully summon the said Defender to compear before me, or my Substitute, in the Court House at *Edinburgh (County Buildings, Lawnmarket), upon Friday, the eleventh day of November, One Thousand Eight Hundred and Fifty-three Years, at Ten of the Clock, Forenoon,* to answer at the Complainer's instance in the said matter, with certification, in case of failure, of being held as confessed, requiring you also to deliver to the Defender a copy of any Account pursued for, and that ye cite Witnesses and Havers for both parties, to compear at the said Place and Date, to give evidence in the said matter; And, in the mean time that ye Arrest in Security the Goods, Effects, Debts, and Sums of Money belonging to the Defender, as accords of Law Given under the hand of the Clerk of Court, *at Edinburgh, the first day of November, One Thousand Eight Hundred and Fifty-three Years.*

J. A. CAMPBELL, *Sheriff-Clerk.*

Citation of Defender.

This summons or complaint being signed by the Sheriff-Clerk, shall be a sufficient warrant and authority to any Sheriff's-Officer for summoning the defender to appear and answer, at the time and place mentioned in such summons of complaint, not being sooner than upon the sixth day after such citation. § 3.

A copy of the said summons or complaint, with the citation annexed, and also a copy of the account, if any, must be served at the same time by the Sheriff's-Officer, on the defender personally or at his dwelling-place, or in case of a company, at their ordinary place of business. § 3.

Citation for Defender.

A. B., Defender, above designed.—You are hereby summoned to appear and answer before the Sheriff in the matter, and at the time and place, and under the certification set forth in the above copy of the summons or complaint against you

This notice served upon the *fifth* day of *November, Eighteen hundred and fifty-three years,* by me.

John Robson, Sheriff-Officer.

The officer must return an execution signed by him, or appear and give evidence on oath of such citation having been duly made. § 3.

Execution of Citation.

Upon the *fifth* day of *November,* One thousand eight hundred and *fifty-three years,* I duly summoned the above designed A. B., defender, to appear and answer before the Sheriff in the matter, and at the time and place, and under the certification above set forth. This I did, by leaving a full copy of the above summons or complaint, with a citation thereto annexed, and a copy of the account for the said defender (in his hands personally, or otherwise as the case may be)

John Robson, Sheriff-Officer.

Witnesses are unnecessary to the citation. § 3.

Decree in Absence.

If the defender does not appear personally or by one of his family; or by such person as the Sheriff shall allow, such person not being an officer of Court, he shall be held confessed, and the other party shall obtain decree against him. § 15.

No procurators, solicitors, nor any person practising the law, are allowed to appear and plead for any party without leave of the Court upon special cause shewn, and on such leave and cause being entered in the Sheriff-Clerk's book of causes. § 14.

But the defender may be heard on a future day, in a certain form and under certain conditions See Chap. VIII. *Reponing.*

In like manner, if the pursuer shall fail to appear personally, or by one of his family, or by such person as may be allowed, not being an officer of Court, the defender shall obtain decree of absolvitor. § 15.

But he also may be heard on a future day; § 16. See *Reponing.*

If in either of these cases a sufficient excuse for delay is stated, or from the absence of witnesses or any other good reason, the Sheriff sees fit to adjourn to the next or any other Court day, he may do so, and ordain the parties and witnesses ther to attend. § 15.

The Pursuer's Evidence—*Preparation of.*

If the pursuer is to attend and prove his case, he must prepare the proper evidence against the Court-day. It is no objection to witnesses that they appear without citation. § 12.

But if they decline to appear without *compulsitor*, the summons of complaint is a sufficient warrant to any Sheriff's-officer for summoning such witnesses and havers as the pursuer shall require, § 3; and if the witness reside in a different county, this warrant must be endorsed by the Sheriff-Clerk of that county.

Form of Officer's Citation to a Witness.

E.F., *residing in No* 10 *Lothian Road, Edinburgh*—You are hereby summoned to appear before the Sheriff of the shire of Edinburgh, or his Substitute, in the Court House at Edinburgh, upon Friday the 11th day of November One thousand eight hundred and fifty-three, at ten of the clock, to bear witness for the pursuer in the summons or complaint at the instance of *A B.*, tailor and clothier in Edinburgh, against *C.D.*, cabinetmaker, residing in Castle Street, and that under the penalty of forty shillings if you fail to attend. This notice served on the eighth day of November 1853 by me,

John Robson, Sheriff-Officer.

Execution of Citation of Witness.

Upon the eighth day of November One thousand eight hundred and fifty-three, I duly summoned E.F., residing in No. 10 Lothian Road, Edinburgh, to appear before the Sheriff of the shire of Edinburgh, or his Substitute, in the Court-House at Edinburgh, upon the 11th day of November One thousand eight hundred and fifty-three, at ten of the clock, to bear-witness for the pursuer in the summons or complaint at the instance of *A.B.*, tailor and clothier in Edinburgh, against *C.D.*, cabinetmaker, residing in Castle Street there. This I did by delivering a just copy of citation signed by me, to the said *E F.* (personally or otherwise, as the case may be.)

John Robson, Sheriff-Officer.

The witnesses or havers must have a citation of at least forty-eight hours; and if a witness or haver fail to appear, he forfeits a penalty not exceeding 40s., unless a reasonable excuse be offered and sustained; and such penalty shall be paid to the party citing him, and be recovered in the same manner as other penalties under the Act. § 12

· The Sheriff may also compel the attendance of the witnesses by letters of second diligence.   § 12.

The Defender's Evidence—*Preparation of.*

Where the defender is to appeal and prove his defence, if it is to be either wholly or partially rested on a counter-account or claim, he must have a copy thereof served by an officer on the pursuer, at least one free day before the day of appearance.   The form of the execution of service is as follows :—

> Upon the *tenth* day of *November* 1853, I gave notice to *A.B.*, pursuer, of the above counter-account (or claim) intended to be pleaded against him by *C D.*, defender, in the small debt action to which the said defender was summoned to appear before the Sheriff at *Edinburgh* upon the 11th day of *November*, at ten of the clock   This I did by leaving a copy of the above account (or notice or claim shortly explaining it) for the said pursuer, in his hands personally, (or otherwise, as the case may be).
>
> *John Robson*, Sheriff-Officer.

Failing such notice, a counter-claim is not allowed to be presented except with the pursuer's consent.   But action is reserved for the same. § 11.

The defender's warrant for the officer citing witnesses and havers is the copy of the summons or complaint served on him, and the same rules as to citation and penalty for not appearing, apply as already mentioned in the case of witnesses for the pursuer.

Trial of the Cause.

, On the parties appearing or being represented, as already explained, on the Court-day, the Sheriff shall hear them *viva voce*, and examine witnesses or havers upon oath, and may also examine the parties, and put them, or any of them upon oath, in case of oath in supplement being required, or of a reference being made; and if he should see cause, may remit to persons of skill to report, or to any person competent to take and report in writing the evidence of witnesses or havers, who may be unable to attend upon special cause shewn (which cause is to be entered in the book of causes kept by the Sheriff clerk), due notice of the examination being given to both parties, and thereupon the Sheriff may pronounce judgment. § 13.

None of the pleadings shall be reduced to writing, or be entered upon any record, unless with leave of the Court first had and obtained, in consequence of any difficulty in point of law, or special circumstances of any particular case; and where such pleadings are reduced to writing, the case shall be conducted according to the ordinary forms and proceedings, and disposed of as if this Act had not been passed. § 14.

By the recent Evidence Act, the parties may be examined on oath as witnesses in the cause; and all objections to witnesses on the ground of interest are abolished.

Decree.

The Sheriff may, if he thinks proper, direct the sum or sums found due to be paid by instalments, weekly, monthly, or quarterly, according to the circumstances of the party found liable, and under such conditions or qualifications as he shall think fit to annex. § 18.

The decree is to be annexed to the summons or complaint, and on the same paper with it. It states the amount of expenses found due, which may include personal charges if the Sheriff thinks fit, and is to be in the following form, or to the like effect. § 13.—

Decree for Pursuer.

At *Edinburgh*, the 11*th* day of November, One thousand eight hundred and fifty-three, the Sheriff of the shire of Edinburgh finds the above designed *C. D*, defender, liable to the pursuer in the sum of Ten pounds fifteen shillings sterling, with three shillings of expenses, and decerns and ordains instant execution by arrestment, and also execution to pass hereon by poinding and sale and imprisonment, if the same be competent, after ten free days.

J. A. CAMPBELL, Sheriff-Clerk.

Decree of Absolvitor.

If the defender prevails, the words after " Edinburgh" will be, " assoilzies the within-designed *C.D.* from the within complaint, and finds the within-designed *A.B*, pursuer, liable to him in the sum of
of expenses, and decerns," &c

Where the pursuer does not return the original Summons, this decree may be written on the copy served on the defender.

Procedure on the Decree.

The decree and warrant, signed by the clerk, is in all cases a sufficient authority for instant arrestment. § 13.

If the party against whom it is given was personally present (when it was pronounced), it is a sufficient authority after the lapse of ten free days for poinding and sale and imprisonment, where competent. § 13.

But if the party was not so present, poinding and sale and imprisonment can only proceed after a charge of ten free days, by serving a copy of the complaint and decree on the party personally, or at his dwelling-place. § 13.

If the person or effects against whom the decree is to be enforced, are situated in another county, the decree, (or an extract thereof), must first be produced to and endorsed by the Sheriff-clerk of such other county. § 19.

Charge on Decree.

C D. above designed—you are hereby charged to implement the decree, of which, and of the complaint whereon the same proceeded, the above is a copy, within ten days from this date, under pain of poinding and sale without farther notice. This charge given by me, on the twelfth day of November 1853, before *Adam Huie, residing in Lawnmarket, Edinburgh.*

JOHN ROBSON, Sheriff-Officer.

Execution of Charge.

On the *twelfth* day of *November*, One thousand eight hundred and *fifty-three*, I duly charged *C.D.* above designed, to implement the above decree within the time, and under the pains therein expressed. This I did by delivering a just copy of the foregoing complaint and decree, and a charge thereto annexed, subscribed by me to the said *C.D.* (personally, or as the case may be), before Adam Huie, residing in Lawnmarket, Edinburgh, witness hereto with me subscribing.

JOHN ROBSON, Sheriff-Officer.

Ad. Huie, Witness.

The effect of the decree lasts for forty years, but if it is not put in force by poinding or imprisonment within a year from its date, or from the date of a charge of payment given thereon, the decree cannot be enforced without a new charge. § 13.

The forms of poinding and sale are given Chapter IX. *voce* Poinding.

The Sheriff-clerk keeps a book of causes, and the other Registers specified in § 17 of the Statute, and causes a copy of the roll of causes to be hung up in the Court room; in the manner specified in § 17.

Appeal and Review.

No decree given by any Sheriff in any cause or prosecution decided under the authority of the Act, is subject to reduction, advocation, suspension, or appeal, or any other form of review, or stay of execution, other than provided by the Act, either on account of any omission or irregularity, or informality in the citation or proceedings, or on the merits, or on any ground or reason whatever. § 30. But provision is made by the recent Statute, § 26, for review by the Sheriff in case of imprisonment on decrees for sums exceeding L 8, 6s. 8d.

It is competent to any person conceiving himself aggrieved by any decree given by any Sheriff in any cause or prosecution, raised under the authority of the Act, to bring the case by appeal before the next Circuit Court of Justiciary, or where there are no Circuit Courts, before the High Court of Justiciary at Edinburgh, in the manner, and by and under the rules, limitations, conditions, and restrictions contained in the before recited Act, passed in the twentieth year of the reign of His Majesty King George the Second, for taking away and abolishing the heritable jurisdictions in Scotland, except in so far as altered by this Act. § 31.

But such appeal is competent only when founded on the ground of corruption, malice, and oppression on the part of the Sheriff, or on such deviations in point of form from the statutory enactments, as the Court shall think took place wilfully, or have prevented substantial justice from having been done, or on incompetency, including defect of jurisdiction of the Sheriff. § 31.

Such appeals are heard and determined in open Court; and it is competent to the Court to correct such deviation in point of form, or to remit the cause to the Sheriff with instructions, or for re-hearing generally. It is not competent to produce or found upon any document as evidence on the merits of the original cause, which was not produced to the Sheriff when the cause was heard, and to which his signature or initials have not been then affixed, which he is only to do if required, nor to found upon, nor refer to the testimony of any witness not examined before the Sheriff, and whose name is not written by him, when the case is heard, upon the record copy of the summons, which he is to do when specially required to that effect. § 3 .

No sist or stay of the process and decree, and no certificate of appeal, can be issued by the Sheriff-clerk, except upon consignation of the whole sum, if any, decerned for by the decree, and expenses, if any, and security found for the whole expenses which may be incurred, and found due under the appeal. § 31.

CHAPTER VII.
Procedure in the Ordinary Court.

At present, and until the recent statute comes into operation on 1st November 1853, the forms of procedure are regulated by 1 and 2 Vict. c. 119, and relative Acts of Sederunt which contain special directions relative to the different steps of process. These provisions continue in force in so far as not inconsistent with those of the new statute. But a question here at once presents itself. In how far is the new statute applicable to processes in dependence previously to the date when it shall come into operation? Viewing the matter in the abstract, there can be no doubt that the new statute does apply. It contains no provision excluding existing cases from its operation; and it expressly declares, that the procedure shall, after 1st November 1853, be in accordance with its provisions, and that the recited Act and Acts of Sederunt, and the existing laws and usages, are repealed, in so far as is necessary to give effect to its provisions.

Practically, however, difficulties will be experienced in applying the new Act to cases in dependence previous to 1st November 1853; difficulties, greater or less, according to the stage at which the process shall then have arrived. In cases where the Record has not been then closed, the application of the new statute will be comparatively easy; but in cases where the process is in a more advanced state, and particularly in cases where proof has been partially led on commission, greater difficulty is to be expected. As, however, there can be no doubt of the general application of the statute to all cases, these must be dealt with as they occur, it being always kept in view by the practitioner that the forms of procedure shall, in all circumstances and cases where practicable, be in conformity with the new statute, and that the previously existing forms are abolished, in so far as necessary to give effect to its provisions.

The Summons.

If the sum pursued for be not above L.12, or if the value of the subject of the suit does not exceed that sum, the procedure is in the Small Debt Court, unless the pursuer prefers the Ordinary Court, subject to the condition, that the Sheriff may modify the expenses to those which would have been incurred by trial in the Small Debt Court. In cases above L.12 the procedure is before the Ordinary Court.

As to the form of the summons, the enactment of the statute is, "That it shall be in the form as nearly as may be of Schedule A, annexed to this Act," § 1 * And the rule of law is, that the forms in the Schedule are equally imperative as substantive enactments.

Turning to Schedule A we find that the form there given consists of what may be termed the instance, viz. the names and designations of pursuer and defender, and the conclusions.

There are four examples given of the conclusions of a Summons.

Where the amount of a bill is pursued for, the conclusion is " To pay to

---

* Throughout this chapter the sections at the end of the paragraphs are those of the recent Act 16 and 17 Vict. c. 80, except when another Statute is mentioned. A. S. 2, is the section of the Act of Sederunt, 10th July 1839.

the pursuer the sum of L.   contained in a bill drawn by the
pursuer, upon and accepted by the defender, dated   ,
and payable   after date, with the legal interest thereof till
payment."

Where delivery of goods is sought, the conclusion is " to make delivery
to the pursuer of   sold by the defender to him."

Where the price of goods is sued for, the conclusion is " to pay to the
pursuer the sum of   for goods sold by the pursuer to the defender, per account commencing the   day of   and ending
the   day of   annexed hereto."

Where damages for slander are sought, the conclusion is " to pay to the
pursuer the sum of   being damages sustained by the pursuer
in consequence of the defender having slandered the pursuer by stating
      ."

These forms are in Schedule A of the Act thrown together, and it is obvious that they are given by way of example of the short and substantive
form in which the conclusions of all Sheriff Court summonses are to be
expressed, rather than as words of style which may not be deviated from
when circumstances require it. Still, however, the enactment of the statute
is, that conclusions shall, as nearly as may be, be in those forms. In all
cases the conclusions must be stated in such a substantive form and manner
that the decree following thereon shall be capable of being extracted without
reference to anything in the Condescendence

We shall, in Chapter IX., give a variety of styles, both of Petitory Summonses, and of such other Summonses and Petitions as are of most common
occurrence. At the close of this chapter we shall treat of procedure commenced by petition ; but we would here suggest, that wherever there is the
slightest doubt as to the competency of procedure by Petition, it will be the
proper and safe course to adopt the form of the Summons. The procedure
after the cause comes into Court, in both cases, is assimilated, and the only
advantage, in point of expedition, attained by commencing by Petition,
is, that the case may proceed during vacation. As the periods of vacation are now distributed otherwise than formerly, and as Sheriffs may now
sign interlocutors in ordinary cases during vacation, and appoint, if necessary, additional Court days therein, the advantage of the summary form
is very greatly diminished. Any expected saving of time is not worth
the risk of adopting a dubious form of proceeding

To illustrate more clearly the new forms of procedure which have been introduced by the statute in question, we shall suppose a case not very complicated in its circumstances, and shall trace the procedure from the summons
onwards, throwing into the next chapter some notice of the various incidental points and matters which are of constant occurrence in the progress of
cases, and leaving for Chapter IX. an explanation of the procedure, statu-

tory or otherwise, suited to what may be called particular forms of action or procedure.

We shall suppose the case of a claim, composed of the price of a horse lent, and alleged to be destroyed by the borrower by bad usage, and of an account for furnishings of clothing.

The following may be the form of the summons :—

Summons.

John Thomson Gordon, Esq Advocate, Sheriff of the County of *Edinburgh*, to Officers of Court, jointly and severally, Whereas it is shewn to me by *A.B., Tailor and Clothier in Edinburgh*, Pursuer, against *C.D., Cabinetmaker, residing in Castle Street there*, Defender ; in terms of the conclusions under written THEREFORE the defender ought to be decerned to pay to the pursuer the sum of L 20 sterling, being the price or value of a brown horse borrowed by the defender from the pursuer on the 29th day of December 1849, which has perished by the defender's fault ; also the sum of L.27, 3s. 6d. sterling, for goods sold by the pursuer to the defender, per account, *commencing on the 30th day of December* 1849, and ending *the 15th day of December* 1852, annexed hereto, with the legal interest on both of said sums *from the date of citation* till payment, with expenses : And my will is, that ye summon the defender to compear in my Court House, at Edinburgh, upon the sixth day next after the date of your citation, in the hour of cause, with continuation of days, to answer in the premises ; with certification, in case of failure, of being held as confessed. And that ye arrest in security the defender's goods, monies, debts, and effects Given at *Edinburgh* the *second* day of *November, Eighteen hundred and fifty-three.*

J. A. CAMPBELL, *Sheriff Clerk.*

(*Account annexed*).

A. B., Dr. to C. D.

1849.					
Dec. 30.	To a fine black cloth dress coat,		L4	4	0
	To a pair doeskin trousers,		2	0	0
1852.					
Feb. 3.	To a black milled venetian cloth lounging coat,		3	3	0
May 1.	To a suit for Master George,		4	11	6
	Do. for Master Thomas,		4	5	0
Dec. 3.	To a fine black cassimere waistcoat,		1	1	0
	To a fine black cloth dress coat,		4	4	0
„ 15.	To a fine fancy fur beaver upper coat, lined with Alpaca cloth, lapped seams,		3	15	0
			L.27	3	6

Where the ground of action is an account of furnishings, it seems imperative that it should be annexed to the summons, though the Statute does not provide that it should be signed or authenticated by the clerk of Court.

It would be clearly erroneous in the case above supposed to put the price of the horse sued for as an article of the account of furnishings, even though the particulars as to borrowing, &c were detailed in the account. In the Small Debt Court it is understood to be the practice to put any kind of claim into the shape of an account, and to insert a mere money conclusion with reference to the account produced. We do not consider that this would be correct practice under the new Statute.

Execution of the Summons.

In order to execution, the summons, with a service copy down to the will, is handed to an officer. The service copy and citation must bear the name of the pursuer's procurator, A S. § 19. If an account is annexed to the summons, a copy of it should be annexed to the service copy. The Statute gives no style of the officer's citation. It may be as follows:—

Officer's Citation to Defender.

C.D., Cabinetmaker, residing in Castle Street, Edinburgh, you are hereby cited to compear in the Sheriff Court House at Edinburgh, on the sixth day next after the date of this your citation, at ele en o'clock forenoon, with continuation of days, to answer to the summons, of which the preceding is a full copy to the will in terms of this citation. Given in presence of Adam Huie, residing in Lawnmarket, Edinburgh, witness in the premises, this *2d day of November* 1853.

JOHN ROBSON, *Sheriff Officer.*
Arthur Angus, Pursuer's Procurator.

The execution is to be written at the end of the summons itself, and where necessary, on continuous sheets, but not on a separate paper, and the Statutory form is declared "Equally valid and effectual in all respects as the larger form of execution at present in use." § 9.

A sheet, though stitched up with the summons, will be considered a separate paper, if part of the summons be not written thereon

The rule of the A. S is—" All executions or returns shall be signed by the officer and the witness who was present at the execution, and shall specify whether the citation was given to the defender personally or otherwise, and if otherwise, shall specify particularly the mode of citation. § 15.

Execution of Summons.

This summons executed by me, John Robson, Sheriff Officer, against C. D., defender, by delivering a copy to him personally, apprehended in presence of Adam Huie, residing in Lawnmarket, Edinburgh, this 2d *day of November, Eighteen hundred and fifty-three*

Ad. Huie, Witness.　　　　　　　　JOHN ROBSON, *Sheriff Officer.*

Where the case occurs of a defender being in a different shire, see Chap. VIII. *voce* Citation.

Non-appearance of Defender, and Decree in Absence.

The Act provides, That where the defender intends to state a defence, he shall enter appearance, by lodging with the Sheriff Clerk, at latest, on the day of compearance, a notice in the form of Schedule C. § 3.

A question on which difference of opinion is likely to arise here presents itself —If notice of appearance is not lodged on the sixth day, can it be afterwards lodged before decree passes? Looking to existing usage, and to the words, "with continuation of days," contained in the form of petitory summons annexed to the Statute, it may be argued that the day of compearance means the sixth day, if a Court-day, and if not, the first Court-day thereafter.

It would be extremely hazardous for a practitioner to put this construction on the Statute. It appears to us that the defender is allowed only six free days to lodge his notice of appearance ; and a talented author, whose contributions to the legal literature of Scotland entitle his opinions to very high respect, has indicated it to be his view that appearance by notice does not seem competent after the sixth day.

The pursuer's procurator having ascertained that no appearance has been entered for the defender, should enrol and lodge his summons before the first Court-day after the sixth day from expiry of the *induciæ*.

The provision of the Act of Sederunt 1839, § 23, that with his summons the pursuer must lodge all the deeds, accounts, and writings on which he founds, so far as in his possession, does not appear to apply where no appearance has been entered.

Hitherto decree in absence could not be obtained after the lapse of year and day from the date of the summons. The instance perished. A new and important provision is now introduced by § 15 of the statute, namely, that " where in any cause neither of the parties thereto shall, during the period of three consecutive months, have taken any proceeding therein, the action shall, at the expiration of that period, *eo ipso*, stand dismissed." Provision is made, however, as to reviving it within the following three, or in certain cases, six months.

This important clause raises some nice questions. It shall be adverted to more fully in the next chapter—*voce Reviving*. Meantime, we observe here, that the pursuer's procurator should keep the clause in view with respect to calling his cause, and that especially if he has used inhibition on the dependence. ~r~*ment has been used, the summons must be called within twen~ days from the compearance; or, if these expire in vacation, the first Court-day, else the arrestment falls. 1 and 2 Vict. 114, § 17, and A. S. § 154.

If the defender does not enter appearance, according to the statutory form, the pursuer is entitled to decree in absence, which will be written on the summons.

The pursuer then gets his account of expenses taxed by the clerk of Court or auditor. The convenient form will be to write it on the summons, and the decree will be as follows :—

> The Sheriff Substitute.—In respect that the defender has not entered appearance, decerns against him, in terms of the foregoing summons, with of taxed expenses.
>
> AND. JAMESON.

Against the decree in absence, the defender may, on certain terms and conditions, obtain himself reponed. See *Reponing*, Chap. VIII. As to amendment of a summons, see *Amendment*.

Entering appearance to Defend.

Where the defender intends to state a defence, he shall enter appearance by lodging with the Sheriff Clerk, at latest on the day of compearance, (See p 32) a notice in the form of Schedule C. annexed to the Act. § 3.

> *Notice of Appearance.*
>
> In the action *A. B* against *C. D.*
>
> *C. D.* designed as cabinet-maker residing in Castle Street, Edinburgh, defender, enters appearance to defend said action.
>
> *C. D.* Defender.
> (or)   *Alfred Bruce*, Agent for Defender.

Meeting with the Sheriff.

Where appearance has been entered, the Sheriff shall, on the first Court-day thereafter, or on any other Court-day to which the diet may be adjourned, not being later than eight days thereafter, hear parties or their procurators on the grounds of action and defence § 3

It is here proper to observe, that any case may, by consent of parties, be removed from the Ordinary Court Roll to the Small Debt Court. The section which provides for this is as follows: "It shall be competent in all civil cases above the value of L 12, competent before the Sheriff, for the parties to lodge in process a minute signed by themselves, or by their procurators, setting forth their agreement that the cause should be tried in the summary way provided in the said first recited Act (the Small Debt Act), and the Sheriff shall thereupon hear, try, and determine such action in such summary way; and in such case the whole powers and provisions of the said first recited Act, namely, the Small Debt Act, shall be held applicable to the said action; provided always, that the parties, or any of them, shall be entitled to appear and plead by a procurator of Court." § 23.

This minute of agreement may be competently lodged at any time after the calling of the cause. There is, however, an obvious expediency in lodging it at an early stage—if possible, at the first calling of the cause or meeting before the Sheriff. Such minute may be in the following terms :—

Minute agreeing to try a case under the Small Debt Act

Minute for *A. B* tailor and clothier in Edinburgh, and *C. D.* cabinet-maker, residing in Castle Street, there.

The parties agree that this cause shall be tried in the summary way provided in the Act 1 Vict c. 41.

> A B *or* ARTHUR ANGUS, *Procurator for A. B.*
> C D *or* ALFRED BRUCE, *Procurator for C. D.*

The Sheriff will then remit the case to the Small Debt Court,—and the interlocutor may be as follows :—

The Sheriff-substitute, in respect of the Joint-minute for the parties, No. of Process, remits this case to the Small Debt Court

> AND. JAMIESON.

But to resume the forms of the Ordinary Court :—

At the meeting with the Sheriff referred to, after notice of appearance has been given, the pursuer explains the ground of action, and the defender the nature of the defence § 3.

In the case of the summons, which we have given above, pursued before the Sheriff of Edinburgh, we shall suppose that there are defences, both preliminary and on the merits. Preliminary—that the defender's residence is not in the county of Edinburgh, but in that of Haddington, and only his place of business in Edinburgh; and on the merits, denial that the death of the horse was occasioned by the fault of the defender,—prescription as to the first two items of the account of furnishings, and overcharge as to the others.

Supposing this explained to the Sheriff, who is satisfied that no farther written pleadings are necessary, "he shall cause a minute, in the form of Schedule D. to be written on the summons, setting forth concisely the ground of defence, which minute shall be subscribed by the parties or their procurators, and the Sheriff shall thereupon close the record by writing under the said minute, " Record Closed," and signing and dating the same. § 3.

Minute at the first calling of Cause where the Defender makes compearance

Edinburgh, 9th November 1853

Act Angus —*Alt.* Bruce.

The defender's procurator stated that the defence was (1) That he resides in Haddington, and that the premises occupied by him in Castle Street, Edinburgh, are used only as a place of business. (2.) He admits that he borrowed a horse from the pursuer, which died, but not by his fault. (3.) That more than three years have elapsed from the date of the first two items of the account, and (4.) That the other items are overcharged. *Pleas—Preliminary—*No jurisdiction. *On merits.*—Not indebted in the value of the horse,—Prescription *quoad* first two items of the account As to the others, overcharge.

ARTHUR ANGUS, *Procurator for Pursuer.*
ALFRED BRUCE, *Procurator for Defender.*

Record Closed.—AND. JAMESON

The case will then proceed in the same way as if the record were closed after condescendence and answers.

We have quoted the clause of the statute with respect to the signing and closing of the record on this minute. The act constitutes the Sheriff sole judge of the necessity or not of further written pleadings. In the event of his thinking none necessary, he is left no choice as to writing the minute, and the agents none as to signing it. The expression in both cases is *shall.*

But should the case occur of the Sheriff being so satisfied, and after causing a minute to be written out, either of the parties, or their agents, refuse to sign it, there is no provision in the act, as to the course to be adopted. Shall the Sheriff certify the refusal, and order a record, by condescendence and answers, and deal with the recusant as in a question of expenses; or shall he treat the refusal as a case of default, and dismiss the action, or decern in terms of the summons, as the case may be; or shall he certify the refusal, and close the record, and proceed either to decide the case or order a proof, leaving to the party his remedy of advocation when competent ?

This question seems to be attended with much doubt, but we incline to think that the Sheriff may adopt any one of the courses mentioned But as he would doubtless, before adopting the last course, grant an adjournment if he should see that expedient, and would make a full minute of the procedure, and of the statement of the objection to close, we consider it not likely that difficulty will arise in this matter.

Making up Record on Condescendence and Defences.

If the Sheriff is satisfied that the record cannot be properly made up without condescendence and defences, he shall pronounce an order for the same
§ 3.

There must now be interlocutor sheets put into process, and the Sheriff at the meeting above-mentioned pronounces the order for condescendence and defences, which will be to this effect :—

> *Edinburgh, 9th November* 1853
>
> The Sheriff-substitute having heard parties (or their procurators) in explanation of the grounds of action, and the nature of the defence, appoints the pursuer to lodge a condescendence, and the defender to lodge defences, in terms of the Statute.
>
>   AND JAMISON

The condescendence is to be lodged with the Sheriff-clerk within six days after the order. § 3.

On failure to lodge the condescendence or defences within the statutory period, the Sheriff shall dismiss the action, or decern in terms of the summons, as the case may be, by default, unless it shall be made to appear to his satisfaction that the failure to lodge such paper arose from unavoidable or reasonable causes, in which case the Sheriff may allow the same to be received, on payment of such sum, in name of expenses, as he shall think just. § 6.

There is, however, a provision for prorogations, as to which see Chapter VIII., *voce* Prorogation

The condescendence must set forth articulately and as concisely as may be, without any argument or unnecessary matter, the facts necessary to found the conclusions of the summons, which the pursuer avers and is ready to prove, together with a note of pleas in law. § 3.

It must be signed either by the party himself, or by a procurator of court, or other person legally authorized to act, and shall state the name and designation of the person by whom drawn, otherwise it shall not be received. A. S. § 63.

In the case above supposed the condescendence may be in these terms —

CONDISCENDENCE for *A. B*, Tailor and Clothier in Edinburgh,—*Pursuer*,

IN THE

ACTION at his instance against *C D.*, Cabinetmaker, residing in Castle Street, Edinburgh,—*Defender*

1. On or about the 29th December 1849, the defender borrowed from the pursuer a brown horse, of the value of L 20 sterling, which died of inflammation next day in the possession of the defender, after having been ridden by him from Edinburgh to Glasgow, within the space of five hours. His death was caused by having been so ridden with undue speed.

2. Of the several dates set forth in the account libelled on, the pursuer supplied, on the order, and for the use and behoof of the defender, the several articles therein mentioned, at the prices therein stated, amounting in all to L.27, 3s. 6d.

8. The value of the horse, and the amount of the account, although frequently demanded. are still resting-owing unpaid.

PLEAS IN LAW.

1. The defender having borrowed the pursuer's horse and caused his death by riding him with undue speed, is liable in the value thereof

2 The articles of furnishing mentioned in the account libelled having been ordered and received by the defender, he is liable in the price thereof.

In respect whereof,

ARTHUR ANGUS, *Procurator for Pursuer.*

Drawn by me.

In the Court of Session where the condescendence is from the first annexed to the summons, and is by the Act declared part of it, as was the case in Sheriff Court procedure previous to the passing of the new Act,—' In ' every thing which is of the essence of the action, whether in the averment ' of what is an essential quality, or what is a proper ground of action, the ' summons and condescendence must be perfect and complete, *ab initio,* and ' no change can be introduced into the revised condescendence which alters ' the summons, or the annexed condescendence, which is part of the sum- ' mons, in such matters. ' Such change can only be by an amendment of ' ' the summons, on leave obtained.' ''—See Dallas and Mann, 14th June 1853, 25 Jur 448 The rule was so expressed by the Lord Justice-Clerk, as to be enforced both in the Court of Session and Sheriff Court. Though this was prior to the passing of the recent Sheriff Court Statute, we consider it proper here to bring it under notice, as requiring the attention of the practitioner when framing the condescendence.

The defender must lodge his defences within ten days after the lodging of the condescendence, setting forth therein articulately his answers to such condescendence. § 3.

Also, where necessary, setting forth articulately, under a separate head, any counter-statements necessary for his defence, which he avers, and is ready to prove, to be framed as concisely as possible, without any argument or unnecessary matter. § 3.

And to the defences shall be appended a note of the defender's pleas in law. § 3

Alongst with his defences, the defender must also produce the deeds and writings on which he founds, so far as the same are in his custody, or within his power, and if they are not within his custody or power, he shall state where he believes them to be, and crave a diligence for recovering them. A. of S 1839, sec. 33.

In the case supposed the defences may be in this form :—

DEFENCES for *C. D —Defender,*

TO THE

CONDESCENDENCE for *A B.—Pursuer.*

1. The borrowing and death of the horse are admitted *Quoad ultra* denied

2. Admitted that the goods were furnished on the defender's order, but explained that the prices thereof, as stated in the account libelled on, are overcharged to the extent of at least one third. More than three years have elapsed from the date of the first two items of the account, and it is not a continuous account.

3. The defender is not resting owing as stated.

DEFENDER'S COUNTER STATEMENT.

1. The defender is a cabinetmaker in Edinburgh, and has a place of business in Castle Street there, but his residence is at Sweethope, in the county of Haddington.

2. The said horse, when borrowed from the pursuer, laboured under a fatal disease, of which the defender was not made aware; and it was under the influence, and in consequence of that disease that he died, without any undue use of him having been made by the defender.

3. The price and value of said horse, even had he been sound, did not exceed the sum of L.13.

PLEAS IN LAW.
Preliminary.

1. No jurisdiction, in respect the defender resides beyond the limits of the county.

On the Merits.

1. The horse having died without any fault on the part of the defender, he has incurred no liability therefor. *Et separatim.* The value put upon the horse by the pursuer is extravagant.

2. The first two items of the account of furnishings, which is not continuous, have undergone the triennial prescription.

3. The goods sued for being overcharged, the defender is not liable in the amount sued for, and is not resting-owing as libelled.

In respect whereof,

ALFRED BRUCE, *Defender's Procurator.*
Drawn by me.

When these papers have been lodged, the Sheriff-clerk shall transmit the process to the Sheriff. § 4.

Meeting with the Sheriff.

The Sheriff, as soon as may be, and at latest within six days after the lodging of the defences, shall appoint the parties or their procurators to meet him; § 4. It may be noticed that the words are, that the appointment shall be made within six days, not that the meeting shall be within six days, though the latter appears to have been intended, if we may judge from the enactment which immediately follows, with reference to the meeting after the lodging of revised condescendence and defences, where the order is to meet within six days.

This meeting before the Sheriff, after lodgment of condescendence and defences, may be adjourned where the Sheriff sees fit, but for no longer period than eight days § 4.

The Statute makes provisions as to several things which may be done at this meeting, or at the adjourned meeting

(1.) Dilatory defences, when stated, are, where possible, to be disposed of at once; or the Sheriff may reserve consideration of them till a future stage of the cause. § 4.

2 If the pursuer is willing to close the record on summons and defences, it is implied that the record must be so closed § 4

3 Where the pursuer is not willing so to close, the Sheriff may, if he thinks fit, order one revisal of the condescendence and defences respectively, § 4, which shall be made on the original papers, unless otherwise directed.

(4.) The sheriff shall allow the pursuer, or his procurator, to put on record, in concise and articulate form, if not already done, his answers to the defender's statement of facts.

Or a simple minute of denial, where that shall be deemed by the Sheriff to be sufficient. § 4.

(5) And shall allow each party to adjust his own part of the record § 4.

(6) And shall strike out of the record any matter which he may deem to be either irrelevant or unnecessary. § 4.

(7) The record shall then be closed by the Sheriff writing on the interlocutor sheets the words, "Record closed," and signing and dating the same § 4.

To apply these provisions to the circumstances of the case which we have supposed. The parties are at issue on the facts out of which the *preliminary* plea arises, namely, the defender having a residence in Edinburgh or not. The Sheriff, therefore, is not in a situation to dispose of that plea.

The pursuer is not in a situation to close on summons and defences, as the defender's counter-statement remains unanswered.

But it seems a case in which issue in fact would be sufficiently joined by the pursuer putting on record answers to the defender's statement of facts. Supposing this, the answers might be as follows—attached to the original condescendence —

Answers for Pursuer to Defender's Statement.

1 Admitted that the defender is a cabinetmaker in Edinburgh and that he has a residence at Sweethope, in the county of Haddington Denied, *quoad ultra*, and explained that the defender has also a residence attached to his place of business in Castle Street, Edinburgh, where he eats, and occasionally sleeps.

2. Denied, and explained that the horse had only a slight cold, of which the defender was informed when he borrowed him.

3. Denied.

In respect whereof, &c.

ARTHUR ANGUS, Procurator for Pursuer.
Drawn by me.

The only point now remaining to be met by the defender is the allegation that he has a residence attached to his place of business in Edinburgh, where he eats and occasionally sleeps. In adjusting the record, the defender must admit or deny this. Supposing him then to amend his counter-statement (on page 38), as follows —

> The defender eats and occasionally sleeps in an apartment attached to his premises in Castle Street, but his family residence is at Sweethope

Such alteration should be made by marginal addition; and marginal additions must be authenticated by the Sheriff's initials, in terms of the provision in § 45 of the Act of Sederunt of 1839, that "All alterations or additions made on the margin of the record, at any period before it is closed, shall be authenticated by the initials of the Sheriff."

After adjusting, the Record is closed by the following words on the Interlocutor sheet —

Edinburgh,   1853.

Record closed.

AND. JAMESON.

It may here be observed, that the Record thus closed may, if the case afterwards goes to appeal on any point, be opened up by the Sheriff <i>ex proprio motu</i>, if it shall appear to him not to have been properly made up. § 16. A. of S. 1839, § 99.

The Sheriff would probably consider that there are now materials for disposing of the preliminary defences, but that the case on the merits required proof

The Sheriff would therefore, of the same date, but by separate Interlocutor, either make avizandum, or appoint a day to hear the parties on the preliminary defence.

Edinburgh,   1853.

The Sheriff substitute makes avizandum with the process.

AND. JAMESON.

OR,

The Sheriff-substitute appoints parties or their procurators to be heard on the   day of   on the preliminary defence.

AND. JAMESON.

Disposing of Preliminary Defences.

The next interlocutor would be one disposing of the preliminary defence; and the Sheriff is to state his grounds, either in the interlocutor, or in a note appended thereto. § 13.

Supposing the plea sustained, the interlocutor might be this :—

Edinburgh,   1853

The Sheriff-Substitute having considered the process (and heard the procurators for the parties, *if so*), finds it admitted that the defender has a residence at Sweethope in Haddingtonshire, and that he resides there with his family, though he may occasionally sleep in the apartment attached to his place of business in Castle Street, Edinburgh. Finds that his residence in Haddingtonshire is his legal domicile, and that he is not subject to the jurisdiction of this Court. Therefore sustains the preliminary plea of no jurisdiction, dismisses the action, and decerns; Finds the pursuer liable in expenses, and remits the account, when lodged, to the auditor, to tax and report.

AND. JAMESON

Note.—(Here the views on which the Sheriff proceeded may be stated.)

Against this interlocutor, if pronounced by the Sheriff-Substitute, the pursuer may appeal to the Sheriff. An interlocutor disposing of a preliminary defence being one of those which may be so appealed under the provisions of § 19.

If he is to do so, he must (§ 16), within seven days from the date of the interlocutor, engross and sign by himself, or his agent, under the interlocutor appealed against, the words—

" I appeal against this interlocutor "

ARTHUR ANGUS, for the Pursuer.

The mode of further prosecuting the appeal is stated below, *voce Appeal.*

On the other hand, supposing the Sheriff-substitute to be of opinion that there is jurisdiction, the interlocutor might be this :—

Edinburgh,   1853.

The Sheriff-substitute having advised the process (and heard parties' procurators, *if so*), Finds it admitted that the place of business of the defender is in Castle Street, Edinburgh, and that the defender eats and occasionally sleeps there, though he has another residence in Haddington, where his family resides: Finds, in respect of his residence in Edinburgh, that he is subject to the jurisdiction of this Court; Repels the preliminary plea stated for the defender; and on the merits allows to both parties a proof of their averments; and appoints the proof to proceed within the Sheriff Court House, Edinburgh, on the day of   at   o'clock.

AND. JAMESON

Note.—(Here the views on which the Sheriff proceeded may be stated)

Against this interlocutor the defender may appeal within seven days, in the same manner as already explained.

There is a third mode of dealing with preliminary pleas, which is, " reserving consideration of them till a future stage of the cause." § 4.

Closing on Minute of Denial.

Let us suppose that in the case we have instanced, the record, in place of being closed on articulate answers for the pursuer to the defender's statement, were closed on a general minute of denial by the pursuer. Such minute will be in this form :—

MINUTE of DENIAL for *A. B.* Pursuer,

IN CAUSA

v.

C. D. Defender.

The pursuer denies the defender's statement of facts, in so far as inconsistent with the condescendence

In respect whereof, &c

Drawn by ARTHUR ANGUS, *Pursuer's Pror*

In this case facts would require to be ascertained in order to dispose of the preliminary defence; the Sheriff would probably, after writing the words " record closed " on the interlocutor sheet, pronounce as follows :—

The Sheriff-substitute reserves consideration of the preliminary pleas; Allows both parties a proof of their averments; and appoints the proof to proceed within the Sheriff Court House, Edinburgh, on the   day of   at   o'clock.
AND. JAMESON.

Against such an interlocutor an appeal to the Sheriff would be competent; not in respect of its reserving the preliminary defences, but as allowing a proof.

Under § 19 of the statute, an interlocutor allowing a proof is one of those which may be appealed to the Sheriff, when pronounced by the Sheriff-substitute. Such interlocutor, in cases above L 40, may also be advocated for trial by jury, in terms of the Act 6 Geo. IV. c. 120, if the right so to advocate with a view to jury trial be not taken away by §§ 24 and 25 of the recent Act; on which question there may be room for doubts, as will be more fully explained in the observations below, *voce Review.*

Suppose the interlocutor allowing proof neither appealed nor advocated, the case would then proceed to proof on the pleas, both preliminary and on the merits; or the Sheriff might order the proof only on the matters involved in the preliminary plea; in which case his interlocutor might be as follows :—

The Sheriff-substitute allows to both parties a proof of the matter of fact on which the preliminary plea of the defender is rested, and appoints the proof to proceed, &c.

In all cases where the preliminary plea is distinct, and in no way involved in the merits, on which there remains behind a case more or less complicated, a proof of the facts connected with the preliminary plea will likely first be ordered. Indeed the Act seems to contemplate this being done even before the record is closed; and in many cases it will be found expedient to adopt that course.

Making up and Closing Record on Revised Conaescendence and Defences.

In the event of the record not being closed in one or other of the modes above stated, at the said meeting or adjourned meeting, in consequence of the Sheriff thinking fit to order revisal, he shall order one revisal of the condescendence and defences respectively, and unless he assign a special reason for directing the contrary, the matter to be added on revisal shall be put upon the original papers. § 4.

It will be observed that power is here given to the Sheriff to allow the revisal to be made by the lodgment of new papers, instead of alterations on, and marginal additions to, the original papers. But where such allowance is given, the Sheriff must assign a special reason for doing so. In most cases the reason will be the extent and importance of the alterations or additions proposed; and it has been well remarked by Mr Sheriff Barclay, that " a revisal by new papers is preferable to tinkering by marginals, which ought to be confined to trivial corrections." The practitioner will, however, keep in view, that when the revisal is to be by new papers, a " special reason " for its being so must be embodied in the order for revisal.

As to the nature of the alterations and additions competent on revisal, it is necessary to keep in view the doctrine enunciated by the Lord Justice-Clerk in the case of Dallas and Mann, 14th June 1853, to which reference has been already made. No change can be introduced into the revised condescendence which alters the ground of action as set forth in the summons and explained in the condescendence. If such change be required, it should be by amendment of the summons, on leave obtained.

The statute prescribes no time for the lodgment of the revised condescendence and answers. But by the Act of Sederunt of 1839, § 59, it is provided that the Sheriff shall, by special order, fix the time within which each paper shall be lodged, except in so far as herein before or after provided, and the clerk shall not receive any paper after the time so fixed, except by consent of the opposite agent written thereon, and subscribed by him A. S. § 59. The Sheriff will therefore fix the time for lodging the revised papers according to circumstances.

It is unnecessary to give any form of revised papers.

As soon as the revised defences are lodged, the Sheriff Clerk shall transmit the process to the Sheriff. § 4.

The Sheriff shall thereupon appoint parties or their procurators to meet him as soon as may be, and at latest six days after lodging of the revised defences. § 4.

This meeting, like the former, may be adjourned, but for no more than eight days. At it the same procedure which has been already mentioned as to adjusting and closing the record, under the Sheriff's correction, shall take place. § 4

It is to be observed, that a closed record may, if the case goes to appeal on any point, be opened up by the Sheriff *ex proprio motu*, if it shall appear to him not to have been properly made up. § 16, and A. of S. (1839) § 99.

Hearing Parties on Closed Record.

It is competent to the Sheriff, on the written consent of both parties, to dispose of the cause upon the papers, without farther statement or argument, § 5; and should that course be followed, the minute of consent may be in this form, the same being written on the interlocutor sheets :—

> Parties crave that the Sheriff shall dispose of this cause on the closed record, without further statement or argument.
>
> In respect whereof, &c

If the parties do not consent, the Sheriff shall hear them or their procurators on the merits of the cause, and upon their respective pleas, or, where he deems it necessary, shall order a proof. § 5.

It will be observed that the hearing may take place at the same diet as the closing of the record; and where the case is simple, the hearing may then advantageously take place. But where the pleas are such as to require preparation, in order to their being properly discussed, it is desirable that the parties, or their procurators, should be heard at an adjourned diet.

After hearing parties, unless the Sheriff deems proof to be necessary, he shall pronounce judgment with the least possible delay. § 5.

Order for Proof.

When the Sheriff, either before or after the hearing, deems proof to be necessary, he shall appoint a diet therefor on an early day; § 5. The form of the interlocutor ordering proof has already been given

This is one of the interlocutors which, if pronounced by the Sheriff-substitute, may be appealed to the Sheriff; § 19. For the mode of entering and prosecuting the appeal, see below, *voce Appeal.*

The proof is appointed to proceed before the Sheriff, but it is provided that it shall be competent, where any witness or haver is resident beyond the jurisdiction of the court, or by reason of age, infirmity, or sickness, is unable to attend the diet of proof, to grant commission to any person competent to take and report in writing the evidence of such witness or haver. § 10.

The statute does not provide any form of application for such commission; neither does it prescribe the time at which it shall be made.

As to the form—The application may be made by motion in court, supported by such evidence, affidavit, or otherwise, as the Sheriff may require. As to the time—the application may competently be made at any time before the proof is closed, yet it is obviously expedient that it should be made at the diet at which the proof is ordered, when that is possible.

It will be observed, however, that the statute does not interfere with the provisions of the Act of Sederunt, as to the obtaining a commission to take the evidence, to lie *in retentis,* of any witness " about to leave Scotland, or whose testimony is in danger of being lost on account of extreme old age or dangerous sickness." A. S. § 73.

Citation for Proof.

A copy, certified by the Sheriff-clerk, of the interlocutor fixing such diet, or of that portion of it which relates to that matter, is a sufficient warrant to any sheriff-officer in Scotland (acting within his own county) to cite witnesses and havers at the instance of either the pursuer or defender. § 11.

But when executed in another county, it must be endorsed by the Sheriff-clerk of such other county, who shall make and date such indorsation. § 11.

Citation of Witnesses and Havers.

James Thomson, weaver, residing at Bannockburn, in the county of Stirling, you are hereby cited to attend in the Sheriff Court of the county of Edinburgh, on the 15th day of December current, at eleven o'clock, within the Court House there, to give evidence for the pursuer in the action at the instance of *A B.,* tailor and clothier in Edinburgh, pursuer, against *C. D,* cabinetmaker, residing in Castle Street there, defender, and that under the penalty of Forty Shillings sterling, if you fail to attend; (if a haver say,) and you are required to bring with you the following books or documents, namely (here specify them.)

Dated this 12th day of December 1853

THOMAS MALCOLM, *Sheriff-Officer.*

Officer's Execution.

Upon the 12th day of December 1853 I duly cited James Thomson, weaver, residing at Bannockburn, in the county of Stirling, to attend in the Sheriff Court of the county of Edinburgh, on the 15th day of December 1853, at eleven o'clock, within the Court House at Edinburgh, to give evidence for the pursuer, in the action at the instance of *A.B.*, tailor and clothier in Edinburgh, pursuer, against *C D.*, cabinet-maker, residing in Castle Street there, defender; (*if a haver say*), and I also required him to bring with him the following books or documents, namely (*here specify them.*) This I did by delivering a just copy of citation to the above effect, signed by me, to the said James Thomson personally (*or otherwise as the case may be.*)

THOMAS MALCOLM, *Sheriff-Officer*

If a witness or haver, duly cited on a citation of at least forty-eight hours, shall fail to appear, he shall forfeit and pay a penalty not exceeding forty shillings, unless a reasonable excuse be offered and sustained by the Sheriff, for which penalty decree shall be given by the Sheriff in favour of the party on whose behalf he was cited; § 11. And farther, the Sheriff may grant second diligence for compelling the attendance of such witness or haver—the expense of which shall, in like manner, be decerned for against the witness or haver, unless a special reason to the contrary be stated and sustained

Although the Statute only makes provision for a citation of 48 hours in all cases, it must be observed, that where the witness does not reside within the county, the citation should be proportionally longer according to the distance. No prudent practitioner will enforce second diligence against a witness whose residence is in another county where the *induciæ* of citation has only been 48 hours,—particularly if the citation has not been a personal one.

Conduct of the Proof.

Before stating the mode in which, under the recent Statute, the proof is to be conducted, we shall here give a summary of the late change in the law of evidence.

These changes have been effected by three Statutes, viz:—

3 & 4 Vict. c. 59 (7th August 1840);
15 & 16 Vict. c. 27 (17th June 1852);
and 16 Vict. c. 20 (9th May 1853).

With respect to the **Persons competent as Witnesses.**

Relationship—as father, mother, son, daughter, brother, sister, by consanguinity or affinity, or uncle or aunt, nephew or niece, by consanguinity of the party adducing the witness, form no objection to the admissibility; nor is it competent to any witness to decline to be examined and give evidence on the ground of any such relationship. 1840, § 1.

Interest—No person adduced as a witness in Scotland, shall be excluded from giving evidence by reason of interest. 1852, § 1.

It shall be competent to adduce and examine as a witness, in any action or proceeding in Scotland, any party to such action or proceeding, or the husband or wife of any party, whether he or she shall be individually named in the record or proceeding, or not. 1853, § 3.

But neither husband nor wife is compelled to give evidence against the other as to any matter communicated during the marriage. 1853, § 3.

> ("But nothing herein contained shall render any person, or the husband or wife of any person, who, in any criminal proceeding, is charged with the commission of any indictable offence, or any offence punishable on summary conviction, competent or compellable to give evidence for or against himself or herself, his wife or her husband, except so far as presently competent." 1853, § 3).

"The adducing of any party as a witness in any cause by the adverse party, shall not have the effect of a reference to oath of the party so adduced;" but it is not competent thereafter to refer the cause, or any part of it, to his oath. 1853, § 5.

None of the enactments of the Act 16 Vict. cap. 20 (1853) apply to any action, suit, or proceeding, instituted in Scotland in consequence of adultery, or for dissolving any marriage, or for breach of promise of marriage, or in any action of declarator of marriage, nullity of marriage, putting to silence, legitimacy or bastardy, or in any action of adherence or separation. § 4

Agency and Partial Counsel.—It is declared "not imperative on the court to reject any witness against whom it is objected that he or she has, without the permission of the court, and without the consent of the party objecting, been present in court during all or any part of the proceedings; but it shall be competent for the court, in its discretion, to admit the witness, where it shall appear to the court that the presence of the witness was not the consequence of culpable negligence or criminal intent, and that the witness has not been unduly instructed or influenced by what took place, during his or her presence, or that injustice will not be done by his or her examination." 1840, § 3.

No person adduced as a witness is excluded by reason of agency or of

partial counsel, or by reason of having appeared without citation, or by reason of having been precognosced subsequently to the date of citation
1852, § 1.

Provided that it shall not be competent to adduce as a witness any person
who shall, at the time when he is so adduced as a witness, be acting as
agent in the action or proceeding in which he is so adduced (except so far as
at present competent); 1852, § 1. This enactment, excluding the agent,
was repealed 1853, § 2.

Infamy.—No person adduced as a witness is to be excluded from giving
evidence by reason of having been convicted of, or having suffered punishment for, crime   1852, § 1.

With respect to the **mode of Examination.**

In Initialibus.—It shall not be necessary for any judge in Scotland, or
for any person acting as commissioner in taking evidence, to examine any
witnesses *in initialibus*   Provided always, that it shall nevertheless be
competent for any such judge or person acting as commissioner, or the
party against whom the witness shall be called, to examine any witness *in
initialibus,* as heretofore.   1840, § 2.

Cross.—It shall be competent for the party against whom a witness is
produced and sworn *in causa,* to examine such witness not in cross only, but
in causa   1840, § 4.

Confidentiality.—Where any person, who is or has been an agent, shall be
adduced and examined as a witness for his client, touching any matter or
thing to prove which he could not competently have been adduced and examined, according to the existing law and practice of Scotland, it shall not
be competent to the party adducing such witness, to object, on the ground
of confidentiality, to any question proposed to be put to such witness on
matter pertinent to the issue   1852, § 1

Previous Statements—It shall be competent to examine any witness, who
may be adduced in any action or proceeding, as to whether he has, on any
specified occasion, made a statement, on any matter pertinent to the issue,
different from the evidence given by him in such action or proceeding
1852, § 3.

And it shall be competent, in the course of such action or proceeding, to
adduce evidence to prove that such witness has made such different statement on the occasion specified. 1852, § 3.

Credibility.—Nothing herein contained shall affect the right of any party,
in the action or proceeding in which such witness (*i. e.* a witness convicted
of crime, or having interest, &c.) shall be adduced, to examine him on any
point tending to affect his credibility. 1852, § 1.

Recal.—It shall be competent to the presiding judge, or other person before whom any trial or proof shall proceed, on the motion of either party, to permit any witness, who shall have been examined in the course of such trial or proof, to be recalled, 1852 § 4.

As to *Conduct of the Proof,* the provisions of the New Sheriff Court Act are these :—

(1) The diet of proof shall not be adjourned, unless on special cause shewn, which shall be set forth in the interlocutor making the adjournment; and the evidence shall be taken, as far as may be, continuously, and with as little interval as the circumstances admit of. § 10

(2) The evidence is to be led before the Sheriff, § 10, who shall take a note of the evidence with his own hand, unless unavoidably prevented, in which case he shall dictate to any competent person he shall select. § 10.

(3.) The note of evidence shall set forth, not by question and answer, but in the form of a narrative—the witnesses examined, and the testimony given by each, and the documents adduced. § 10.

(4) And any evidence, whether oral or written, tendered and rejected, with the grounds of such rejection § 10.

(5.) And a note of any objections taken to the admission of evidence, whether oral or written, which had been allowed to be received. § 10.

(6) The note of the evidence given by each witness shall be read over to him by the Sheriff, and signed by the witness, if he can write, on the last page, in open court, before the witness is dismissed. § 10.

(7.) The Sheriff's note of the evidence shall be forthwith lodged in process. § 10.

(8) The Sheriff Clerk shall mark the documents admitted in evidence, and also separately any documents tendered and rejected. § 10.

(9.) The Sheriff is also empowered to remit to persons of skill or other persons to report on any matter of fact; and where such remit shall be made, of consent of both parties, the Sheriff shall hold the report to be final and conclusive with respect to the matter of such remit. § 10.

(10.) The proof shall be taken "in open Court." § 10.

The words "in open Court" here employed seem to us to imply that the procedure shall be in public—in the Ordinary Court, at least some place which is known to the public as the place where such proceedings are conducted,—and not merely in "an apartment to which all feeling interest may have access during the proof." In expressing this opinion, however, we find ourselves differing from the experienced author formerly referred to, who has indicated his opinion of the statutory meaning in the words we have here quoted.

The Sheriff is "to take a note of the evidence with his own hand, unless unavoidably prevented," &c　In carrying out this provision, we would respectfully suggest the practical expediency of having the "proofs" written on sheets of paper uniformly ruled, and having lettered margins　Practitioners should also be enjoined, when having the proofs transcribed for reference, to write the copy on similarly ruled and lettered paper—page for page　The strict adoption of this course would promote uniformity in all the Sheriff Courts of Scotland, and greatly facilitate reference by both the Bench and the Bar.

The Sheriff may allow oral argument during the leading of the proof where it is necessary, taking a note of authorities cited, where required by either of the parties ; and a note of the argument where he shall himself see fit. § 12.

Appeal During the Proof.

With two exceptions, which will be noticed below, no interlocutor of the Sheriff-substitute on the admissibility of evidence can be appealed to the Sheriff prior to the closing of the proof. § 17.

But on the proof being declared closed, or within seven days thereafter, it is competent to appeal against all or any of such interlocutors. § 17.

In the event of such appeal being taken, the provisions under sec. 16 as to the mode of appeal and supporting it, come into operation.

And the Sheriff shall pronounce such judgment on the appeal as shall be just, and shall appoint any evidence which he may think ought not to have been rejected, to be taken before the case shall be advised on its merits. § 17.

The exceptions above referred to, and as to which the Sheriff's judgment also is declared subject to review, § 18, though the mode does not seem to be specified, are these :—

If a person, whether party to the cause or not, plead confidentiality with reference either to documentary or oral evidence, such person may take an appeal to the Sheriff at the time in open court. § 18.

The same provision applies in the case of any person not a party to the cause, who may object to produce writings, whether on pleas of alleged hypothec or otherwise. § 18.

In either of these cases the appeal shall be minuted by the Sheriff-substitute, and thereupon such part of the proceedings as may be necessary for the disposal of such appeal, or as the Sheriff may require, shall be transmitted to the Sheriff, who shall dispose of the same summarily, but may appoint a hearing before giving judgment. § 18.

But such appeals, in the two cases last mentioned, shall not be held to remove the cause from before the Substitute as regards any point or points not necessarily dependent upon the interlocutor or judgment appealed from As to all such points the cause may be proceeded with as if no such appeal had been taken § 18.

In all interlocutors by the Sheriff-substitute or Sheriff, deciding on the admissibility of evidence, or on any plea of confidentiality, or in a note appended thereto, the grounds of judgment must be stated. § 13.

Hearing Parties after Proof.

The parties, or their procurators, are entitled to be heard orally when the case shall be ripe for judgment, and on the import of any concluded proof. § 12.

No written argumentative pleading is competent; but the Sheriff shall, if required by either of the parties, take a note of the authorities cited in the course of the oral argument, and also where he shall see fit, of the argument, and such notes shall form part of the process § 12.

Decree after Proof.

The Sheriff is then to decide the case with the least possible delay. § 5.

If he disposes, in whole or in part, of the merits of the cause, or disposes of a dilatory defence, or sists process, or gives interim decree, he is required to set forth in the interlocutor, or in a note appended to and issued along with it, the grounds on which he has proceeded. § 13.

In all cases of proof it is the duty of the Judge to separate his findings of fact from those in law.

Every decree for expenses pronounced after the passing of the Act shall be held to include a decree for the expense of extracting the same. § 14.

The Sheriff-substitute or Sheriff may correct any merely clerical error in any of his judgments at any time before the proceedings have been transmitted to the Judge or court of review, not being later than seven days from the date of such judgment. § 20.

Appeal to the Sheriff.

What Interlocutors may be Appealed.

Until an interlocutor has been pronounced disposing in whole or in part of the merits of the case, it is not competent to appeal to the Sheriff against any interlocutor of the Sheriff-substitute, with the following exceptions, viz. :—

An interlocutor disposing of a dilatory defence.
Or sisting process.   } § 19.
Or allowing a proof.
Or on admissibility of evidence to the extent above stated.

It is provided, however, that in every case in which an appeal is taken against any interlocutor, it shall be competent to appeal also against all or any of the interlocutors previously pronounced, whether before or after the date of closing the record, or whether the record has been closed or not. § 19

But it may be doubted whether, under the provisions of sections 16 and 17, appeals as to the admissibility of evidence are not limited to the period specified in § 17.

The Sheriff shall pronounce such judgment on the appeal as shall be just § 19.

It shall be competent for the Sheriff, if he thinks fit, to pronounce interlocutors in time of vacation, in all causes, whether summary or not. § 44.

It shall be lawful for any Sheriff to pronounce and sign any interlocutor, judgment, or decree, when furth of his sheriffdom. § 47

Appeal to the Sheriff.

Mode of Entering and Prosecuting.

The party who proposes to appeal against any judgment of the Sheriff-substitute, shall, within seven days from the date thereof, engross and sign by himself or his agent, under the interlocutor appealed against, the words, " I appeal against this interlocutor." § 16

Thereafter it is competent for the appellant to lodge, within eight days, a reclaiming petition against the said judgment, which petition the Sheriff Clerk shall forthwith transmit to the Sheriff, who may order answers thereto, and shall thereafter dispose of the appeal; § 16. It would appear that the word " thereafter" means after expiry of the seven days, and not after the engrossing of the minute of appeal, as there is no provision that such minute shall be dated.

Or the party appealing may intimate, by notice lodged with the Sheriff-Clerk within the said eight days, his desire to be heard orally before the Sheriff, in which case the Sheriff shall hear the parties or their procurators on such appeal, and shall dispose of it § 16.

The Sheriff may, in cases requiring despatch, order a reclaiming petition and answers instead of the oral hearing

But it is not competent both to receive a reclaiming petition, and hear the parties orally. § 16.

If within eight days no reclaiming petition shall be lodged, and neither party shall desire to be heard orally before the Sheriff, the Sheriff may proceed to dispose of the appeal without farther argument. § 16.

As already stated, the Sheriff, when the cause is before him on any point, may open up the Record *ex proprio motu*, if it shall appear to him not to have been properly made up. § 16.

As to the effect of neither party taking any proceeding in an action for three consecutive months, see Chapter VIII. *voce Reviving.*

Review by the Court of Session.

An important question in the construction of the Act, and affecting the matter of review, here again presents itself, viz. whether the provisions, with respect to review, apply to cases in dependence prior to the 1st of November next, or only to cases instituted after that date. Our views upon the general question have been already explained. As there is no saving clause in the statute as to depending cases, we are of opinion it applies to them, and that where they do not exceed in value L.25, they cannot be brought under review of the Court of Session, unless on those special grounds of corruption, malice, &c which render judgments under the Small Debt Act liable to such review.

There were under the former system of procedure two modes of review by the Court of Session, viz appeal to the Circuit Courts, and advocation, suspension, and reduction, in the Court at Edinburgh.

Appeal to the Circuit Courts.

Appeal to the next Circuit Court of the Justiciary Circuit within which the court whose sentence was appealed from was situated, was, by 54 Geo. III. chap 67, competent in any case where the value did not exceed L 25. That right of appeal, unless to the extent already referred to, is now taken away. It is declared that it shall not be competent, except as hereinafter specially provided, to remove from a Sheriff Court, or to bring under review of the Court of Session, or of the Circuit Court of Justiciary, or of any other court or tribunal whatever, by advocation, appeal, suspension, or reduction, or in any other manner of way, any cause not exceeding the value of L.25 sterling, or any interlocutor, judgment, or decree pronounced, or which shall be pronounced in such cause by the Sheriff. § 22.

Advocation.

There were three kinds of advocation competent, viz —

(1.) By 50 Geo. III. chap. 112, § 36, advocations of interlocutory judgments of the Sheriff might be brought on the grounds of incompetency, including defective jurisdiction—personal objection to the judge, and privilege of party; also of contingency. In these cases no leave of the inferior judge was necessary. In the following cases such advocation was competent only with leave of the inferior judge, viz. on the ground of legal objection to the mode of proof, or with respect to some change of possession, or to an interim decree for a partial payment.

By the new statute it is declared, § 24, that it shall be competent in any cause exceeding the value of L.25, to take to review of the Court of Session—

1. Any interlocutor of a Sheriff sisting process.
2. And any interlocutor giving interim decree for payment of money.
3. And any interlocutor disposing of the whole merits of the cause, although no decision has been given as to expenses, and although expenses, if such have been found due, have not been modified or decerned for.

But it shall not be competent to take to review any interlocutor, judgment, or decree of a Sheriff, not being an interlocutor of one or other of those descriptions. § 24.

It is then declared that the provisions of 50 Geo. III. chap. 112, and 6 Geo. IV. chap. 120, "are, in so far as inconsistent with this enactment, repealed." § 24.

The procedure in advocations of interlocutory judgments was as follows: After caution had been found (where caution was necessary) the note of advocation was presented in the Bill-Chamber, with a statement of facts and pleas annexed. If the note was passed by the Lord Ordinary in the Bill-Chamber, intimation thereof was made, and after fifteen days the note might be called, and then enrolled in the weekly printed roll of the Court of Session.

(2.) Another species of advocation was that allowed by 6 Geo. IV. chap. 120 (Judicature Act) § 40. The words of the act are: that in all " cases originating in the inferior court, in which the claim is in amount above L.40 sterling, as soon as an order or interlocutor allowing a proof has been pronounced in the inferior court (unless it be an interlocutor allowing a proof to lie *in retentis*, or granting diligence for the recovery or production of papers), it shall be competent to either of the parties who may conceive that the case ought to be tried by jury, to remove the process into the Court of Session by bill of advocation, which shall be passed at once, without discussion and without caution."

In these advocations no caution was necessary. The note had no statement of facts or pleas appended, and it was presented in the Bill-Chamber, and then transmitted to one of the depute-clerks of Session.—See Corry, 12th July 1842, 4 D. 1514. A certificate by the clerk of the note being lodged, written on a copy thereof, stopped procedure in the inferior court, and fifteen days after intimation, it might be called, and thereafter enrolled in the weekly roll.

Some doubts are entertained whether this kind of advocation is not abolished by the recent statute. It appears to us that it is not abolished. The expression in § 24 differs from that in § 22. In the latter it is that it shall not be competent " to *remove from a Sheriff Court*, or to bring under review," &c. In the former it is simply that " it shall not be competent to *take to review* any interlocutor," &c. Such advocations, however, are for the purpose of having the interlocutor *not reviewed*, but expressly carried into effect —in a way and manner which the party thinks preferable to any competent in the Sheriff Court. The object in fact is " to remove" the case from that court. These advocations, and the privileges under them, are not abolished in express terms. To hold that they are so, by implication, seems to require a very unnatural construction of the words of the act; and, moreover, that view, unless it be supposed that the mode of trial in question is abolished, involves the practical inconvenience, that the case, after having been disposed of on a proof taken before the Sheriff, might be brought up to the Court of Session for a jury trial, while the last Court of Session Act 13 and 14 Vict. cap. 36, § 32, provides a different mode of procedure in advocations, where there has been a concluded proof in the Court below. The true view of section 24 seems to be, that it is intended to regulate advocations at interlocutory stages, and not those which bring up the whole process.

(3.) The third kind of advocation hitherto competent was the advocation of final judgments, and of this class is the interlocutor disposing of the whole merits of the cause, though there has been no decision on the question of expenses, or though they have not been taxed.

In this kind of advocation the procedure differs from that in advocations with a view to jury trial. The note is in the first place lodged with a depute or assistant clerk, and is called and enrolled without passing through the Bill-Chamber, and it is necessary that caution be previously found in the inferior court.

By the 13th and 14th Vict. chap. 36, two enactments were made respecting advocations, viz. (1.) That such advocations as were presented on juratory caution should not proceed unless a *probabilis causa* was reported, § 34 : (2.) That in advocations where a record had been made up and closed, and a proof had been led and concluded before the inferior judge, the Lord Ordinary should at the first calling, on motion by either party, appoint the papers to be boxed for the Judges of the Inner House, and report the cause to the Inner House. § 32.

By the recent Sheriff Court Statute it is enacted, that all advocations which shall come to depend before the Court of Session, *may* be brought in the first instance before one or other of the Divisions (*i. e.* Inner Houses) of the Court of Session, or, by consent of both parties, before any Lord Ordinary in the Outer House ; in which last case the judgment to be pronounced by such Lord Ordinary shall be final, and shall not be subject to review by the Inner House, or by appeal to the House of Lords. § 25.

By this enactment the consent of both parties seems requisite to the taking of a case before the Lord Ordinary. Unless, therefore, such consent be given (in which event the judgment to be pronounced will be final) it seems imperative to bring all advocations, whether of interlocutory or final judgments, at once into the Inner House, unless in the case of advocations with a view to jury trial, if such be still competent.

The form of the minute by which parties may consent to the advocation being brought before the Lord Ordinary as the ultimate Judge, which should be annexed to the note of advocation, may be as follows:—

JOINT MINUTE for *A. B. Advocator* and *C. D. Respondent.*

The parties consent that the above advocation shall be brought before Lord   , Ordinary, in the Outer House.

The expression "*such* Lord Ordinary," seems to imply that he is to be named by the parties.

Suspension.

The procedure in this mode of review continues unaltered by the recent statute, except that it is excluded in cases not exceeding L 25, and its application to Removing under the new forms is saved.—See Chap. IX., *voce Removing.*

Of Procedure commenced by Petition.

We refer to what we have stated, p. 29, with respect to commencing by summons or petition. The summons is the more advisable mode, except where a petition is clearly competent, and despatch greater than that of the ordinary court is required.

The statute declares that " in all applications before the Sheriff, which are at present commenced by petition, and   not otherwise regulated by this act, the petition shall be as nearly as   be in the form of Schedule E " annexed to this act; " and thereafter t   cedure under such petition shall, as nearly as may be, be the same .   ahefore provided in regard to ordinary actions." § 7.

In Chapter IX. we shall give forms of petitions applicable to particular kinds of procedure, and shall here only give a petition according to the statutory form in an ordinary case.

PETITION

A B   [*design*]

v

C. D.   [*design.*]

Unto the Sheriff

The petitioner *A. B.* humbly sheweth ;

That in consequence of the said *C D.* wrongfully and unwarrantably withholding and refusing delivery of the documents after mentioned belonging to the petitioner, the present application is necessary.

> May it therefore please your Lordship to grant warrant on the said *C. D.* for delivery to the petitioner of the following documents (*here specify them*), and generally of all title-deeds and other papers in the hands of the said *C D* belonging to the petitioner; and to find the respondent liable in expenses.
>
> According to Justice, &c.

Drawn by   (Signed)   *A B* Petitioner.
              (Or)   ARTHUR ANGUS, Agent for Petitioner.

The Statute says nothing as to the order by the Sheriff on a petition, or how it shall be brought into Court. It only prescribes the form of the execution of service. We think that the clear intendment of the Statute, is that the Sheriff shall pronounce, not as hitherto an order for answers, but an order for appearance, written on the petition, as follows :—

Sheriff's Interlocutor.

Edinburgh, 1st November 1853.

The Sheriff-substitute appoints the defender to compear within the Sheriff Court house at Edinburgh, upon Friday the 10th day of November current, at ten o'clock forenoon, with continuation of days, to be heard in defence, and appoints a copy of the foregoing petition and of this deliverance to be served on the said defender by an officer of Court, 48 hours previously.

AND. JAMESON.

For the first interlocutor in sequestration cases and the like, see the next Chapter.

A copy of the petition and deliverance will then be served by an officer of Court. The Statute gives the form of execution. It must be written on the petition (see above, page 31), and is as follows :—

Officer's Execution.

This petition served by me, *John Robson,* sheriff-officer, upon *C. D.* respondent (*state whether personally or otherwise*) in presence of *Adam Huie, residing in Lawnmarket, Edinburgh,* this first day of November eighteen hundred and fifty-three years, between the hours of   and   o'clock afternoon.

John Robson, Sheriff-officer

Ad. Huie, witness.

According to our view, the respondent must appear by himself or his agent at the time mentioned in the deliverance, and the petitioner and he must then be prepared to explain the grounds of the action and defence, as at the first meeting before the Sheriff in ordinary actions, in terms of § 3 of the Statute.

Thereafter the proceedings will be conducted as in ordinary actions, § 7, but with that dispatch which is at present given to summary cases.

CHAPTER VIII.
Incidental Points.

Abandoning an Action.

There appears to be nothing in the recent statute to interfere with the rule of the Act of Sederunt, that " it shall be competent to the pursuer before any interlocutor of absolvitor" (or leading to that result—Findlater, 24th May 1839) " is pronounced, to enter on the record an abandonment of the cause on paying full expenses to the defender, and to bring a new action, if otherwise competent "   A. S. § 61.*

The abandonment here referred to is usually made by a Minute in the following terms —

Minute Abandoning an Action.

Minute for *A. B*, tailor and clothier in Edinburgh, *pursuer*, against *C. D*, cabinetmaker, residing in Castle Street there *defender*.

The pursuer craved the Court to allow him to abandon the present action at his instance against the defender, on payment of expenses, and reserving to him right to bring a new action, if so advised.

In respect whereof,

A. B., Pursuer.

Or ARTHUR ANGUS, Agent for Pursuer.

The Sheriff's interlocutor on this Minute may be as follows —

The Sheriff-substitute, in respect of the Minute for the pursuer, No. of process, dismisses the action, reserving right to the pursuer to bring a new action if so advised : Finds the defender entitled to expenses, and remits the account, when lodged, to the auditor to tax and to report   AND. JAMESON.

Should a new action be raised before the expenses are paid, the pursuer will not be allowed to proceed with it until payment of those expenses.

There appears nothing to prevent the Sheriff, instead of at once pronouncing the interlocutor, dismissing the action, and remitting the account for taxation, to find in the first place the expenses due, and order them to be taxed, and when they are paid, to dismiss the action.

---

* Where in this Chapter sections only are quoted, they are those of the statute 1853, 16 and 17 Vict. c. 80. The sections prefixed A. S. are those of the Act of Sederunt, 10th July 1839.

In a case where the interlocutor following on a qualified Minute of abandonment bore, " assoilzies the defender,", in place of dismissing the action, under the reservation of a right to bring a new one, the Court held that there was a clerical error in the interlocutor, and no *res judicata*.— Sheriff *v.* Brodie, 24th May 1836.

As to taking no procedure in a cause within three months, in which case it is to stand as *eo ipso* dismissed, but under certain provisions as to revival; § 15 See Chap. IX., *Reviving.*

Adjourning.

Certain diets of meeting with the Sheriff, &c. which are to take place at periods fixed by the statute, may be adjourned, as has been explained in in the last chapter. But a diet of proof is not to be adjourned except on special cause shewn and set forth in the interlocutor.

Advocation.

At the close of last chapter we have explained the three kinds of advocation.

The rules as to caution and juratory caution are contained in the A. S §§ 114 and 121 et seq. As to intimating the note of advocation and transmitting the process, *ib.* §§ 127 and 128. And, pending advocation of interlocutory judgments, the Sheriff may regulate all matters respecting interim possession. § 130.

Amendment of Libel.

Occasion for this will more rarely occur under the new form of summons, which consists only of instance and conclusions, without statement or *media concludendi.* Still blunders may occur in the instance or conclusion. And for the decisions which have been given, we refer to the works of Mr Shand, Mr M'Laurin, and Mr M'Glashan, and need only call attention to the clause of the recent statute.—" That it shall be competent for the Sheriff, where a cause is before him on any point, to open up the record *ex proprio motu*, if it shall appear to him not to have been properly made up." § 16.

When amendment is necessary, the party applies by motion, on which the Sheriff either grants leave *de plano* to amend, or allows a minute of amendment to be lodged and seen, on which he will hear parties, and then allow or refuse the amendment The Interlocutor, if pronounced by the Sheriff-substitute, is not subject to appeal at this stage.

It was enacted by the A. S. that no libel shall be amended after citation is given thereon, except by authority of the Sheriff; § 11. And " when a libel is amended in absence of the defender, a copy of the amendment must be served upon him in the same manner and upon the same induciæ as the original libel." § 13.

In the Court of Session, where the condescendence is attached to and forms part of the original summons, the question was lately discussed as to the extent of change which could be introduced into the revised condescendence, excepting by amendment of the summons on leave obtained. The Lord Justice-Clerk, in delivering his opinion in the Second Division, announced the rule which, after consultation with the whole other Judges, was laid down, and to be enforced, viz "That in everything which is of the essence of the action, whether in the averment of what is an essential quality, or of what is a proper ground of action, the summons and condescendence must be perfect and complete *ab initio*, and that no change can be introduced into the revised condescendence which alters the summons or the annexed condescendence (which is part of the summons), in such matters Such change can only be by an amendment of the summons on leave obtained." Accordingly, in the action in which this was announced, which was one of damages against a party for maliciously and falsely stating calumnious matter to the Procurator Fiscal, it was held that a want of probable cause was of the essence of the action, and could not be introduced by way of revisal of the condescendence; Dallas *v* Mann, 14th June 1853; 25 Jur 448 The rule was stated as to be enforced also in the Sheriff Court, but this announcement was prior to the change which the statute prescribes in the form of the summons.

Appeal.

The matters of appeal from the Small Debt Court, or from the Substitute to the Sheriff, or from the Sheriff to the Court of Session, have been discussed in the former chapters.

Argument, Written and Oral.

The recent statute abolishes all written argument, except only in a reclaiming petition, in carrying out appeal from the Substitute to the Sheriff, where the appellant adopts that mode in place of oral argument The words are,—" The parties or their procurators shall be entitled to be heard orally when the cause shall be ripe for judgment, and on the import of any concluded proof, and at any other stage of the cause when argument may be necessary, and shall be appointed by the Sheriff; and it shall not be competent, at any stage of the cause, to receive any written argumentative pleading, excepting as herein after provided" (*i e.* reclaiming petition). § 12

But the Sheriff shall, if required by either of the parties, take a note of the authorities cited in the course of the oral argument. § 12.

And also, where he shall see fit, of the argument. § 13.

And such note shall form part of the process. § 12.

Arrestment.

As already seen, arrestment may be used on the clause authorizing it in the will of the summons, given p. 30 above. As to other warrants for arrestment, also the mode of using it, and having it loosed or recalled, the procedure belongs to the next chapter, where it shall be stated, *voce Arrestment.*

Asleep and Wakening.

Hitherto a process, after being in Court, fell asleep when it was allowed to lie over for a year and day without any judicial proceeding. A new enactment now seems to supersede this rule, and cases in which no proceeding has been taken for three consecutive months, are, except where the right under the action has been acquired by a third party, to stand dismissed, but under provisions as to reviving § 15. See below, *Reviving.*

Borrowing Processes.

Procurators of Court, and qualified agents resident within the jurisdiction of the Court, are alone entitled to borrow any process, by themselves or their clerks duly authorized, and for whom they are responsible by the ordinary compulsitors of the law —A S § 159. But it must be observed that, according to the recent Act, parties themselves are allowed to appear at every stage for themselves, and to sign their papers.

The Statute 1 and 2 Vict. c. 119, § 16, directs that an inventory of the process shall be kept by the clerk, in which the borrowing and returning of processes shall be entered, and no process shall be given up by the clerk without a receipt or such inventory. See also A. S. § 163, which directs that a separate inventory shall accompany the proceedings.

Caption for Process.

Where a process is unduly kept up by the agent of either of the parties, a caption, which is warrant to officers of Court to apprehend and incarcerate the agent or clerk who granted the receipt till it is returned, is granted by the Sheriff on application of the opposite agent after intimation. The form is as follows :—

The Sheriff of   shire grants warrant for apprehending and imprisoning in the prison of   the person of   writer in   and (if a clerk subscribed the receipt)   his clerk, until they return to the clerk the process *A.B* against *C.D.*

Payment of the dues of the caption and officer's fee for executing, was, before the abolition of imprisonment for small debts, part of the warrant.

If the party against whom a process-caption is issued has any good objection, he ought to apply to the Sheriff, and not, in the first instance, to present a note of suspension in the Bill-Chamber.

Forcing back the process, however, may often be effected by enrolment, and notice may be given that production of the process will be demanded when the cause is called. And on failure the Sheriff may award a penalty or amand. See below, *voce Interlocutor Sheets*.

Circumduction.

Where a party failed to lodge a paper which had been ordered, or after a proof had been allowed, there was undue delay to proceed with it, it was the practice in some Sheriff Courts to pronounce circumduction, and hold the party as confessed; in others to send the case to the Sheriff, with a certificate by the Clerk of Court of default. There is no enactment relating to circumduction in the recent statute. By § 10 thereof, evidence is to be led at the diet appointed for proving; and the diet is not to be adjourned unless on special cause shewn; and the proof is to be taken as far as may be continuously. The statute seems to point at a procedure similar to that in the Jury Court. The Sheriff's notes will bear the *res gestæ*, and special enrolment for circumduction appears unnecessary, except in the case where a commission has been granted and not reported   See A S. § 81.

Citation.

Forms of execution and citation, both as regards parties and witnesses, have already been given   Where parties reside in a different county, all warrants of citation, when endorsed by the Sheriff-clerk of that county, have equal effect as in the county where issued. Letters of supplement, however, remain competent. One witness to every execution by an officer (except of a poinding) is sufficient   1 and 2 Vict c 119, §§ 23 and 24, and the A. S §§ 16, 72.

Conjoining Processes.

Under the former practice it was generally necessary, in order to conjoining processes, that they should be between the same parties, and closely connected with each other, and that one should not be in a greatly more advanced stage than the other, nor one for a liquid and the other for an illiquid claim. There is nothing in the new statute to interfere with the continuance of such rules.

Decree.

The procedure in cases of decree by default, and the provisions as to the Sheriff setting forth the grounds of his judgment in certain decrees, and that a decerniture for expenses includes the expense of extract, have already been mentioned in the course of the ordinary procedure.

Interim Decree.—No interim decree can be extracted without a special allowance therefor; it is otherwise in the Court of Session   An interlocutor granting interim decree can be appealed.

Delay to proceed with a Cause.—See *Revising*.

Confessed—*Holding as.*

If in the summons, defences, or in the condescendence and answers, a statement of fact within the opposite party's knowledge be averred by one party and not denied by the other, the latter shall be held as confessed. A. S. 55. This provision still applies; and where proof is by writings in the hands of the opposite party, who has been cited as a haver to produce them, and he fails to exhibit and depone on the day appointed, he shall be held as confessed upon the point offered to be proved by such writings.   A. S. § 70

Diligence for Recovery of Writings.

Either at the first meeting with the Sheriff, or with his condescendence, the pursuer ought to produce all writings on which he founds, so far as in his custody or within his power, and the defender, on the other hand, should produce in like manner with his defences.   But where documents are not within the power of either party wishing to recover and found upon them, either by reason of being kept up by his opponent, or by being in the hands of a third party, he must apply to get them.

The provisions of the Act of Sederunt are as follows :—

" If the mean of proof be by writings alleged to be in the other party's hands, a day shall be assigned to that party for producing them, or to depone thereanent as in an exhibition; or a diligence may be granted against him as a haver; and in case he shall fail to exhibit or depone on the day appointed, he shall be held as confessed upon the point offered to be proved by such writings."   § 70.

When the mean of proof is by writings not in the party's hands or by witnesses, a day shall be assigned for recovery of such writs, or for proving by witnesses, and diligence shall be granted to that effect, to be reported against the day assigned.   § 71.

It is not stated in the Act of Sederunt at what stage of the case diligence may be granted for the recovery of writings. That must plainly be left to the discretion of the Judge with reference to the circumstances of each case. Unless the party is apparently fishing to make up a case, it appears expedient to grant a diligence before the closing of the record, that the statements of parties may set forth more perfectly the true facts. See *Miller, 8th March* 1849.

A specification of the writings called for must be lodged.

If the haver whom it is proposed to examine be within the jurisdiction of the Sheriff, it would appear to be in accordance with the spirit of the recent statute that the Sheriff should take the examination himself. In such case the interlocutor may be as follows :—

Interlocutor Allowing a Diligence.

The Sheriff-substitute grants diligence against havers for recovery of the writings in the specification, No.   of process, and appoints the examination to proceed within the   upon the day of   at   o'clock.

AND. JAMESON

A copy of this interlocutor, certified by the clerk, is a sufficient warrant to any Sheriff-officer acting within his own county, to cite the havers. § 11.

If the havers reside beyond the jurisdiction of the Sheriff, or are unable to attend the diet through age, infirmity, or sickness, it is declared competent to the Sheriff to grant commission to any person to take and report in writing the evidence of such haver; § 10. In that case the interlocutor may be as follows :—

Interlocutor granting Diligence and Commission

The Sheriff-substitute grants diligence against havers for the recovery the writings in the specification, No.   of process, and grants commission to Robert Baird, writer in Glasgow, to take the examination of the said havers, and receive their exhibits, to be reported by the day of

AND. JAMESON

Upon obtaining this interlocutor the agent will lay the process before the Commissioner, and get a diet fixed. The interlocutor granting the diligence having been, where necessary, endorsed by the Sheriff-clerk of the county, a copy of it, accompanied with notice of the day and hour fixed by the Commissioner, and copy of the specification, or such part of it as applies to the haver to be examined, will be served by an officer of that county.

Such citation must be given at least forty-eight hours before the time of compearance. § 11

The penalty of the haver's failure to attend is a forfeit of not less than 40s. in favour of the party in whose behalf he was cited, unless a reasonable excuse be offered and sustained by the Sheriff. § 11.

The following may be the form of the

Deposition and Report of Examination of Havers.

At Glasgow, the 30th day of November 1853, there was presented to Mr Robert Baird, writer in Glasgow, commission dated the   of day

November 1853, granted by the honourable the Sheriff of Edinburgh, in an action depending before the said Sheriff, at the instance of *A B*, tailor and clothier in Edinburgh, pursuer, against *C. D*, cabinet-maker, residing in Castle Street there, defender, to examine havers in that cause, of which commission the said Robert Baird accepted, and appointed   , clerk to Messrs C. and R. Baird and Muirhead, writers, Glasgow, as clerk to the said commission, to whom he administered the oath *de fideli administratione*.

Appeared.

Mr *L. M*, writer in Glasgow, agent for the pursuer; and *N. O*, writer in Glasgow, agent for the defender.

Whereupon compeared John Thomson, residing in Glasgow, who being solemnly sworn, and called upon to exhibit or produce in terms of article first of the copy specification herewith produced, and now docqueted and subscribed by him and the commissioner as relative hereto, depones and exhibits (here describe shortly the documents produced), and the same are now docqueted and subscribed by the haver, commissioner, and clerk, as relative hereto (If the documents are excerpts from books, say), depones and exhibits a book (describing it) containing therein certain entries of the description called for, and copies of said entries having been taken therefrom, and the excerpt having been compared by the commissioner therewith, and found to be correct, the same is now docqueted and subscribed by the haver, commissioner, and clerk, as relative hereto. Being called on to exhibit in terms of article second of said specification, depones and exhibits, &c (*as before*). Depones, I have no other of the documents called for, and I have not destroyed or away put the same, and I do not know or suspect where or in whose possession the same or any of them may be. All which is truth, as I shall answer to God.

JOHN THOMSON.
R. BAIRD, *Comr.*
                , *Clerk.*

What is written on this and the   preceding pages, is the report of the commission mentioned on the first page hereof.

Humbly reported by   R. BAIRD, *Comr.*
                , *Clerk,*

Diligence upon a Decree.

In the Small Debt Court.—The forms of diligence by poinding and sale are given under the head Poinding.

In the Ordinary Court.—The forms are elsewhere given. It may be noticed here, that if any step of diligence has been taken on a decree in absence, prior to the statutory application to be reponed, the Sheriff may, in the course of the proceedings in the cause, decern in favour of the pursuer for the expense of such charge or diligence, or such part thereof as shall be just. § 2.

J

It is also provided, that a certificate by the Sheriff-clerk, with whom a reponing note in the statutory form has been lodged, and the expenses decerned for, consigned, shall operate as a sist of diligence.   § 2

Disjoining of Processes.

It is competent to disjoin processes which it may appear to the Sheriff ought not to have been conjoined, or when there is reason for their no longer continuing conjoined.

Expenses.

On the issue of a cause, the general rule is to award expenses to the successful party, even though the question may be difficult.   The ground of this is, that that party has been found in the right, and the old ground of mulcting the opponent in respect of a litigious spirit is exploded.   See cases of Kirkpatrick, 10 D. 367; and Torbet, 11 D. 694.

By the Act of Sederunt, a party, although he has been found entitled to expenses generally, is not allowed to include in his account the expense of any particular part or branch of the litigation in which he has been unsuccessful, or which has been occasioned by his own fault.   § 107.

Where there was nimious and unreasonable procedure on both sides, no expenses were found due to either party; but it was observed, that the proper course would be to give each party his expenses, so far as he had been successful; Lowrie, 12 D. 167.

A great many decisions on questions of expenses have been reported within the last few years   These will be found in the Digests, *voce* Expenses.

Where in the course of a cause interim expenses are awarded to either party, he is entitled to have them paid before the case proceeds; and by the Act of Sederunt, there is no claim for repetition thereof at the end of the cause.   A S. § 108.

A party abandoning a case with the view of raising a new action, is bound to pay the expenses before his new action can proceed.   When, through neither of the parties having taken any proceeding in a cause during the period of three consecutive months, the action stands *eo ipso* dismissed, there is power to either party to revive on cause shewn, or on payment to the other party of the preceding expenses incurred in the cause   § 15.   See *Reviving.*

A decree for expenses includes a decree for the expense of extracting it, § 14; and where diligence has been done on a decree in absence, the expense thereof may, on the defender being reponed, be decerned for in the cause.   § 2.

Where a decree is given for expenses, the Sheriff, if he see cause, may, upon the application of the procurator who conducted the suit, allow the decree for expenses to go out and be extracted in the name of such procurator. A. S. § 106.

Taxation of Expenses.

The amount of expenses to be given in any decree, whether in absence or *in foro*, shall always be taxed before extract A. S. § 105.

If either party object to the auditor's report, "it shall be competent, within forty-eight hours after an account has been taxed, to lodge a note of specific objections to such taxation, which the Sheriff shall dispose of, with or without answers, as he shall see cause." A. S § 109.

The following is the form ·—

NOTE of OBJECTIONS to AUDITOR'S REPORT,

IN CAUSA

A. B, Tailor and Clothier, Edinburgh—*Pursuer;*

AGAINST

C. D, Cabinetmaker, residing in Castle Street, Edinburgh—*Defender.*

The pursuer objects to the auditor's report, inasmuch as it disallows the following items—[here quote from the account the charges disallowed, and the disallowance of which is complained of.]

In respect whereof, &c.

The note of objections, and answers, if ordered, must be without argument, as there can be little doubt that the 12th section of the Statute, abolishing all written argument, applies at this stage of the cause; and any discussion on the auditor's report will in future take place orally upon the note of specific objections.

It is farther provided by the Act of Sederunt, that no reclaiming petition shall be competent against any interlocutor regarding the taxation or modification of accounts of expenses, nor shall any appeal be competent against any such interlocutor unless lodged within forty-eight hours from its date. § 109.

It is thought that the provisions as to appeal contained in the 19th and 16th sections of the Statute, are not intended to apply to interlocutors regarding the taxation or modification of expenses, and that the above rules of the Act of Sederunt limiting the time for appealing, are not altered by the Statute. But the point may be doubtful.

Taxation of an Agent's Account against his Client.

An agent, either during the dependence of a process or after it is out of Court by an extracted decree, may by summary application to the Sheriff before whom the cause depends or has depended, have the account claimed by him audited and taxed, and a similar privilege is accorded to the client from whom the account is claimed.   A. S. § 110 and 112.

Such procedure, however, is not competent where liability for payment of the account is disputed by the client, in which case the agent is bound to proceed by an ordinary action, A. S § 112.

The form of such application is as follows :—

PETITION.

Unto the Sheriff of the County of Edinburgh,

Arthur Angus, Writer in Edinburgh ;

AGAINST

A. B , Tailor and Clothier in Edinburgh.

The petitioner, *Arthur Angus*, humbly sheweth—
That the petitioner was employed by the said *A. B.* to conduct an action at his instance against *C D.*, cabinetmaker, residing in Castle Street there, which is now in dependence before your Lordship—(or which was recently in dependence before your Lordship)   That he has incurred an account of expenses amounting to the sum of L.10, 6s. 8d. herewith produced.

> May it therefore please your Lordship to remit the said account to the auditor of Court to tax the same, and to report , and thereafter to find the said *A. B.* liable to the petitioner in the taxed amount thereof, and to decern against him therefor, with expenses.

In respect whereof.

Drawn by   (Signed)   ARTHUR ANGUS.

The form of the petition where the client is the party applying for the taxation is similar *mutatis mutandis*.   A S. § 110

Although the account claimed should be below L 12, the application will be presented by either party in the Ordinary Court, not in the Small Debt Court.

Such application must be served on the party, the period of intimation being at least seven days   A. S. § 110

On its being produced in Court with such service of intimation, it shall be forthwith granted   § 110.

The said account shall thereupon be audited and taxed, and the " parties shall have it in their power to state objections to the report, all in manner above provided." A S. § 110.   The manner provided is the lodging of specific objections within forty-eight hours, as above stated, and so forth.

The sum so ascertained as the amount of the account shall form the only charge against the client, and a precept or decree on a charge of fifteen days may issue therefor, provided always that the judgment of the Sheriff shall be liable to review in common form A. S. § 111. Review by the Court of Session is now of course excluded, if the amount of the account as claimed (whatever be the amount as taxed) does not exceed L.25

Fees.

The fees in the Small Debt Court which are exigible by the clerk, officer, and crier, are engrossed in the Small Debt Statute. § 32

With respect to fees of practitioners and others in the Ordinary Court, these were regulated by Acts of Sederunt, 6th March 1833 and 2d June 1837. In cases to which the jurisdiction of the Sheriff is extended by 1 and 2 Vict. c 119, Court of Session agents may practise, but at no higher fees than those of the Sheriff Court agents 1 and 2 Vict c 119, § 33

By the recent statute—" The Court of Session shall be, and is hereby authorized and required to frame, from time to time, a table or tables of fees for business in the Sheriff Courts of Scotland, and such table or tables of fees so framed, shall be submitted to the Secretary of State for the Home Department, and, if approved of, shall form the rule of professional charge for business performed in such Courts " § 49. It is presumed, that " business in the Sheriff Courts of Scotland" will be held to include the business of the Small Debt Court, at least, will include the charges that may apply to cases which, of whatever amount, may be removed by consent of parties from the ordinary to the Small Debt Court under § 23.

As the Act of Sederunt contemplated by the statute is not yet passed, we regret that the future table of fees cannot be included in this work As the length of written papers can no longer gauge the rate of professional remuneration for Court business ; and as the mode in which the business of Sheriff Courts is to be henceforth conducted will demand an increased amount of attention and skill, especially in the preparation for oral debate, it may be expected that the fees will be fixed on a liberal principle

With respect to Sheriff-clerks (not now paid by salary) whose emoluments may be affected by the operation of the Act, they are empowered either to require that they should be paid by salary in terms of 1 and 2 Vict. c. 119, or may apply to the Commissioners of the Treasury for compensation , and those who are now paid salaries, may have the same adjusted by the Treasury § 41.

Imprisonment .

Is competent for debts above L.8, 6s. 8d. For the warrant in the Small Debt Court, see *supra*, p 25. If a decree pronounced in the Small Debt Court be put to execution by imprisonment, a petition to the Sheriff for suspension and liberation is competent. See Chap. IX. *Suspension.* The warrants on Ordinary Court decrees and decrees of registration are regulated by 1 and 2 Vict. c. 114, § 1, *et seq*

Interlocutor Sheets.

In all defended cases, the interlocutors of Court must be written on a separate sheet or sheets of paper, and not on the pleadings of parties, A. S 162. It greatly facilitates procedure when the principal interlocutor sheets are retained by the clerk of Court (as in the Sheriff Court at Glasgow), and a certified copy only accompanies the proceedings.

Interpretation of Words.

The interpretation clause of the statute is § 50. which provides, that unless where the context is repugnant to such construction.

The word	*shall include*
Sheriff,	Sheriff-substitute
Tenant,	Sub-tenant.
Lease,	Sub-lease

The interpretation clause of 1 and 2 Vict c 119, is § 34, and that of the Small Debt Act, § 37.

Irritancy—*Landlord's*

An extension of the Sheriff's jurisdiction is provided by the recent statute, to the effect of making it competent for a landlord, in a lease of longer endurance than twenty-one years, to proceed by ordinary action before the Sheriff, where the rent has run two years in arrear, and to obtain a warrant to have the tenant removed from his possession , which warrant may be executed the first term of Whitsunday or Martinmas four months after it is issued by the Sheriff, and is to have the effect of a decree of irritancy of the lease, § 32. The procedure in such a case is detailed below, Chapter IX.—*Removing and Irritancy.* It seems doubtful whether the clause applies to subjects where the yearly value exceeds L.25

Irritancy—*Superior's*

The jurisdiction of the Sheriff is also extended so as to enable a superior, whose vassal is two years in arrear of his feu-duties, and where the subject does not exceed the yearly value of L. 25, to proceed by ordinary action before the Sheriff, to have the vassal removed from his possession, which warrant may, in like manner, be executed at the first term of Martinmas or Whitsunday occurring four month after the warrant is issued by the Sheriff, and which warrant so exceed has the effect of a decree of irritancy *ob non solutum canonem*, § 32. The form of procedure in this action is given below, Chapter IX.—*Removing and Irritancy.*

Judicial Examination.

By the late Evidence Act (1853), § 6, it is provided, that nothing herein contained shall alter or affect the authority or practice of Courts in Scotland as to judicial examination; and by the A. S. § 66, the Sheriff has power to order both parties, or either of them, to confess or deny facts specified by the Sheriff, or to attend personally for examination, and answer such interrogatories as the Sheriff or Commissioner shall think proper. In practice, such examinations are seldom ordered, except in cases where the Sheriff is satisfied that there is an attempt to evade or conceal, and in cases of filiation. The party is not put on oath. See observations on the law of allowing judicial examination of parties in the cause, *A B.*, 23d *December* 1843, 6 D. 342; and the subsequent cases of Barrie, 6 D. 102; Cowper, 9 D. 909; M'Kenzie, 10 D. 611; Little, 24th Jan. 1845, 17 Jur. 148

Judicial Reference.

A judicial reference may be made at any stage of the process, and may either refer the whole matter in dispute, or certain points, as may be agreed on. It is done by a minute lodged in process.

Minute of Judicial Reference.

Joint Minute for *A B*, tailor and clothier in Edinburgh, and *C.D*, cabinetmaker, residing in Castle Street, there.

The parties hereby agree judicially to refer the whole cause to John Porson, woollen merchant in Edinburgh, and crave the Sheriff to interpose his authority thereto.

(Signed)   *A B.*
(„)   *C.D.*

This minute should be signed by the parties themselves, unless their agents hold an express mandate to sign for them. The Sheriff will interpone his authority by interlocutor in the following form —

Interlocutor

Edinburgh,   *December* 1853.

The Sheriff-substitute interpones his authority to the Joint Minute of judicial reference, No.   of Process.

AND. JAMESON.

If a record has been made up in the cause, it will be held to be the subject of the reference. Before pronouncing judgment, the referee should issue notes of his intended award. As the judicial reference does not take the case out of Court, the referee may either pronounce an award or report the terms of the judgment he thinks should be pronounced, in which last case a decree conform will be pronounced. The judge may, before interponing his authority, hear parties upon any objections in point of irregularity or non-exhaustion of the reference, or going beyond it, and may remit again to the referee to open up the award and correct any irregularity. But the Court will not otherwise disturb the judgment on the merits. The referee may (where the whole cause has been referred) decide the point of expenses without special power thereanent, and he has been allowed to include in the expenses a fee to himself, if it should be the pleasure of the Court to find him entitled to remuneration.

It would seem to be clear that the provision in the recent Statute, as to a cause standing dismissed when no procedure has been taken by either of the parties for three consecutive months, will apply to a case before a judicial referee; and should such delay occur, there might be still more difficulty than in a case not so referred in getting the action revived, and again remitted to the referee, or the previous remit continued.

Lis Alibi

Is a preliminary defence, consisting of an objection to a case proceeding, in respect that the same matter is under judicial discussion elsewhere. As we do not observe anything in the recent Statute or in the Act of Sederunt calling for observation as to using this plea, we do not think it necessary to make any remarks on or.

Mandate.—(*Agents.*)

The rule of the Act of Sederunt is: A procurator appearing for a defender must produce along with his defences either a written mandate from the defender, or the copy of citation given to the defender, A. S. § 30. In like manner it is presumed, that on entering appearance, or at the first meeting held with the Sheriff, if the pursuer or his agent call for a mandate in favour of the defender's agent, it must be produced.

Mandatory.

The law of mandatory, in the case of parties who are abroad, remains unaltered by the recent statute.

Oath, Reference to—

The following is the form of a

Minute of Reference to Oath

MINUTE for *A. B.*, Tailor and Clothier in Edinburgh ;

IN ACTION AT HIS INSTANCE AGAINST

C. D., Cabinetmaker, residing in Castle Street there.

The pursuer hereby refers the whole cause to the oath of the defender.

ARTHUR ANGUS.

In all cases where the oath of party is required, the party by whom the reference or deference is made, must either subscribe along with his procurator the paper in which the requisition is made, or sign a separate writing to that effect to be produced along with the paper, or judicially adhere to the reference or deference in presence of the Sheriff or the Commissioner. A. S. § 84.

If the pursuer has previously examined the defender as a witness in the cause, as allowed by the recent Evidence Acts, it is not competent thereafter to refer the cause, or any part of it, to his oath. 16 Vict. c. 20, § 3.

This oath must be taken by the Sheriff, but if he cannot attend, or in any case of special emergency, he may appoint a Commissioner   A. S. § 79

If the party fail to appear upon the day assigned, and if no satisfactory reason be given for his absence, and the Sheriff do not see cause to prorogate the diet, the term shall be circumduced against him, and he shall be held as confessed, and either decerned against, or avizandum made with the cause as the nature of the case may require. A. S § 79.

Oath of Calumny.

If at ~ ~ ~ the oath of calumny be insisted for when the party from ~ ~ ~ is ~ ~ ~ manded is not present, it shall not be allowed unless upon consignation of a sum not exceeding forty shillings nor under five shillings, to be fixed by the Sheriff, and if he see cause to be forfeited to the other party, in case the oath is afterwards passed from, or is negative. besides payment of what shall be awarded by the Sheriff as travelling charges and other expenses occasioned by the oath of calumny being insisted on. A. S § 92.

Poor's Roll.

The procedure to enable a party to be placed on the poor's roll, in order either to prosecute or defend an action, is given Chap. IX.—voce Poor's Roll Cases.

Productions.

The provision of the Act of Sederunt is, that along with the summons the pursuer must produce the deeds, accounts, and other writings on which he founds, so far as the same are in his custody, or within his power, or state where he believes them to be.   A. S. § 23

With the condescendence or defences parties must produce all writings in their custody or within their power not already produced, on which they mean to found, but when books of business are founded on, excerpts therefrom may be produced in the first instance, the books themselves being produced in the course of the proof, if required. A. S. § 51.

In the Court of Session the record is often closed, under reservation to parties to produce documents within a specified number of days; and that course would also seem competent in the Sheriff Court.

The penalty of withholding writings or documents which ought to have been previously produced, is, that the Sheriff may find the party in fault liable in the whole, or such part of the expenses previously incurred as may appear proper, and give interim decree therefor   A. S. § 52.

No new production can be received with either a reclaiming petition or the answers.   A. S § 57

Prorogations.

By the Act of Sederunt, the clerk is prohibited from receiving any paper after the time fixed by the Sheriff for lodgement, except of consent of the opposite agent written thereon, and subscribed by him: A. S § 59.   And on failure the Sheriff may close the record and either give judgment, allow a proof, or otherwise dispose of the cause as he shall think fit.   A. S. § 59

The provision of the statute § 6, as to failure to lodge papers, has been cited in discussing the ordinary procedure.   By the same section the periods appointed for lodging any paper, or for transmitting any process to the Sheriff, or for closing a record, may always be once prorogated by the Sheriff, without consent, on special cause shewn, and may always be prorogated by written consent of parties, with the approbation of the Court; and in every interlocutor prorogating on special cause shewn the time for lodging any paper, the nature of such cause shall be set forth, and a definite time shall be therein fixed within which the paper is to be lodged; § 6

Protestation.

Under the existing practice the defender may, on the pursuer's failing to appear and insist, obtain protestation extractable on the expiry of seven free days (or where arrestments have been used, in forty-eight hours), and after protestation is extracted the instance falls, A. S. § 25 to 28   Under the recent Act, by which, on the first Court day after the notice of appearance to defend has been given, the Sheriff shall hear parties, there is no provision for the case of the pursuer not producing his summons and appearing   It would therefore seem, that in such circumstances such meeting can take place only if the pursuer produces the summons; and failing his doing so, that the defender, on production of the copy summons served on him, may obtain protestation on any Court day.

Remitting to Ordinary Court, and vice versa.

The cases in which such remits may be made are explained elsewhere, and will be found in Small Debt Act, § 4 and 27, and Recent Statute, § 23.

Removing Tenants and Vassals.

The procedure will be found in the next chapter, *voce Removing*

Repeating an Action.

Where it is necessary for a defender, in order to maintain a defence, to plead it by way of action, he raises a summons, and without its being executed or called, produces it, and an interlocutor is pronounced holding it repeated The necessity of such procedure, however, is often obviated by the pursuer consenting to hold the requisite action as repeated, in order not to delay the progress of his case This is done by a minute lodged in process.

Reponing or Hearing (in Small Debt Court.)

Where a decree has been pronounced in absence of a defender, it is competent for him, upon consigning the expenses decerned for, and the farther sum of ten shillings to meet farther expenses, in the hands of the clerk, at any time before a charge is given, or in the event of a charge being given, before implement of the decree has followed thereon, provided in the latter case the period from the date of the charge does not exceed three months, to obtain from the clerk a warrant signed by him, sisting execution till the next court-day, or to any subsequent court-day to which the same may be adjourned, and containing authority for citing the other party, and witnesses and havers for both parties; and the clerk is bound to certify to the Sheriff, on the next court-day, every such application for hearing and sist granted , and such warrant being duly served upon the other party, personally or at his dwelling-place, in the manner provided in other cases by the act, is an authority for hearing the cause 1 Vict c 41, § 16.

And in like manner, where absolvitor has passed in absence of the pursuer or prosecutor, it is competent for him, at any time within one calendar month thereafter, upon consigning in the hands of the clerk the sum awarded by the Sheriff in his decree of absolvitor as the expenses for the defender and his witnesses, with a farther sum of five shillings to meet farther expenses, to obtain a warrant signed by the clerk for citing the defender and witnesses for both parties , which warrant being duly served upon the defender in manner provided in other cases by the act, is an authority for hearing the cause as provided in the case of a hearing at the instance of the defender, the said sum of expenses awarded by the Sheriff, and consigned as aforesaid, being in every case paid over to the other party, unless the contrary shall be specially ordered by the Court; and all such warrants for hearing shall be in force, and may be served by any Sheriff-officer in any county, without indorsation or other authority than the Act; 1 Vict. c. 41, § 16.

Reponing (in Ordinary Court.)

The defender may obtain himself reponed against a decree in absence (for failure to enter appearance) whether extracted or not at any time before implement has followed thereon, or against such part thereof as may not have been implemented. § 2

This procedure is independent of the suspension of charges on decrees of registration for sums not exceeding L 25, provided by 2 Vict. c. 119, § 19.

It becomes a matter of importance what is *implement*. If a poinding were completed on the decree, the poinder can proceed to sell and pay himself. It has been held that such completed poinding would be implement, and bar reponing. Horning and charge do not preclude reponing; 1 and 2 Vict. c. 119, § 18, and A. S § 115. Nor does it appear that imprisonment would bar Neither would arrestment, unless followed by a decree of forthcoming

In order to be reponed, the defender must consign into the sheriff-clerk's hands, along with a reponing note, the sum of expenses decerned for. § 2.

Form of Reponing Note

Edinburgh, 11th November 1853
In the action *A. B.* against *C. D.* the defender craves to be reponed against the decree in absence, dated the 10th November 1853 [add where necessary so far as not implemented] The expenses decerned for are consigned with the Sheriff-clerk.
A B , *Defender*
(or) ALFRED BRUCE, *Agent for Defender*

A copy of this note must at the same time be delivered, or transmitted through the post-office to the pursuer or his agent in the action. § 2.

A certificate by the Sheriff-clerk that such note has been lodged shall operate as a sist of diligence. § 2

The Sheriff pronounces a judgment reponing the defender, and appoints the whole consigned money to be paid over to the pursuer, unless special cause be shewn to the contrary § 2. The following may be the

Interlocutor.

Edinburgh, 14th November 1853.
The Sheriff-substitute, in respect of the reponing note lodged for the defender, repones him against the decree in absence, authorises and ordains the clerk of Court to pay to the pursuer the sum of
of expenses consigned, and decerns.
AND. JAMESON.

The cause shall thereafter proceed as if appearance were made therein of the date of such judgment (*i. e.* 11th November, in the case supposed.)

There is no limit by the statute to the time within which such reponing may take place. It is plain that the provision of § 15, as to a case standing dismissed, has no application here. The words, " unless special cause be shewn to the contrary," imply the pursuer's right to be heard before the defender is reponed—a right which will only be insisted in where there is a dispute whether the decree has been implemented, and if so, to what extent.

Any expensess of diligence incurred prior to the application to be re-poned, may be afterwards decerned for in the cause. § 2

Res Noviter.

It is competent to either party, before final judgment in a cause, to apply either by motion in Court, or by a short note without argument, for leave to lodge a statement of any matter of fact or any document *noviter veniens ad notitiam*, or emerging since the record was closed. A. S § 58.

The Sheriff thereupon appoints the said party, within a time to be specified, to give in a condescendence, stating, in the first place, the facts which he alleges to have newly come to his knowledge, or to have emerged since the record was closed ; and secondly, and *separatim*, setting forth the circumstances under which they have only recently come to his knowledge or emerged ; and, if he see cause, appoints the other party, within a spe-cified time, to answer the latter part of the said condescendence. A.S § 58.

Upon the said answers being given in, the Sheriff, either upon proof or otherwise, determines whether or not the said matter *noviter veniens ad notitiam*, or as having emerged since the record was closed, ought to be added to the record, and pronounces an interlocutor accordingly, at the same time determining or specially reserving the point of expenses , and in case he is of opinion that the said facts ought to be added to the record, he appoints the opposite party to answer the first part of the said condescendence ; and the Sheriff thereafter of new closes the record upon the additional papers. A. S. § 56.

Restriction of the Libel.

This is still competent as formerly, and is done by lodging a minute in process

Reviving.

Unless a summons is regularly executed within a year and day of its date, and called in Court within a year and day of compearance, the in-stance perishes, and it cannot be revived.

According to the form of process hitherto in use, a process, after being in Court, fell asleep when it was allowed to lie over for a year and day without any judicial proceeding. This is now superseded by the recent statute, which enacts, that " Where, in any cause, neither of the parties thereto shall, during the period of three consecutive months, have taken any proceeding therein, the action shall, at the expiration of that period, (eo ipso) stand dismissed." § 15.

Without prejudice nevertheless to either of the parties, within three months after the expiration of such first period of three months, but not thereafter, to revive the said action, on shewing good cause to the satisfaction of the Sheriff why no procedure had taken place thereon, OR, upon payment to the other party of the preceding expenses incurred in the cause § 15

Whereupon such action shall be revived and proceeded with in ordinary form, with power to the Sheriff, if he shall see fit, to disallow such expenses, or any part thereof, in the accounts of the agent of either party against his client. § 15.

But there is the following exception :—" Provided always that nothing herein contained shall apply to cases in which the right under such action has been acquired by a third party, by death or otherwise, within such period of six months" § 15   In such case there may be a wakening.

By the former practice a judicial act, such as an interlocutor renewing the last interlocutor, was sufficient to keep a process awake, and such an interlocutor falls within the words taking " any proceeding therein." At the same time it must be observed that prorogations by the Sheriff of the periods for lodging any paper, and for transmitting any process to the Sheriff, or for closing a record, can only be made once, except by written consent of parties § 6

Sisting Process.

An interlocutor sisting process, if pronounced by the Sheriff-substitute, may be appealed to the Sheriff, and a Sheriff's interlocutor sisting process may be advocated.

Supplementary Summons.

A supplementary summons may still in certain cases be required   There is nothing in the recent statute declaring it incompetent

Taxation of Expenses—See *Expenses*

Tender.

A tender, in order to have the effect of subjecting the opposite party to expenses subsequent to its date, must be pure, absolute, and unqualified— See Gunn, 17th March 189, 11 D. 106, and other recent cases as to the effect of tender on the question of expenses; Carnegie, 13th Feb. 1849. Logan, 6th March 1850; and Allan, 1st July 1851

CHAPTER IX.

Particular Actions.*

With reference to the rules which we have stated in the two preceding chapters, as applicable to the ordinary course of procedure in the Sheriff Court, we shall, in this last chapter, treat of what may be termed Particular Actions—namely, those in which the styles of the summons or petition, and more or less of the after procedure, differ from the ordinary procedure which we have exemplified in Chapter VII

Adjudication.

We need not enter upon the subject of adjudications, because although they are, to a certain extent, and within narrow limits, competent before the Sheriff (see page 10), yet in practice they are seldom, so far as our observation has gone, pursued before the Sheriff, but before the Court of Session. Should any practitioner intend to raise any of those kinds of adjudication which are competent before the Sheriff, he will find the subject fully and ably handled by Mr Parker in his valuable treatise on Adjudications, to which forms of summonses are appended, which can, by a slight alteration, be adapted to the Sheriff Court.

Aliment.

As stated in the chapter on Jurisdiction, page 8, actions of aliment may be instituted, heard, and determined in any Sheriff Court in Scotland. 1 Will. IV. chap. 69, § 32

If, however, an action for aliment be brought at the instance of a woman against her alleged husband, should he deny the marriage, it has been held that instead of allowing the proof to be taken incidentally in the Sheriff Court, process should be sisted until the pursuer shall instruct her marriage in a declaratory action before the Court of Session —Cameron v Innes, 25th January 1711, Dict 7405

But in an action for the aliment of a child born of a married woman, but said to be illegitimate, against which the defender, the alleged father, who was not the husband, pleaded *pater est quem nuptiæ demonstrant*, the Court of Session held that the question, whether the defender was the father of the child, to the effect of subjecting him in aliment, could be decided in the inferior court, such decision, however, being no bar to the child afterwards bringing a process to declare its legitimacy.

The following may be the form of a

---

* Throughout this Chapter, where Sections alone are cited, they are those of the recent Statute 16 & 17 Vict c 80 A S. § is the Section of the Act of Sederunt, 10th July 1839.

Summons of Aliment, a Son against his Father.

———— ———— Esquire, advocate, Sheriff of the county of ———— ————,
to officers of Court, jointly and severally.—Whereas it is shewn unto me by
A B design) pursuer, against C D. (design) defender, in terms of the conclusions underwritten THEREFORE the defender ought to be decerned to pay to
the pursuer, his lawful son, who is unable to earn a livelihood for himself, and
whom the defender refuses to receive into his house, the sum of L 25 sterling yearly, in name of aliment, and that by two equal portions, beginning the
first payment thereof on the first day of October last, as for aliment from the
1st of April last, to that date, and the next payment at the 1st day of April
next for the six months preceding, and so forth half-yearly during the pursuer's lifetime (or as the case may be, or until the defender receive and
support the pursuer under his own roof), with interest on each term's payment
from the time the same is payable until payment, with expenses of process.
AND MY WILL is that ye summon the defender to compear in my Court-house
at Edinburgh, upon the sixth day next after the date of your citation, in the
hour of cause, with continuation of days, to answer in the premises, with certification in case of failure of being held as confessed, and that ye arrest in
security the defender's goods, monies, debts, and effects —Given at Edinburgh
the second day of November eighteen hundred and fifty-three years.

———— ————, *Sheriff-Clerk.*

Summons of Aliment at the instance of a Wife against her Husband.

———— Sheriff, &c *(as above)*—Whereas it is shewn to me by A. B (design her)
wife of C. D (design him) pursuer, against the said C D defender, in terms of
the conclusions under written Therefore the defender ought to be decerned to
pay to the pursuer, whom the defender has deserted, and left without the means
of subsistence, the sum of L.   &c as in the preceding style

In the case of a mother pursuing for the aliment of an illegitimate
child, the form of petition has hitherto occasionally been resorted to But
the more correct form of proceeding is by a summons It is declared by
§ 147 of the Act of Sederunt 1839, that actions of aliment brought in
the form of a summons are to be entitled to the privileges of summary
processes in every respect The following may be the form of a

Summons of Filiation and Aliment.

———— Sheriff, &c. *(as above)*—Whereas it is shewn to me by A. B (design) pursuer, against C. D. (design) defender, in terms of the conclusions under written
Therefore the defender ought to be decerned to pay to the pursuer the following
sums of money as his proportion of the inlying expenses and aliment of an illegitimate male child, of which the pursuer was delivered on the   day of
last, and of which the defender is the father, viz. L 1, 10s of inlying expenses ; *Item,* L 5 sterling for nursing, clothing, and aliment to said child
for the first year after its birth ; *Item,* L.4 sterling of aliment for each
year thereafter, aye and until said child shall arrive at the age of ten years
complete, said sums of aliment to be payable quarterly per advance, with
the legal interest of said sum of inlying expenses from and since the
day of   and of each quarter's aliment from and since the
time it has fallen or may hereafter fall due, quarterly until paid ; but super-

seding execution on said decreet until each quarter's aliment be first come and bygone, and reserving to the pursuer to apply for additional aliment on the expiry of said ten years, if said child shall then be unable to earn its own subsistence, also to make payment of expenses of process AND MY WILL IS, &c

Arrestment.
Small Debt Forms.

The Small Debt Statute, § 6, provides that the pursuer of any civil cause, including maritime civil causes and proceedings, may use arrestment on the dependence in regard to any money, goods, or effects, to an amount or extent not exceeding the value of L 8, 6s 8d now L 12, owing or belonging to such defender, in the hands of any third party, either within the county in which such warrant shall have been issued, or in any other county or counties

But if the warrant is used in any other county, it must be first indorsed by the Sheriff-clerk thereof § 6.

The form both of the schedule, and execution of arrestment, are given in the statute, schedule (C) It is unnecessary to repeat them here One witness to the execution is sufficient. § 21

The Small Debt Statute farther enacts, that the wages of labourers and manufacturers shall, so far as necessary for their subsistence, be deemed alimentary, and in like manner as servants' fees, and other alimentary funds not liable to arrestment. § 7

Any arrestment laid on under the authority of the Small Debt Act shall, on the expiry of three months from the date thereof, cease and determine without the necessity of a decree or warrant loosing the same, unless such arrestment or warrant shall be renewed by a special warrant or order, duly intimated to the arrestee, in which case it shall subsist and be in force for the like time and under the like conditions as under the original warrant, or unless an action of forthcoming or multiplepoinding shall have been raised before the expiry of the said three months, in which case the arrestment shall be in force until the termination of such action. § 6

Ordinary Court Forms.
Arrestment on the Dependence

If the summons do not contain a warrant for arresting (which every summons may do, A S § 12), the clerk is authorized to issue separate precepts of arrestment upon there being produced to him a libelled summons not containing a warrant of arrestment, or a petition with pecuniary conclusions, A. S. § 153.

The precept shall always set forth the ground of application for the arrestment, and no blank warrant of arrestment shall be granted upon any pretence whatever, A. S § 153

Supposing the summons, of which we have given the style at page 30, had not contained a warrant of arrestment, and the pursuer wished to arrest, the clerk of court would issue a precept in the following form :—

Precept of Arrestment

—— Sheriff, &c.—Whereas it is humbly meant and shewn to me by A B, tailor and clothier in Edinburgh, complainer, against C. D. cabi-

L

netmaker, residing in Castle Street there, defender, that the complainer has raised an action against the said defender, concluding (*take in the conclusions*). Therefore it is my will that ye arrest in security the defender's goods, monies, debts, and effects.—Given at Edinburgh the 4th day of November 1853

—— ——, *Sheriff-Clerk.*

This is a very much abbreviated form of the precept of arrestment at present in use, but it seems quite clear that such shortened form is authorised by the statute

The agent instructs the officer to what extent he should arrest. The sum is generally to an extent which will safely cover debt and expenses.

The following is the officer's

Schedule of Arrestment.

By virtue of a warrant of the Sheriff of the shire of Edinburgh, given under the hand of the Clerk of Court at Edinburgh, the 4th day of November 1853 years, for arrestment on the dependence of an action raised before the said Sheriff at the instance of *A B* tailor and clothier in Edinburgh, against *C. D.* cabinetmaker, residing in Castle Street there, I hereby fence and arrest in the hands of you *H. H.* residing in No 99 Queen Street, Edinburgh, all sums of money owing by you to the said defender, or to any other person for his use and behoof, and all goods and effects in your custody belonging to the said defender, and that to an amount or extent not exceeding the sum of L   , all to remain under sure fence and arrestment at the complainer's instance, until due consignation be made, or until sufficient caution be found, as accords of law   This I do on the second day of November 1853, before Adam Hure, residing in Lawnmarket, Edinburgh, by delivering a copy of this execution to you personally (or as the case may be.)

JOHN ROBSON, *Sheriff-Officer.*

The execution will be the usual echo of this schedule, commencing with the date on which the arrestment was used.

Should the warrant of arrestment require to be used in a different county from that in which it is issued, endorsation by the Sheriff-clerk of that county is necessary.

If the officer executes the warrant of arrestment contained in the summons, by arresting the defender's effects, he must forthwith return an execution of arrestment to the clerk; A S § 18

Where arrestment is used upon any libelled summons before executing the warrant of citation, " such arrestment shall be effectual, provided the warrant of citation shall be executed against the defender within twenty days after the date of the execution of the arrestment, and the summons be called in court within twenty days after the diet of compearance ; or when the expiry of the said period of twenty days falls within the vacation, provided the summons be called on the first court-day next thereafter, whether such court-day be one of those authorized to be held in vacation, or in the ensuing session ; and if the warrant of citation shall not be executed, and the summons called in manner above directed, the arrestment shall be null, without prejudice to the validity of any subsequent arrestment duly executed in virtue of the said warrant" 1 and 2 Vict. c. 114, § 17, A. S. and A. S 154.

Arrestment on Decree.

Besides arrestment used on the dependence, arrestment may be used on any Sheriff-Court decree. It is provided by 1 and 2 Vict, chap 114, § 9, that extracts proceeding on decrees of Sheriffs, or proceeding on any extract of Sheriffs' decrees proceeding on any deed, decree-arbitral, bond, protest of a bill, promissory-note, or banker's note, or upon any other obligation or document on which execution may competently proceed, recorded in the Sheriff Court Books, the extractor shall insert a warrant to charge and arrest.

Where a debtor or obligant's moveables are within the territory of any other Sheriff, such extract may be presented for concurrence in the Bill-Chamber of the Court of Session, or in the court of such other Sheriff, with a minute; 1 and 2 Vict, chap 114, § 13, in the following terms.—

(Place,)   *Nov.* 1853.

Warrant of concurrence by the Sheriff of   is craved at the instance of *A. B.* (design), for executing the within warrant against the within designed *C. D*

, *Procurator.*

The Sheriff-Clerk subjoins his concurrence thus.—
     Nov. 1853.   Fiat ut petitur.

Sheriff-Clerk.

Where arrestment is wanted to be executed in the hands of a person furth of Scotland, the warrant of concurrence is from the Bill-Chamber, and the execution is at the Record Office of Edictal Citations, 1 and 2 Vict. c. 114, § 18

Any party acquiring right to an extract of a decree or act of the Sheriff, may also obtain warrant to arrest. In that case, he presents to the Sheriff-Clerk the extract, with a minute endorsed (Ibid, § 12) in the following terms:—

Minute by Assignee, &c.
     Edinburgh,   *Nov.* 1853.

Warrant is craved to arrest, at the instance of *E F.*, corn-dealer in Edinburgh, as assignee of *A. B.*, tailor and clothier in Edinburgh, conform to assignation produced herewith, dated the   day of November 1853.

ARTHUR ANGUS, *Procurator.*

The assignation, confirmation, or other legal evidence of the acquired right, must be produced. *Ibid,* § 12.
The Clerk writes the deliverance thus:—

Edinburgh, November 1853.   Fiat ut petitur.

J. A. CAMPBELL, *Sheriff-Clerk.*

Loosing or Recal of Arrestment.
Small Debt Forms.

When an arrestment shall be used on the dependence, the defender may have it loosed on security in the following manner.—

He lodges with the Sheriff-Clerk of the county in which such arrestment shall have been used, a bond or enactment of caution, by one or more good and sufficient cautioners, to the satisfaction of the Sheriff-Clerk, in the following form, § 8.—

Bond or Enactment of Caution for Loosing Arrestment.

At Edinburgh, on　　　　day of November one thousand eight hundred and fifty-three, compeared *E. F* (design him), who hereby judicially binds himself, his heirs, executors, and successors as cautioners, acted in the Sheriff Court Books of the shire of Edinburgh, for *C. D.,* common debtor, against whom arrestment was used at the instance of *A B.,* in the hands of *H. H.,* on the second day of November, in virtue of a warrant of the Sheriff of Edinburgh, dated the first day of November last, that the sums of money, goods, and effects owing or belonging to the said common debtor, arrested as aforesaid, shall be made forthcoming as accords of law

Thereupon the clerk grants a certificate in the form specified in the Small Debt Act, Schedule C, narrating that caution had been found, and bearing, " warrant for loosing" the said arrestment is hereby granted accordingly.

This certificate operates as a warrant for loosing any arrestment used in any county on the dependence of the same action.

The intimation is made by an officer in the form prescribed by the Schedule C, who returns an execution also in the form there given.

Or, the defender may have the arrestment loosed, on consigning, in the hands of the Sheriff-Clerk of the county in which the arrestment was used, the amount of the debt or demand, with 5s. of expenses in cases of actions for sums below £5, and 10s in cases of higher amount.

In this case the clerk grants a certificate varied only to the effect of narrating that the common debtor made sufficient consignation in the hands of the Sheriff-Clerk of Edinburgh, in order to the loosing

Or, if the defender produces evidence to such Sheriff-Clerk of his having obtained decree of absolvitor in the action, or of his having paid the sums decerned for, or the amount of the debt or demand, and expenses, when no decree has yet been pronounced, he may obtain a certificate § 8.

In Ordinary Court.

An arrestment may be loosed by the arrester discharging the arrestment, or, " it shall be competent for any Sheriff from whose books a warrant for arrestment has been issued on the petition of the debtor or defender, duly intimated to the creditor or pursuer, to recal or to restrict such arrestment, on caution or without caution, as to the Sheriff shall appear just, provided that the Sheriff shall allow answers to be given in to the said petition, and shall proceed with the further disposal of the cause in the same manner as in summary causes, and his judgment shall be subject to review in the Court of Session;" 1 and 2 Vict. chap. 114, § 21.

The petition may be to restrict the arrestment, on or without caution, or it may be to recal without caution, as nimious and inept.

Petition for Recal and Arrestment

Unto the Sheriff of the County of

　　　　A. B. (design)

　　　　　against

　　　　C D (design)

The petitioner, *A. B*, humbly sheweth, that, on the   day of
     , the said *C. D.*, respondent, by virtue of the warrant of arrestment
contained in a summons dated   at his instance against the
petitioner (or otherwise, as the case may be), caused the sum of £
due to the petitioner by *H H* (design), to be arrested, though the respondent had ample security for the payment of his debt (*or had previously arrested more than sufficient to cover his debt, or otherwise, as the case may be*).

> May it therefore please your Lordship to grant warrant for recal of said
> arrestment, and to find the respondent liable in expenses.
> According to Justice, &c.
>
> *Petitioner's Procurator.*

If it be thought necessary to offer caution, the following words may be
added above the prayer.—

The petitioner is ready to find such caution as your Lordships may order

According to the provisions of the recent statute, as explained above,
p. 57, the Sheriff's deliverance will not be an order for answers, but for
compearance. See the form of deliverance there given. The service and
execution will also be as there given.

If the Sheriff should order caution, the bond is inserted in the Sheriff
Court Books.

Arrestment to Found Jurisdiction.

Where a person is resident out of Scotland, and is not otherwise amenable to the jurisdiction of Scotch courts, but has funds and effects in this
country, he may be made liable to the jurisdiction by attaching those
funds and effects in the hands of the parties in Scotland who possess them.
This warrant to arrest *ad fundandam jurisdictionem* is obtained by a petition
to the Sheriff, which may be in this form.—

> Unto the Sheriff, &c. (as above).

The petitioner, *A B*, humbly sheweth,

That the said *C. D*, defender, is owing the petitioner the sum of L.100 sterling, contained in a bill dated 1st January 1853, accepted by the defender to
the petitioner for value, and payable ten days after date, which bill is herewith produced· That the said *C D.* is a foreigner, and has no domicile in
Scotland; but he has debts and effects in this country, which he intends to
withdraw to the pursuer's prejudice

> May it therefore please your Lordship to grant warrant for letters of
> arrestments *jurisdictionis fundandæ causa*, authorising the arrestment,
> within your Lordship's jurisdiction, of all debts and effects therein
> situated, indebted or belonging to the said *C. D.*, all to remain under
> sure fence and arrestment, at the petitioner's instance
> According to Justice, &c.

The warrant and precept is generally granted on this petition without
answers. In order to lay a *nexus* on the funds, the pursuer, after having

raised his action in the Court of Session, must arrest on the dependence of that action. The summons in the Court of Session must bear, after the word defender, "against whom arrestments have been used *ad fundandam jurisdictionem*, in terms of," &c.

Arrestment of Workmen or Apprentices.

Where a workman or apprentice deserts his service without finishing his engagement, or giving the agreed on notice or warning, he is liable at common law to be imprisoned until he find caution to return and work out his contract. See this subject fully treated of in Mr Fraser's valuable work on the Law of Domestic Relations, vol ii, p. 683, *et seq*

The procedure before the Sheriff is by petition. As this complaint is of a penal nature, the short form of petition given in the schedule of the recent statute does not seem applicable The following form will suffice for illustration :—

Unto the Sheriff of the County of Edinburgh,
A. B , carpet manufacturer in Edinburgh,
against
C. D , residing in Causeyside, Edinburgh.

The petitioner, A. B , humbly sheweth,

That, on the   day of   , the said C D contracted with the complainer, to serve him as a manufacturer in his workshop situated in   for six months from said date. That the said C. D. entered on his service with the complainer, and continued to work to him in his said workshop till the   day of this present month of   1853. That upon the said last-mentioned day, the said C. D. absented himself from his said service, without just cause, and has not since returned thereto

May it therefore please your Lordship to appoint this Petition to be served upon the said C. D., and to summon him to appear before you within a certain short space, to answer to the said complaint, and upon the same being admitted or proven, to find that the said C. D. is bound to return to his service with the petitioner, and to continue thereat till the expiry of the term of his contract, farther, to ordain him to find sufficient caution acted in your Lordship's Court books, that he shall so return ; and failing his finding such caution, to grant warrant to imprison him in the prison of Edinburgh, therein to remain until he shall find such caution, reserving always to the petitioner his claim of damages against the said C. D. for breach of engagement, and non-implement of the said contract, and to him his defences as accords ; and farther to find him liable in the expenses of this application and procedure to follow hereon.

According to Justice, &c.

Drawn by   ALFRED ANGUS, *Procurator.*

Should the Sheriff find the facts in the Petition proved, the Interlocutor may be as follows :—

Interlocutor

The Sheriff-substitute having considered the complaint at the instance of *A. B.* carpet manufacturer in Edinburgh, against *C. D.* residing in Causeyside, Edinburgh, declaration of the said *C. D.,* proof for both parties, and whole process · Finds it proved that the said *C D.* contracted to serve the said *A B.* as a carpet manufacturer for six months from the   day of   in his manufactory in
Street, Edinburgh ; finds it proved that the said *C. D.* absented himself, and still continues absent from his said service in the said workshop without cause · Therefore ordains the said *C. D.* upon intimation of this interlocutor, to find sufficient caution acted in the Books of Court, that he shall return to said service, with certification farther, Finds him liable in expenses, of which allows an account to be given in, and when lodged, remits to the auditor to tax and report

Cessio Bonorum.*

The procedure whereby an unfortunate debtor obtains protection against imprisonment for debts previously contracted was prior to 1836 competent only in the Court of Session   In that year, the Act 6 and 7 Geo. IV. c. 56 was passed, making the process competent also in the Sheriff Court If the petition be presented to the Court of Session, a remit is made to the Sheriff. The statute referred to, and relative Act of Sederunt, 6th June 1839, regulate the whole procedure. There is nothing in the late Sheriff Court Act applying to cessio, excepting that any incidental petitions in the case may be in the shorter form now introduced.

As the above mentioned Statute and Act of Sederunt contain full directions respecting the form of the procedure, we shall only notice the leading points, referring our readers to the Statute and Act of Sederunt themselves.

The process may be raised either by a party liable to imprisonment, in prison, or liberated from prison. § 2.

The form of the petition is given in Schedule A of the Act of Sederunt It is as follows :—

Unto the Sheriff of the county of
The Petition of (*giving the full name and designation, and present place of residence, and specifying the jail, if the debtor has been or is incarcerated*)

Humbly sheweth,
That the petitioner has been charged, and that a warrant to imprison has been issued against him at the instance of   , for not making payment of the sum of L.   contained in a

(*or*) That he is liable to imprisonment under a Small Debt decreet, obtained against him at the instance of   for the sum of L.

(*or*) That he is in prison, in respect of a civil debt amounting to L
at the instance of

(*or*) That he has been imprisoned, and afterwards liberated, in respect of a

---

* The sections cited at the end of the paragraphs under the head of *Cessio,* are those of 6 and 7 George IV. c. 56, and the A. S. is 6th June 1839

civil debt, amounting to L.   at the instance of
, (*specifying the debt, and the particular circumstances of its constitution by a bill, decreet, or otherwise.*)

That the petitioner is unable to pay his debts, and is ready to surrender his whole means and estate for behoof of his creditors. That his inability to pay his debts has not been occasioned by fraud; but has arisen solely from misfortunes and losses, to be particularly specified in the state of his affairs, subscribed by himself, and to be produced in the hands of the clerk of Court. That the following is a list of the petitioner's real or pretended creditors, viz. (*stating their names on separate lines, with a progressive number for the sake of reference.*)

That there is herewith produced the schedule of an expired charge for payment of the said debt; (*or*) a copy certified by the clerk of the Small Debt Court, of the warrant on which he is liable to imprisonment; (*or*) a certificate from the keeper of the prison of the imprisonment of the petitioner, and the date thereof, and of the liberation (*if such there were.*)

That the petitioner is farther desirous to obtain a warrant of (*liberation and*) interim protection against the execution of diligence, and is ready to find sufficient caution, acted in the Sheriff Court Books of the county of
      to the amount of   , for which
will become his cautioner

May it therefore please your Lordship to grant warrant for the requisite intimation or citation, and on the expiry of the *inducix*, and on the petitioner finding such caution, to grant authority for his liberation, and interim protection against the execution of diligence; thereafter, on resuming consideration of this Petition, and advising the whole cause, to find that the petitioner is entitled to the benefit of the process of cessio bonorum and to grant decreet accordingly, and to appoint such person as your Lordship shall think proper trustee, who shall take the management and disposal of his estate for the general behoof of his creditors, all in terms of the Statute and Act of Sederunt made thereanent.

According to Justice, &c

The productions mentioned in the petition must be made therewith. § 3.

On the petition being presented, the Sheriff grants warrant, appointing the debtor to publish the statutory notice in the Edinburgh Gazette for the app nce of his creditors on not less than 30 days' notice, and within five days after such publication, either to send a copy thereof by letters, post paid, to all the creditors, (the letter containing the name of the petitioner's agent), or to cite them in terms of law, and also order the petitioner to appear in Court on the day of compearance for public examination. If the petitioner prays for interim protection from diligence, or for liberation, that prayer is to be specially intimated in the Gazette notice and letter to creditors. A S § 4.

Six days prior to said diet, the petitioner must lodge with the Sheriffclerk, a state of his affairs subscribed by himself, and all his books, papers, and documents relating to his affairs, along with the evidence of the intimation to his creditors. If the petitioner has been under seque/tration, and not discharged, he must produce a certificate by the trustee and commissioners on his sequestrated estate, as to his having made a fair surrender of his means, and complied with the requisites of the Bankrupt Statute ; A. S. § 10.

At the diet for examination, if the petitioner is in jail, the Sheriff may grant warrant for bringing him for examination ; § 15. The agent for any opposing creditor must produce the letter sent, or citation given to that creditor, or a mandate. A. S. § 18.

If the petitioner apply by incidental petition for protection or liberation from prison, he must set forth the name of a cautioner, and the amount of caution offered, which must be intimated to the agent of the opposing creditors, and the amount of caution is fixed by the Sheriff, and a bond granted. The form of the bond is given in the A. S. schedule B. Protection may be granted before the expiry of the *induciae—Anderson*, 20th *Feb.* 1849.

At the diet for examination the Sheriff hears parties.

If there be an objection that all creditors have not been called, the objector must produce a list of those alleged to be not called, and re-examination may be ordered, new notice being given to all the creditors.

The bankrupt on his examination may be called on to give all necessary explanations as to the state of his affairs, his funds and documents, and causes of his insolvency. Mr Alexander in his Digest of the Bankrupt Act, gives a formula of interrogatories in a bankrupt's examination, which agents for creditors opposing a cessio may usefully consult.

The Sheriff may adjourn the diet, if he thinks fit, and order an amended state of affairs, if he judges that necessary.

After the examination, parties are heard *viva voce*, and the Sheriff makes notes of the objections and answers, which he signs, and these form part of the process, A S. § 15.

The Sheriff may allow the opposing creditors a proof, and they are not precluded by the debtor having been put on oath, from proving their case, A. S. § 12. When the Sheriff does allow a proof, it is recommended that he specifies in his interlocutor the facts to be proved. § 13.

In finding the petitioner entitled to the benefit of cessio, the Sheriff may attach the condition that the decree shall not be extractable or available as a protection for such time as shall appear proper, as a punishment for any delinquency committed. And where the Sheriff grants decree under such limitation, or when he refuses decree *hoc statu*, he must state the grounds of his decision. § 6

When decree of cessio is granted, whether *de plano* or under limitation, the petitioner must take the oath in the form of schedule C. of the Act of Sederunt.

A Reclaiming Po ion within six days is competent, § 7 ; and the Sheriff may allow answers, A. S. 17 If the reclaimer intimate his desire in the petition that should the Sheriff-substitute be disposed to refuse it, it may be laid before the Sheriff, it shall accordingly be transmitted to the Sheriff. § 7.

A Reclaiming Note to the Court of Session is competent within ten days from the date of the judgment, or if more than one, the last of the judgments of the Sheriff complained of, and is lodged with the clerk of that division under whose review it is intended to bring the cause   § 8.

If the Court be not sitting, the Reclaiming Note is disposed of by the Lord Ordinary on the Bills, after hearing parties *viva voce* If not brought to a termination before him, it goes, when the Court meets, to the Inner-House.

If disposed of by the Lord Ordinary on the Bills, the judgment may be brought under review by a reclaiming note, lodged within ten days after the date of the judgment

Agents in the Court of Session may practise in all processes of cessio before Sheriffs.   § 21.

The decree of cessio operates as an assignation to the trustee named in it for behoof of the creditors, but it is in the option of the creditors to require the debtor to execute a disposition.   § 16

Choosing Curators.

When a minor wishes to put himself under curators, the procedure is regulated by the Act 1535.   It is by edict, on which citation is given to two of the minor's next of kin on his father's, and two of the next of kin on the mother's side, by personal service, or service at their respective domiciles, and to all others having interest by edictal citation, or citation at the head burgh of the county where the minor has his heritable property, or, failing his having heritable property, where he resides.

"Edicts for choosing curators, summonses for curators giving up inventories, multiplepoindings, transumpts, wakenings, and cognitions, may be executed by delivering a copy citation before one witness, containing the names of and designations of the pursuer and defender, and bearing the extent and special grounds of the pursuer's claim without any copy of the summons;" A. S. § 14. Now, however, that summonses are in such an abridged form, it may be better to have a full copy of the summons served. By § 21 of the same Act of Sederunt, it is provided—" That in the case of libels or edicts for choosing curators, and of summonses for giving up inventories, defenders shall be cited to appear on the tenth day after date of citation, if a court-day, or if not, on the first court-day thereafter, with continuation of days ," and by § 22, "That when the defender is a minor, his tutors and curators shall be called edictally upon the same *induciæ* as the principal defender."   If there be not two existing nearest of kin on the side of either father or mother, a practice has sometimes prevailed of serving a copy of the edict on the Officers of State.

The edict or summons will be in the usual style as above, p. 80, the defenders being designed as next of kin on the father's or mother's side ; and the conclusion will be,

Therefore the said defenders ought to be summoned, warned, and charged, and my will is that ye summon, warn, and charge the said *C. D.* &c., defenders, personally, or at their dwelling-places, and all others having interest, edictally, by open proclamation at the market cross of Edinburgh, all to compear in my Court-house at Edinburgh, on the tenth day next after the date of your citation, in the hour of cause, with continuation of days, to answer in the premises: That is to say, to hear and see curators duly elected, nominated, chosen, and decerned to the said minor, *tam ad lites quam ad negotia*, by whose advice and consent he may do and perform all his affairs: And such curators being elected and chosen, the foresaid nearest of kin to concur with the said curators in making up a just and true inventory of the said minor's means and estate; and to subscribe three duplicates thereof, and to see everything done thereanent, as by the Act of Parliament, 28th June 1672, entituled, "Act anent Pupils and Minors or their Tutors and Curators," is directed, or else to allege a reasonable cause to the contrary, with certification that I or my substitute will concur or delegate some fit person to concur with the said curators in making up the said inventories; subscribe the duplicates thereof; interpone my authority thereto, ordain them to be recorded in my Court-books, and acts, one or more, to be made out thereupon, making mention of the production of the same; and in general, to see everything done thereanent that is prescribed in the Act of Parliament. Given at ———, the first day of November, eighteen hundred and fifty-four years

——— ————, *Sheriff-Clerk*

Cognition.

A creditor who has not had his debt constituted before the death of his debtor, must, if required by the executor confirmed, constitute the debt by an action *cognitionis causa* and for payment. This action may be before the Sheriff, and in this form:—

Action Cognitionis Causa, and for Payment.

——— Sheriff, &c. (as on page 80). Whereas it is shewn to me by *A. B.* (design), pursuer, against *E. F.* (design), defender, executor decerned and confirmed to the deceased *C. D.* in terms of the conclusions under-written: Therefore the defender, as executor foresaid, ought to be decerned to pay to the pursuer the sum of L.51, for groceries sold by the pursuer to the said deceased, per account commencing the 1st day of January 1852, and ending the 6th day of January 1853, annexed hereto, with interest from date of citation, and with expenses. AND MY WILL IS, &c.

Where there has been no executor decerned and confirmed, and the proceeding is intended to found an application for confirmation as executor-creditor, a case which frequently presents itself, it is a Summons purely *cognitionis causa*, and therefore it does not contain the conclusion for payment. It would appear, however, that it must be preceded by a charge to confirm. Turnbull, 27th June 1850; 12 D. 1097. The following is the form of the Summons of Cognition:—

——— Sheriff, &c (as on p. 80). Shewn to me by *A. B.* (design), against *E. F.* (design) and *G. H.* (design), nearest in kin of the deceased *C. D.* in terms of the conclusions underwritten. Therefore the said *E. F.* and *G. H.* defenders, as nearest in kin foresaid, ought and should be called for their interest, and the pursuer ought to have my decree *cognitionis causa*, finding and declaring the sum of L.51 sterling, being the amount of an account for grocery goods sold and delivered by the said pursuer to the said deceased *C. D.*, as per account commencing on the 1st day of January 1852, and ending on the 6th day of January 1853, annexed hereto, with interest thereon .

and expenses, to be a just, true, and lawful debt due by the deceased to the pursuer; and that the pursuer has a right and interest in his means and estate for payment thereof, &c.

All the next in kin to the deceased must be called in the action, and when decree is obtained, the pursuer may raise edict as executor-creditor thereon, and proceed to confirm in that character.

Consistorial Cases.

The forms which are now of most frequent occurrence before the Sheriffs, *quâ* Commissaries, relate to the confirmation of executors, the securing repositories and inventorying the effects of deceased parties, before and after interment, and generally to the administration of the effects of deceased persons.

Confirmation of Executors.

Claimants are preferred to the office of executor in the following order:—
(1.) person named in testament; (2.) general disponee; (3.) next in kin; (4.) widow; (5.) creditors; and (6.) special legatees.

The proceedings must be before the Commissary of the district where the deceased had his principal domicile. If he died furth of Scotland, but having property within it, the proceedings are before the Commissary of Edinburgh.

Edict of Confirmation.

———— Sheriff, &c. (as on page 80.)

Whereas it is shewn to me by *A. B.* (design). pursuer, against the executors, testamentars, spouse, bairns, and intromitters with the goods and gear of umquhil *C. D.* (design), who died at Glasgow on the 1st day of November 1853, and against all others having, or pretending to have interest in the said matter, defenders, in terms of the conclusions underwritten. Therefore the said defenders ought to be summoned to see executors-dative decerned and confirmed to the above named defunct, in and to the personal estate of the said defunct *C. D.* at the time of his death, and my will is, that ye summon the defenders to compear in my Court-House at Glasgow, upon the tenth day after the date of your citation, &c.

Procedure after raising Edict.

Although it is not intended here to enter at any length into the subject of the c___rmation of executors, we shall notice shortly the general course of proced___ ___llowing upon such an edict as that given above.

The edict being served against all and sundry, by execution at the door of the parish church of the parish in which the deceased had his domicile, or where he had no domicile, or was abroad with an intention of remaining, in which case the edict must be raised before the Commissary of Edinburgh, at the market-cross of Edinburgh, and the parish-church door of Saint Giles. The edict may be called in the ordinary court after the lapse of nine free days after citation.

Under the provisions of the new statute, any party intending to compete with the pursuer of the edict for the office of executor, will require to give intimation of his intention so to do, by lodging notice with the Sheriff-clerk at latest on the day of compearance or ninth day.

The edict being called, and appearances entered to compete, the case will proceed like an ordinary action, and the Sheriff Commissary will decern in the competition. If no appearance be made, the Sheriff Commissary will decern, and allow the claimant eight free days to find caution and confirm.

Caution being found, warrant will be granted for confirmation, which, being extracted, vests the moveable estate in the executor-dative, and authorises him to sue for and recover it.

Such is the course of procedure in the appointment of an executor-dative. When an executor has been nominated in the will or testament of the deceased, there is no necessity for the edict or decree of decerniture following thereon. The deed of nomination is sufficient evidence of the nominee's title to the office; and on his producing this, with an inventory, on oath, of the deceased's moveable estate, he will obtain without waiting for a court-day, extract-decree of confirmation, which vests him in the estate as executor-nominate.

When the party confirming does so as executor-creditor of the deceased, his title, which is obtained by edict *qua* creditor, and completed by extract, authorizes him to administer to the estate, and, in questions with other creditors, to retain so much of the property confirmed as will be sufficient to pay the expenses of confirmation, and the amount of his own claim or debt

Applications for confirmation by *executors-creditors* must be advertised by notice in the Edinburgh Gazette, at least once, and a copy of the Gazette must be produced in evidence

Petition for Warrant to Seal Repositories.

Unto the Sheriff, &c. (as on page 84).

The petitioner *A. B* humbly sheweth,

That *C. D.* died on the   day of   current, never having been married, and it is as yet uncertain how he has left his affairs, or whether he has left any will or testament relative to the settlement and distribution of his estate.

That the petitioner is the only brother of the said *C. D.*, and, as such, his nearest in kin.

That it is expedient that the household furniture and personal effects of the said *C. D.* should, in the meantime, be protected and saved.

May it therefore please your Lordship to grant warrant to *E. F.* licensed auctioneer in Glasgow, at sight of *G. H.* notary-public there [or to clerks of Court] to secure and seal up the repositories of the said *C D*, and thereafter to open the said repositories, and make an inventory and valuation of the contents thereof; and also an inventory and valuation of the household furniture and other effects in the dwelling-house of the said *C. D.*, so that the same may be forthcoming and accounted for to the heirs, executors, or other representatives of the said *C. D.*

According to Justice, &c.

Drawn by   ROBERT BAIRD, *Pror.*

On such an application the Sheriff's deliverance will be as follows :—

Glasgow, 1853.

The Sheriff-substitute having considered the foregoing petition, grants warrant to *E. F.* licensed auctioneer in Glasgow, at sight of *G. H.* designed in the petition, to examine and seal up, as craved.

Having executed the warrant, the auctioneer should annex a certificate to that effect. which may be in these terms :—

Glasgow, Nov. 1853.

In terms of the above warrant, I, *E. F*, licensed auctioneer in Glasgow, passed to the house lately occupied by the said deceased *C. D.*, and did there, in presence, and in sight of *G. H.* notary-public in Glasgow, seal up and secure the repositories of the said *C. D.*

(Signed)   *E. F.* Licensed Auctioneer
     G. H. Notary-Public.

The forms of application for warrant again to open the repositories, and to inventory and value as craved in the petition (which may be by minute or incidental petition in the process), and of the subsequent procedure, will readily present themselves.

Adherence.

By Will. IV. cap. 69, § 53, all actions of declarator of marriage, &c. can be brought and insisted in only before the Court of Session. This act did not include the process of adherence which remained with the Commissaries of Edinburgh against parties domiciled within their restricted territory, until their office become vacant, after which it passed to the Sheriff of Edinburgh. The Sheriffs of counties, by Geo. IV. cap. 97, are competent to actions of adherence against parties resident within their territory. See Lothian on Consistorial Actions. The following is the style of a

Summons of Adherence.

—— Sheriff, &c as on page 80.
Shewn to me by Mrs   otherwise *B.* presently residing in
     wife of *A. B* (design him) pursuer, against the said *A. B.* defender, in terms of the conclusions underwritten. Therefore the defender, who has deserted the pursuer, ought to be decerned to adhere to the pursuer as his lawful wife, her society, fellowship, and company, and to treat, cherish, and entertain her at bed and board, and to perform the other conjugal duties as becometh a husband to his wife, and to cohabit with the pursuer, and nowise leave or desert her company in time coming ; and the said defender ought to be decerned to make payment to the pursuer of the expenses of process ; and my will is, &c.

Count, Reckoning, and Payment.

This action is resorted to where a party has funds in his hands belonging to the pursuer, arising out of intromissions of one kind or another, whether as a cash-keeper, factor, or manager, or as intromitter with effects of a deceased debtor.

In the Small Debt Act there is no form of the summons of count, reckoning, and payment. If, therefore, a claim under L.12 arises out of intromissions, the course must be to obtain an ordinary petitory summons for a sum as a balance.

In the ordinary court procedure there is a style of a summons of count and reckoning given in Schedule A, as follows :—

Against a Cash-Keeper.

———— Sheriff, &c. (as on page 80). Therefore the defender ought to be decerned to produce before me a full account of his intromissions as cash-keeper to the pursuer, that the true balance due to the pursuer thereon may be ascertained, and the defender should be decerned to pay to the pursuer such sum as may be found to be the true balance on said account, with the interest which may be due thereon; and if he fail to produce such account, the defender should be decerned to pay to the pursuer the sum of L.   ,* which should, in that case, be held to be the balance due, with interest thereon from the   day of   , with expenses.

Against a Factor, Commissioner, or otherwise

———— Sheriff, &c. (as on page) 80. Therefore the defender ought to be decerned to produce before me a full account of his intromissions as factor, agent, commissioner, or otherwise, for the pursuer, between the   day of   and   day of   , that the true balance due, &c. (as above)

For a Share of an Executry.

———— Sheriff, &c. (as on page 80). Whereas it is shewn to me by A. B. (design), one of the four brothers of the deceased C. D. and one of the nearest in kin of the said deceased C. D. against E. F. (design), executor appointed by the said deceased C. D. and intromitted with his moveable means and estate, defender, in terms of the conclusions underwritten . Therefore the defender ought to be decerned to produce before me a full account of his intromissions with the moveable means and estate of the deceased C. D., that the true balance due to the pursuer, as one of the four next of kin as aforesaid, may be ascertained; and the defender should be decerned to pay to the pursuer such sum as may be found, &c. (as above).

Damages.

There are a great variety of grounds of action of damages. The following will sufficiently exemplify the conclusions :—

For Breach of Contract.

———— Sheriff, &c. (as on page 80): Therefore the defender ought to be decerned to pay to the pursuer the sum of L.2000 sterling, being damages sustained by the pursuer, in consequence of the defender's breach of contract, through refusal or delay to deliver to the pursuer 500 tons of No. 1 Gartsherrie pig-iron, conform to contract entered into between the pursuer and defender, through the medium of E. F metal-broker in Glasgow, on the first day of January eighteen hundred and fifty three, with expenses.

For Failure to Implement Contract.

———— Sheriff, &c. (as on p. 80) Therefore the defender ought to be decerned to pay to the pursuer the sum of L.100 sterling, as the loss and

---

* The sum here mentioned would appear to fix the jurisdiction. See *Lamb* v. *Henderson,* (Glasgow circuit) 4th October 1849. 2 Broun, 311.

damage which the pursuer has sustained by the defender's failure to implement an agreement, whereby the defender sold to the pursuer, at Glasgow, upon the 1st day of October 1853, four tons of Peruvian guano, at the price of L.9 per ton, &c

For Spoliation.

———— Sheriff, &c. (as on page 80): Therefore the defender ought to be decerned to make payment to the pursuer of the sum of L 100 sterling, being damages sustained by the pursuer in consequence of the defender having seized, or caused to be seized and taken, from the pursuer's possession, in a park at Morningside, near Edinburgh, ten milch cows, the property of the pursuer, and having illegally detained them, &c.

For Bodily Injury.

———— Sheriff, &c. (as on page 80). Whereas it is shewn to me by *A. B.* (design) against *C. D* proprietor of the coach called the Highflyer, betwixt Edinburgh and Moffat, defender, in terms of the conclusions underwritten. Therefore the defender ought to be decerned to pay to the pursuer L 1000 sterling, being damages sustained by the pursuer, in consequence of bodily injuries occasioned by the upsetting, on the 3d day of November 1853, of the said coach betwixt Edinburgh and Moffat, through the fault of the defender, his servants, or others in his employment, and for whom he is responsible, &c.

For Defamation.

———— Sheriff, &c. (as on page 80): Therefore the defender ought to be decerned to pay to the pursuer the sum of L 1000 sterling, being damages sustained by the pursuer, in consequence of the defender having, on the   day of   , and within the Royal Exchange, Glasgow, and in presence and hearing of *E. F.*, and *G* (design them), slandered the pursuer, by stating that he was a knave and a cheat.

It must be kept in view, that wherever malice or want of probable cause is of the essence of the action, as in cases of privilege, the Summons must be set forth that the words or act was so said or done.

Exhibition.

Where a party who requires exhibition of deeds or papers is the party entitled to the possession of them, the proper form of compulsitor seems to be by petition. The schedule E of the statute containing the forms of petitions seems to apply to such a case.

We have given the form of such a petition in Chapter VII. at page 56. There is no doubt, however, of the competency of a summons of exhibition, and if that form be preferred, the conclusions may be as follows:—

Summons of Exhibition and delivery of Writs.

———— Sheriff, &c. (as on page 80). Therefore the defender ought to be decerned to exhibit and produce before me the whole writs, titles, and evidents of the lands of   belonging to the pursuer, and particularly the following (here describe them), and all others in the defender's possession relating to said lands unvitiated and uncancelled, at least in such condition as they were in when the defender received the same; and the said writs should be decerned and ordained to be given and delivered up to the pursuer, to be used and disposed of by him as his own proper writs and evidents in all time coming; and the defender ought to be decerned to pay to the pursuer expenses of process, &c.

In title deeds a clause by granter of the deed, obliging himself and his heirs and successors to make previous titles forthcoming on all necessary occasions, on receipt and under penalty for redelivery, is of frequent occurrence. Supposing the grantee or his successors had occasion to enforce such an obligation, it would probably be competent by petition. But we shall give the conclusions of a summons suited to such a case.

Summons of Exhibition.

—— Sheriff, &c (as on page 80). Therefore the said defender ought to be decerned to make forthcoming, exhibition, and delivery to the pursuer of the following writs (here specify them) in terms of the obligation contained in a disposition by *J. H.* his author and predecessor, in favour of
dated the   day of
and of which obligation the pursuer is now in right, and that on a receipt and obligation to return the same within a reasonable time, and under a suitable penalty.

Exhibition ad deliberandum.

This is an action at the instance of an apparent heir for exhibition of the writs connected with his ancestor's estate, to enable him to judge whether he ought to take up the succession.

This action is now scarcely ever resorted to, as it is always in the power of an heir to expede service by limitation.—See below, *voce Service.* Should circumstances occur where this action is to be resorted to, the variation in the form given above will suggest itself.

Forthcoming.
Small Debt Forms.

The jurisdiction of the Small Debt Court extends to cases of forthcoming by the 9th section of the statute quoted above, page 5.

Summons of Forthcoming in Small Debt Court.

—— Sheriff, &c. (as on page 80). Whereas it is humbly complained to me by *A. B*, (design him) upon and against *H. H.* (design him) arrestee, and *C. D.* (design him) common debtor; that the said common debtor is owing to the complainer the sum of L.10, 15s. sterling, and 4s. 6d of expenses, contained in a decreet at his instance, obtained before me, dated the 11th day of November 1853 years, and that the complainer, on the 2d day of November 1853 years, by virtue of my warrant, dated the 1st day of November 1853 years, arrested in the hands of the arrestee all sums of money owing by him to the said defender, or to any other person for his use and behoof, and all goods and effects in his custody belonging to the said defender, and that to an amount or extent not exceeding the value of L.12 sterling, which ought to be made forthcoming to the complainer · Therefore the arrestee, and the said common debtor for his interest, ought to be decerned and ordained to make forthcoming, pay, and deliver to the complainer the money, goods, and effects arrested as aforesaid, or so much thereof as will satisfy and pay the said sums of L.10, 15s. and 4s 6d. owing to the complainer as aforesaid Therefore it is my will, &c.

This summons is signed by the Sheriff-clerk of the County in which the arrestee resides, and is a warrant for summoning the arrestee and the common debtor to appear and answer at the Sheriff-Court of that county not sooner than the sixth day after the date of citation, and also for summoning witnesses and havers for all parties

The arrestee and the common debtor must be cited to appear on the same court-day. The citations and executions are the same with those given above, p 22.

Where the common debtor does not reside, and is not found within the county in which the action is brought, he may be cited by any other Sheriff-officer in any other county to appear in a Sheriff-Court of the county where the arrestee resides, but not sooner than the twelfth day after the date of citation, and the warrant must be endorsed by the Sheriff-clerk of that other county § 9.

The style of the decree for the pursuer is given in the Small Debt Act, Schedule D If it be money that is arrested, it is ordained to be paid to the pursuer; if goods, warrant is granted to sell the same, or as much thereof as will pay the pursuer his debt, and the expenses of process and of sale.

In the Ordinary Court.

No form of the summons is given in the statute. It may be as follows —
Summons of Forthcoming.

——, Sheriff, &c (as on p. 80). Shewn to me by *A. B.* (design), pursuer, against *H H* (design), arrestee, and *C. D.* (design), defenders, in terms of the conclusions under written . Therefore the said *H. H.*, defender, arrestee, ought to be decerned to make payment and deliverance to the pursuer of the sum of L 100, or such other sum or sums as may be owing by him to the said *C D.*, and arrested in his hands on the   day of November 1853, at the instance of the pursuer, AT LEAST of such part thereof as shall satisfy and pay the pursuer the principal sum of L 47, 3s. 6d., interest thereof from the   day of   , and of L.   of expenses of process, and   as dues of extract,—all contained in a decree, obtained before me at the pursuer's instance, dated the   day of   , and the said defender, principal debtor, ought to be decerned to pay expenses of process. And my will is, &c.

Interdict.

The procedure in the case of interdict is by petition, and there are a great variety of circumstances in which there may be occasion to apply for it. The conclusion of the petition will be directed against the respondent, or those in his service or employment, doing the thing which is complained of.

To take a case of alleged nuisance, such as a candle manufactory, against which interdict is sought, the petition for interdict will be in this form ·

Petition for Interdict against a Nuisance.

Unto the Sheriff of the county of

       A B. (design)

against

C. D. (design).

The petitioner, A B., humbly sheweth,

That the petitioner is the proprietor of the dwelling-house, No.   of Street, Edinburgh. That the respondent is the proprietor of the steading immediately adjoining thereto on the south, and is in the course of converting the buildings thereupon into a candle manufactory, with the intention of manufacturing candle therein, to the nuisance of the petitioner and the neighbourhood.

> May it therefore please your Lordship to grant warrant for interdicting the said C. D., his servants, and all others employed by him, from making a candle manufactory on his foresaid premises, or manufacturing candle thereupon, and to find the respondent liable in expenses.
> According to Justice, &c.

Or an action of declarator and damages might be resorted to, for a style of which, see below, *Nuisance*

Interdict, a Landlord v. his Tenant.

Unto the Sheriff, &c. (as above).

That the petitioner, by lease dated the   day of   , let to the respondent the farm of   , situated in the parish of   , of which farm the petitioner is proprietor. That the respondent is in the course of putting down shafts, and making other operations on the said farm for other purposes, with the intention of working and disposing of coal, or other minerals, situated therein, without any right so to do

> May it therefore please your Lordship to grant warrant for interdict against the said C. D., his servants, workmen, and all others employed by him, from sinking shafts, and from all other operations on the said farm, with the view of searching for, using, or disposing of any coal, or other minerals situated therein, and to find the respondent liable in expenses.
> According to Justice, &c.

A Landlord against the Removal of his Tenant's effects.

Unto the Sheriff of the county of

A. B. (design), house-factor in Edinburgh, factor for   , and one of the trustees of the late C. D., merchant there;

against

E. F., auctioneer in Edinburgh.

The petitioner humbly sheweth, that G. H., residing at No.   Princes Street, Edinburgh, is tenant under the petitioner, as factor and trustee fore-

said of the house, No.   Princes Street, for the year current from Whitsunday 1853 till Whitsunday 1854, at the rent of L 80 sterling, payable
half-yearly, and no part of said rent has yet been paid.

That the said *E F.*, as acting for himself, or for some party to the petitioner
unknown, has announced a sale of the furniture and effects in said house,
over which the petitioner has a right of hypothec.

> May it therefore please your Lordship to grant warrant for interdict against
> the said *E. F*, and all others, from selling or otherwise interfering
> with said furniture and effects, until the petitioner's said rent is paid,
> or judicial security found for the same, and to find the said *E. F.*
> liable in expenses.
>
> According to Justice

Against the sale of effects illegally poinded.

Unto the Sheriff of the county of

A B. and Co., general dealers in Edinburgh,

against

C. D, merchant in Edinburgh

The petitioners humbly show, that the said *C. D.* having wrongously and unwarrantably poinded the following effects (here enumerate them) belonging to
the petitioners, and in their premises, on an alleged warrant or diligence
directed against *E. F*, a partner of the petitioner's firm, and threatening to
sell the same.

> May it therefore please your Lordship to grant warrant for interdict against
> the said *C. D.* from selling, or in any way interfering with said
> effects, and to find the said *C. D.* liable in expenses.
>
> According to Justice.

Breach of Interdict.

The complaint for breach of interdict is of a penal nature, and the shorter
form of petition introduced by the recent statute does not therefore seem to
apply to it. The following may be the form :—

Unto the Sheriff of the County of

A B. [*design*] with concurrence of *M. L.* procurator-fiscal of the county of

v.

C. D.   (*design.*)

The petitioner *A. B.* humbly sheweth,

That, on a petition presented to your Lordship for interdict at the petitioner's
instance against the respondent, your Lordship was pleased to grant interdict
against the respondent, interdicting and prohibiting (here specify the nature
of the interdict.) That notwithstanding of the said interdict, and in the knowledge of it, the said *C. D.* (here state the particulars of the breach) whereby
the said *C. D.* has been guilty of breach of said interdict.

May it therefore please your Lordship to order service of this petition on the
said *C. D.*, and to ordain him to lodge answers thereto, if so advised, within
a short space ; and thereafter, on advising this petition with or without an-

swers, to grant warrant for the apprehension and examination of the respondent, and to find him liable to the petitioner in the sum of L.100 sterling, in name of damages: And also to find and amerce the respondent in the sum of L   as a fine for behoof of the public for contempt of Court, and to grant warrant to officers of court to imprison him in the prison of   till he pay such fine, but not exceeding such time as to your Lordship shall seem proper, or to inflict such other punishment as to your Lordship shall seem just, also to find the respondent liable in expenses.

According to Justice, &c.

Maills and Duties.

The action of maills and duties is resorted to by a proprietor infeft, or by disponees or adjudgers, for obtaining payment of the rents or profits of heritable subjects

———— Sheriff, &c. (as on page 80).—Shewn to me by *A. B.* (*design*) pursuer, against *C. D.* (*design*) principal debtor, and against the following persons, tenants or occupants of the subjects specified and described in the bond and disposition in security after mentioned, viz. *E. F. G. H.* defenders, in terms of the conclusions under written. Therefore the said *E. F. G. H.* &c. ought and should be decerned to pay to the pursuer of the rents, maills, and duties of their several possessions of the foresaid subjects and others, and that during their possession thereof respectively, with the legal interest thereof from and after the respective terms at which the same are or shall become due, and until paid, viz. the said *E F.* of the sum of L 20, being the rent due and payable by him at the term of (here specify unpaid rent past due, or current) and the like sum half-yearly thereafter during his possession, with interest as aforesaid, the said *G. H.* of the sum of, &c. specify (*in like manner,*) at least, of so much of the said rents as will satisfy and pay the pursuer the principal sum of L 750, interest thereof from the term of Martinmas 1852, liquidate penalty, and termly failures, all specified and contained in a bond and disposition in security, granted by the said *C. D.* to and in favour of the said *A. B.*, his heirs and assignees dated 15th, and recorded in the Particular Register of Sasines for the shire of Lanark the 17th day of May 1852; and further the said *C. D.*, principal debtor, and any also of the other defenders appearing to oppose the conclusions of the present summons, ought to be decerned to make payment to the pursuer of expenses of process. And my will is, &c.

Maritime Actions.

We refer to what we have stated in chapter III. p. 12, as to the Sheriff's jurisdiction in Admiralty cases.

The enumeration in the Statute of Maritime causes relating to civil matters seems, both comprehensive and specific; but various nice questions have arisen, illustrative of the difficulties that may sometimes present themselves, in deciding whether an action is maritime or not. And Mr Smith, in his book on Maritime Practice, gives sound advice, when he thus concludes his short chapter, entitled, Description of Cases Strictly Maritime, thus: " *In dubio*, therefore, wherever the practitioner entertains the slightest doubt as to a case being maritime or not, the safest course is to assume that it is not, and proceed accordingly."

Moreover, there is not now the inducement that there formerly was, to have the action considered and treated as a maritime one. Until the passing of 1 and 2 Vict. chap. 119, it was held in practice that the pursuer of a maritime action was entitled at the very outset of his case to insist on the defender finding cation *de judicio sisti et judicatum solvi*. While, on the other hand, the defender, who had found such caution, was entitled to demand that the pursuer should, in his turn, find security *de damnis et impensis*. This is now materially changed, in so far as it affects parties domiciled in Scotland, by § 22 of the 1 and 2 Vict. cap 119, which declares "That, in maritime causes or proceedings raised and brought before any Sheriff Court in Scotland, caution *judicatum solvi*, or *de damnis et impensis* snall not be required in any such cause or proceeding, from any party who shall be domiciled in Scotland, any law or practice to the contrary notwithstanding, unless the judge shall require it, on special grounds, to be stated in the interlocutor requiring the same, or in a note annexed thereto."

There is generally no substantial difference in the form of the conclusions of maritime and those of ordinary summary actions. Special forms of actions on bills of lading, charter-parties, for seamen's wages, &c. may therefore be here dispensed with.

The following forms are, however, somewhat peculiar :—

PROCESS OF SET.

When part owners differ among themselves in regard to the affairs of their ship, or when one of them desires to free himself from joint ownership with the rest, the object is accomplished by the process of set.

It is raised at the instance of the dissatisfied part-owner, who, in the first place, proposes to his co-owners to have the vessel sold by auction, and the proceeds divided. If this is declined, he then makes offer by letter or protest, either to sell his shares at a price which he names, or to buy theirs at the same rate. If this proposition is also declined, he then can proceed in Court by summons in the following form :—

———— Sheriff, &c. (as on page 80) Whereas it is shewn to me by *A. B.* (design) owner of thirty-two sixty-fourth parts of the ship Fly of Glasgow, pursuer, against *C. D* (design) owner of sixteen sixty-fourth parts of the said vessel, and *E. F.* (design) also owner of sixteen sixty-fourth parts of said vessel, in terms of the conclusions under written . Therefore it ought to be found and declared, that the parties having differed as to the employment of the said ship, and that as the pursuer is contented to sell, let, and dispose of his half of the said ship or vessel, her float-boat, furniture, and apparelling whatsoever, to the said *C. D.* and *E. F.* for the sum of L.250 each, they, the said *C. D.* and *E F.*, each ought to accept thereof, or otherwise the said *C. D.* and *E. F.* ought to be decerned each of them, to sell, set, and give over to the pursuer their respective fourth shares of the said vessel, and pertinents at the above-mentioned rate of L.250 for each fourth share as aforesaid, upon payment to them of the said sums; or otherwise the said ship or vessel with her float-boat, apparelling, and appurtenances, ought and should be publicly rouped and sold by warrant of Court, and the free proceeds, after deduction of all expenses, divided among the parties, agreeably to their respective rights and interests, and the defenders ought to be found liable in expenses of process.—And my will is, &c.

ARRESTMENT OF A VESSEL

When under an action against the owners of a vessel, it is intended to arrest and to prevent her departure by dismantling, a special warrant is inserted in the will of the summons. It is in these terms —

Warrant to Arrest.

And that ye arrest in security the defender's said vessel, the Fly of Glasgow, and all other ships, barques, boats, goods, monies, debts, and effects, tackle, sails, rudders, and anchors from the said vessel (the same being always in a safe harbour), to remain under sure fence and arrestment, and if need be, that ye charge all judges, magistrates, officers of Her Majesty's army and navy, and others whom it effeirs, to concur with and assist you in putting hereof to due and lawful execution.

It is proper to observe, that a warrant to arrest and dismantle in the above terms, is not necessary for the mere purpose of arresting the ship. The ordinary warrant of the statute to arrest "goods, monies, debts, and effects," executed in the usual way, is sufficient to authorise the arrestment of a ship to remain in the harbour of   under sure fence and arrestment until caution be found. *Clark and Others* v. *Loos,* 17th June 1853. The inserting of the special warrant to arrest and dismantle, will therefore only be resorted to when there is fear that the vessel will be removed, and it is intended to dismantle as well as arrest.

SALE OF AN ARRESTED VESSEL.

The ship being arrested, and if necessary dismantled, cannot sail until a bond of caution be lodged with the Sheriff-clerk, who thereupon will grant a certificate for the loosing of the arrestment, and uplifting and restoring of the articles that may have been removed from the ship. Should this not be done, the pursuer, after obtaining decree in his action, may proceed by a process of sale on the arrestment.

The following is the style of the summons of sale :—

——— Sheriff, &c. (as on page 80) Shewn to me by *A. B.* (design), pursuer, against *C D.* shipmaster, residing in   , part owner of vessel Fly of Glasgow, and *E. F.* (design), the other part owner of said vessel, defenders, in terms of the conclusions under written: Therefore the vessel Fly of Glasgow, with her boats and apparelling, as she now lies arrested in the harbour of Glasgow, ought to be publicly rouped, and the proceeds of sale, or as much thereof as will satisfy and pay to the pursuer the sum of L 200 sterling, with the sum of L.   of interest and expenses of process, all contained in a decreet obtained before me at the instance of the pursuer against the defenders, on the   day of   , together with the expense of using the said arrestment, and of this process of sale and whole procedure to be had thereon ; and all concerned ought thereafter to compete their preferences in the residue of said proceeds (if any), us accords.—And my will is, &c.

The rest of the procedure in the process of sale consists of the recovery of the ship's papers, particularly her certificate of registry from the party holding the same, or failing such recovery, getting, under application to the Board of Customs, a copy of the said certificates taken from the Custom-house books, and getting a remit to inventory the ship and her appurtenances; the minute for and authority to advertise the same for sale; the conditions of sale, minutes thereof, and the authority to the collector and comptroller for registering the purchaser as owner.

If a vessel has been put back to port by stress of weather, a petition of the following description is sometimes presented:—

Petition to report on a Vessel and her " Stowage."
Unto the Sheriff of the county of
A. B. shipmaster,
AGAINST
The ship *Fly* of Leith, at present lying in the river Clyde, off Greenock,

The petitioner A. B. humbly sheweth—

That on or about the 11th day of June current, the petitioner sailed from Greenock with the said vessel, she being then under the command of *M. N.* who was afterwards drowned, bound for New York, with passengers and a cargo of iron, bleaching-powder, and other merchandise—all properly dunnaged and stowed.

About the 15th day of June current the said vessel encountered a violent storm, accompanied by a heavy sea, during which she lost her top and top-gallant masts, with the whole sails and gear thereto pertaining, and sustained other very considerable damage, and was in such imminent peril that the petitioner, for the general safety, was obliged to throw overboard a part of said cargo.

For the safety of the passengers, crew, and ship, and cargo, the petitioner put back with the vessel to Greenock, where he arrived early this morning.

For the satisfaction of the passengers, the petitioner is desirous of having the opinion of competent parties as to the stowage of the cargo of the said vessel, and as to her capability of carrying to New York the cargo on board safely and conveniently.

May it therefore please your Lordship to grant warrant authorising *C. D.* and *E. F.*, both shipmasters in Greenock, to examine the stowage of the cargo of the said vessel, and to ascertain the quantity of cargo on board of her, and thereupon to report as to the state of the stowage, and as to the capabilities of the ship to carry the said cargo to New York safely and conveniently; or do otherwise in the premises as to your Lordship shall seem proper.

According to Justice, &c.

On such a petition the Sheriff's deliverance may be as follows:—

" *Greenock,* 18th *June* 1851.—The Sheriff-substitute having considered the foregoing petition, grants warrant to, and appoints *C. D.* and *E. F.*, both shipmasters in Greenock, to pass, examine, ascertain, and report, all as craved "

Petition for Warrant to Land, Store, and Sell Unclaimed Goods.

Unto the Sheriff of the county of

A. B ship owner in Leith,

AGAINST

The shipper or consignee of " Whitestone," on board said vessel

The petitioner *A. B.* humbly sheweth—

That on the 19th of June 1854 the petitioner's ship, the Fly of Leith, arrived here, having on board, and as part of a cargo shipped at Smyrna, two hundred tons or thereby of an article called Whitestone, to be delivered at said port of Leith " unto order," on payment of freight at the rate of seven shillings per ton, conform to master's copy of said bill of lading, herewith produced.

That the ship has been in a discharging-dock since the above date, but no one has applied for said Whitestone, and it is still on board, and the petitioner does not know to whom to deliver it.

That the ship is chartered and about to proceed on a new voyage, and must be cleared preparatory to receiving a new cargo.

May it therefore please your Lordship to grant warrant for landing and storing, and thereafter for selling the said Whitestone, and for applying the proceeds, first, in paying the cost of this procedure, and, second, of the freight and charges, reserving to the petitioner his claim against the shipper or consignee for any deficiency between the proceeds of sale and the amount of said cost, freight, and charges.

According to Justice, &c.

The Sheriff's deliverance on such a petition will probably be a warrant to land and store, accompanied by an order (before granting warrant to sell) for intimation by advertisement in an advertising paper of general circulation, and in one or more local papers having fair circulation in the county or place. These advertisements to certify that unless appearance is entered within   days from the date of the publication in which they appear, warrant of sale would be granted as craved

The commodity being landed and stored, and the advertisements inserted, and the   days expired, the petitioner will produce copies of the publication containing the advertisements, with a short minute (which may be written on the petition) narrating his implement of the order, and a certificate by the Sheriff-clerk (which may be indorsed on the petition) that no notice of appearance has been given.

On resuming consideration of the application, with the additions, the Sheriff may be expected to grant warrant to sell by public roup the commodity, or as much of it as will pay the said cost, freight, and other charges, pointing out the manner in which the sale is to be previously notified, and ordaining the petitioner to lodge a report of the sale, with an account of costs, in the hands of the Clerk of Court within fourteen days after it, and remitting the account of costs to the auditor for taxation.

The sale being carried through in the manner ordered, and the costs taxed, the petitioner lodges report with vouchers. If there be a surplus (and there may be a small one, although the warrant is only to sell " so much, &c.") it should be consigned in Court. If a deficiency, the petitioner should in his report crave special reservation of his claim against the shipper and the consigners

On such report, &c the Sheriff may close the procedure by a deliverance in these terms :—

> *Edinburgh, 28th July* 1854 —The Sheriff having considered the foregoing report of sale, and whole previous procedure, approves thereof (if there be a craving for reservation of claim he will here add, " and reserve as therein craved") and decerns.

Meditatio Fugæ.

When a creditor believes on reasonable grounds that his debtor is going abroad, with the view of avoiding payment of his debt, he may present a a petition to the Sheriff or a Magistrate, within whose jurisdiction the debtor is at the time, with the view of caution being obtained *de judicio sisti;* in other words, that the debtor shall abide action by the creditor for his debts.

The whole law and practice in this subject has been fully and ably put into the hands of the profession by Mr Barclay, first in his Notes on *Meditatio Fugæ,* published in 1832, and in his Digest of the Law of Scotland, with reference to the office and duties of a Justice of the Peace, recently published.

We need only therefore sketch the procedure referring to these works for details and authorities. The form of the petition is not materially changed, nor is the subsequent procedure affected by any of the rules introduced by the recent statute.

The creditor's claim may be contingent, but it must be specific, and must be above L.8, 6s 8d.

The following is the form of the

Petition.

(Date.)

Unto the Sheriff of the County of Edinburgh,

A. B (design him.)

v.

C. D. (design him.)

The petitioner A. B. humbly sheweth ;

That the said C D. is justly due and owing to the petitioner the sum of L.   (here state the amount of the debt, and how due, whether by account, bill, or otherwise), conform to   herewith produced

That the petitioner intends immediately to raise (or has raised) an action against the said C. D. for payment and recovery of the said debt, interest, and expenses of prosecution.

That the petitioner has been credibly informed, and in his conscience believes, that the said C. D. is presently in *meditatione fugæ,* and about to leave Scotland, whereby the petitioner will be defrauded or disappointed of said debt and consequents.

May it therefore please your Lordship to take the petitioner's oath to the verity of the averments made in this petition, and thereon to grant warrant to apprehend and bring the said *C D* before you for examination, and thereafter to commit him to the prison of   , therein to be detained until he find sufficient caution, acted in your Lordship's court-books, *de judicio sisti*, in any action for payment of the said debt and consequents which may be raised against him, within six months, at the instance of the petitioner (or in the said depending action), for payment of said debt and consequents, and in case the said *C. D.* has left your jurisdiction, to recommend to all other judges and magistrates to concur in your said warrant.

According to Justice, &c

A. B.

(or)   ALFRED ANGUS, *Agent for Petr.*

Upon this petition being presented, the Sheriff will pronounce a deliverance, ordaining the creditor to appear and depone.

Edinburgh,   1853.

The Sheriff-substitute having considered the foregoing petition with productions, ordains the petitioner to appear and depone to the verity of the statements therein made, and to condescend on his grounds for believing the defender to be in *meditatione fugæ.*   AND. JAMESON

Form of Deposition of Creditor.

Edinburgh,   *Nov.* 1853.

Compeared the within designed *A. B*, and he being solemnly sworn and examined, Depones,—That what is contained in the within petition is truth, and especially that the debt therein mentioned is justly due by the said *C. D.* to the deponent: That the deponent has been credibly informed, and believes in his conscience, that the said *C. D.* is in *meditatione fugæ,* and about immediately to leave Scotland and to go to Australia, or some other place abroad, whereby the deponent will be defrauded or disappointed of his said debt, and being specially interrogated on the grounds of his belief, Depones,—(here the particulars of the deponent's information, and from whom received, will be stated).—All which is truth, as the deponent shall answer to God

A. B.

AND. JAMESON.

If the Sheriff sees sufficient reason to grant warrant to apprehend the debtor for examination, the following may be the interlocutor :—

Warrant to Apprehend for Examination.

Edinburgh,   *Nov.* 1853.

The Sheriff-substitute having resumed consideration of the petition, with the oath of verity thereto by the petitioner, grants warrant to apprehend *C. D.* designed in said petition, and bring him for examination, and recommends to all judges and magistrates to concur herein.   AND. JAMESON.

This warrant may be executed on Sunday.

When the debtor is apprehended, he undergoes an examination, which must be in presence of the Sheriff. If, after the examination, the Sheriff finds it necessary to order a proof, his interlocutor will be as follows.—

Edinburgh,   *Nov.* 1853.

The Sheriff-substitute having resumed consideration of the petition, with the oath of the petitioner, and declaration of the debtor, in respect of the denial by the defender of any intention to leave the Kingdom, allows the petitioner a proof *pro ut de jure* of all facts and circumstances in support of his petition and oath, that the defender is in *meditatione fugæ*. Allows the defender a proof in the same way, of all facts and circumstances in opposition to that statement, and allows both parties conjunct proofs ; grants diligence against havers and witnesses to both parties, and assigns to-morrow, at one o'clock afternoon, for the petitioner proceeding with his proof, and, in the meantime, grants warrant for committing the said *C D.* to the

prison of   , until he find caution acted in the books of Court, *de judicio sisti,* in the present petition, and that he shall abide the final deliverance to be pronounced therein.

AND. JAMESON.

The debtor can now be liberated by getting a responsible party to grant a bond of caution *de judicio sisti.* Such bond is prepared by the Clerk of Court, and he alone is judge of the sufficiency of the caution, unless where the creditor consents to the cautioner being accepted, and this bond continues in force until the decree in the action be extracted.

But if such caution be not found, the proof for both parties will proceed before the Sheriff on the day and hour fixed, after consideration of which he will either grant or refuse the prayer of the petition. When the prayer of the petition is granted, the following deliverance will be pronounced —

Edinburgh,   *Nov.* 1853.

The Sheriff-Substitute having resumed consideration of the petition and productions, the deposition of the petitioner, the declaration of the defender, and proof adduced for both parties ; circumduces the term for proving ; finds the complaint proved, grants warrant to apprehend *C. D.* within designed, and to commit him to the prison of   , therein to be detained until he find caution acted in the books of Court, *de judicio sisti,* in the depending action mentioned in said petition, (or in any action for payment of the debt mentioned in said petition, to be brought against him at the petitioner's instance, in any competent court within six months from this date) Finds the petitioner entitled to expenses, modifies the same to the sum of L   , for which, with the clerk's dues of extract, decerns against the defender.

AND. JAMESON.

On the other hand, where the petitioner has failed in his proof to satisfy the Sheriff of the debtor's intention to leave the country, he will pronounce as follows :—

The Sheriff-substitute having resumed consideration of the petition and productions, the deposition of the petitioner, the declaration of the defender, and proof adduced for both parties; finds the complaint not sufficiently proved; dismisses the same, Finds the defender entitled to expenses, modifies the same to L.   , for which, with the clerk's dues of extract, decerns against the pursuer. AND. JAMESON.

Molestation and Damages.

Where a party is molested in the possession of his property, an action of molestation is competent. The following may be the style of the

Summons.

———— Sheriff, &c. (as on p. 80). Shewn to me by *A B.* heritable proprietor of the lands and others after mentioned, pursuer, against *C D.* (design), and *E. F.* (design), in terms of the conclusions underwritten: Therefore the defender ought to be decerned to desist and cease from troubling and molesting the pursuer in the possession of All and Whole (here describe the property), in all time coming, and they ought to be decerned to pay to the pursuer the sum of L.100 sterling, being damages sustained by the pursuer in consequence of their having molested and interfered with him in the possession of the said property, with expenses.—And my will is, &c.

Unless it be the object of the pursuer both to prevent the molestation and to recover damages, a petition for interdict would be competent, and sufficiently answer the purpose.

Multiplepoinding
In Small Debt Court.

The procedure in the Small Debt Court, in the case of multiplepoinding, is prescribed by § 10 and Schedule E. of that Statute. The fund held and claimed must not exceed L.12. See remark *infra*, p. 111.

We may notice, that this is one of the instances in which parties may often avail themselves of the power of having the case remitted of consent from the Ordinary to the Small Debt Court. It often happens that all parties in such case wish expedition; and in the Small Debt Court they may, if disposed to be content with the Sheriff's judgment as final, have the summary form of trial, whatever be the pecuniary amount involved

For the form of the summons we refer to Schedule E (p. 60, App. of this volume).

The action is to be brought before that Sheriff Court, to the jurisdiction of which the holder of the fund or subject shall be amenable. 1 Vict c. 41, § 10.

The claimant and common debtor are to be cited in manner enacted by Act to be followed in small-debt summonses of forthcoming, &c. Ib. § 10

If the process be raised in name of the holder by another party, the holder shall be cited. Ib. § 10.

The Sheriff may, where, and as he sees fit, order further intimation or publication of the Multiplepoinding by advertisement in any newspaper, or otherwise Ib. § 10.

It is provided that no judgment preferring any party to the fund or subject *in medio*, shall be pronounced at the first calling of the cause, or until

due intimation has been given, such as may appear satisfactory to the Sheriff, in order that all parties may have an opportunity of lodging their claims.
§ 10.   The following is the form of a

Claim in a Multiplepoinding

I. *E F* (design) hereby claim to be preferred in the Multiplepoinding raised in
name of *A B.* against (mention the defenders), for L.   of principal due to
me by, conform to (state generally the ground of debt, whether by bond, bill,
or account, &c. as the case might be,) with interest from   , and
expenses.   (Signed)   *E. F.*

Quoad ultra, the Sheriff tries the case according to the summary forms
provided as to other cases in the Small Debt Court.   § 10.

In the Ordinary Court.

The form of the multiplepoinding in the ordinary Court is given in Schedule A. annexed to the recent Statute.   It may be raised either by the
holder of the fund or subject arrested, or by a claimant in name of the
holder.   In either case it must be stated in the body of the summons who
is the real raiser of the action. § 8.   The following is the form of a

Summons of Multiplepoinding raised by the holder.

———— Sheriff of the county of   To officers of Court, jointly and severally.
Whereas it is shewn to me by *A. B* (*design him*) pursuer, and real raiser,
against *C D.* (*design him*) common debtor, *E. F* (*design*) and *G. H.* (*design*)
all defenders, alleged creditors of the said *C. D.* in terms of the conclusions
underwritten : THEREFORE, it should be declared that the pursuer holder of
a fund *in medio,* viz. the sum of L.500 sterling, owing by the pursuer to the
said *C. D*, being the price of   bags of flour purchased by the pursuer
from the said *C D.* on the   day of   ; and that the pursuer is
liable only in once and single payment of the fund to those having right
thereto ; and the defenders should produce their claims, and the pursuer
should be decerned to pay the said fund, deducting his expenses of process
in such way as may be just, and such of the defenders as may be found to
have no right, should be prohibited from troubling him in time coming. And
my will is, &c. (as on page 80.)

This summons is executed like any other.   By the A S. § 103, where the
holder of the fund is the real raiser, he shall state in his summons, or in a
precise and articulate condescendence, to be lodged at the calling, the
amount and particulars thereof ; and also any claim or lien which he may
think he has thereon.

At the first calling, the Sheriff pronounces an order for claims within a
short space. § 8.

It is competent for any number of parties whose claims in such action
depend upon the same ground, to state such claims in the same paper. § 8.

The claimants shall state their respective claims in the forms of condescendences, with the conclusions to be drawn from the facts as stated in the
shape of Notes of pleas, producing therewith their grounds of debt, and other
writings for instructing their claims. A. S. § 104.

As soon as the parties, who shall appear and claim an interest in the fund, shall have lodged their claims, or have had an opportunity of doing so, the Sheriff shall appoint the parties or their procurators to meet him. § 8.

At this meeting, the Sheriff shall allow each party to adjust his own part of the record, and to meet the averments of any other claimant, so far as necessary, and the procedure at such meeting, and in the after progress of the cause, shall be, as nearly as may be, the same as provided with reference to ordinary actions, after defences have been lodged. § 8.

There is a provision in the A S. that the Sheriff may, if he see cause, appoint a common agent, whose duties are similar to those of a common agent in a ranking and division in the Court of Session.

The procedure, when the summons is raised by a claimant in name of the holder of the fund, somewhat differs from that already noticed. The following may be the form of a

Summons of Multiplepoinding raised by a Claimant in name of the holder.

———— Sheriff, &c.—Whereas it is shewn to me by *A. B.* (design) against *C D.* (design) common debtor, *E. F.* design and *G. H.* (design) all defenders, alleged creditors of the said *C. D.*, the said *E. F.* being the real raiser of the action, in terms of the conclusions underwritten. THEREFORE it ought and should be declared that the pursuer is the holder of a fund *in medio* (here it will be stated, in so far as the particulars are known to the real raiser, and then the summons will proceed in the style above given)

In this summons A. B. is only the nominal pursuer, therefore it must be served upon him as well as upon the other defenders, and an execution of service returned; A S. § 102. At the first calling of the cause, or on or before the seventh day thereafter, if a court-day, the nominal pursuer must put in a precise and articulate condescendence of the fund, or lodge objections as his defences against the summons served as a claim against him, otherwise he shall be held as confessed, or a condescendence of the fund may be ordered from any of the claimants; A.S. § 103

By the recent Statute, the Sheriff shall, at the first calling of the cause, where no defences are stated, or where defences are stated and repelled, at the first calling thereafter, pronounce an order for claims. § 8.

If, therefore, the nominal raiser intends to state objections and defences, it appears he must state them at the first calling of the cause, and such defences will in the general case fall to be disposed of before the competition commences

With respect to the Court to which multiplepoindings are competent, and questions of appeal and review, we refer to *Matheson* v. *Monkland Iron Company*, 17th September 1849, J. Shaw, i. 266, where it was held by the Circuit Court at Glasgow, that in a multiplepoinding it is the amount admitted by the common debtor, and not the amount claimed by the respective 'compearers, that determines whether an appeal is competent to the Circuit Court.

Nuisance.

Summons of Interdict and Damages on account of Nuisance.

———— Sheriff, &c (as on page 80.)—Therefore the defender ought and should be interdicted, prohibited, and discharged, from carrying on the business of a soap manufacturer, on or within the buildings and premises lying upon the south side of the road or street called Thistle Street, and directly behind, and within a few yards of the pursuer's property and dwelling-house, or, at least, from carrying on the said manufactory in such a way as to occasion annoyance to the pursuer, and ought to be decerned to pay to the pursuer the sum of L.   sterling, of damages already sustained by him, his family, and his property, during the year 1851 and 1852, and subsequent thereto, by the foresaid works, with the legal interest of the said sum from the date of citation to follow hereon, and thereafter until paid.—And my will is, &c.

Petitory.

For Money Lent

———— Sheriff, &c (as on p 80) THEREFORE the defender ought to be decerned to pay to the pursuer the sum of L 50, being money lent by the pursuer to the defender at his request on the 15th day of November 1853, with the legal interest, &c

Another Form

———— Sheriff, &c. (as on p 80) THEREFORE the defender ought to be decerned to pay to the pursuer the sum of L.   being money lent by the pursuer to the defender, conform to receipt or acknowledgment, dated the   day of   , with the legal interest, &c.

For Money received on the Pursuer's Account.

———— Sheriff, &c. (as on p. 80) THEREFORE the defender ought to be decerned to pay to the pursuer the sum of L.50, or such other sum, less or more, received by the defender from $E F$ merchant in Falkirk, on or about the first day of January 1853, for and on account of the pursuer, &c

For Freight.

———— Sheriff, &c. (as on p. 80) THEREFORE the defender ought to be decerned to pay to the pursuer the sum of L.50 for the freight of goods shipped by the pursuer's vessel, the " Mary Jane," from Glasgow to Belfast, payable on the 10th September last, per account annexed hereto, &c.

For Carriage.

———— Sheriff, &c. (as on p 80) THEREFORE the defender ought to be decerned to pay to the pursuer the sum of L 50 for the conveyance of goods, from Glasgow to Edinburgh, by the pursuer, on the defender's employment, per account dated the 1st day of October 1853, annexed hereto, &c.

For Board and Lodging.

———— Sheriff, &c. (as on p. 80) THEREFORE the defender ought to be decerned to pay to the pursuer the sum of L.25 for board, lodging, and washing furnished by the pursuer to the defender, per account commencing the 15th day of May, and ending the 11th day of November 1853, annexed hereto, &c.

For a Professional Account.

———— Sheriff, &c. (as on p. 80) THEREFORE the defender ought to be decerned to pay to the pursuer the sum of L 35 for professional business performed, and disbursements made by the pursuer on the defender's employment, per account commencing the 1st February 1852, and ending 31st December 1852, annexed hereto &c.

For Work done and Materials supplied.

—— Sheriff, &c. (as on p. 80.) THEREFORE the defender ought to be decerned to pay to the pursuer the sum of L.50 for mason work done, and materials provided therefor by the pursuer in the empolyment of the defender, per account commencing   annexed hereto, &c.

Poinding and Sale.
Small Debt Forms.

When decree is obtained in the Small Debt Court, poinding and sale can, if the party was present, proceed after the lapse of ten free days; but if he was not present, there must be a charge of ten free days, 1 Vict. c. 41, § 13. The form of appraisement and sale is provided, *ib* § 20 The poinded effects are appraised by two persons, and forty-eight hours thereafter are sold at the cross or the most public place of the nearest town or village, on previous notice of at least two hours by the crier. But the Sheriff may, by a general regulation or special order in any particular case, appoint a different hour or place, or longer or different kind of notice Any surplus of price, after payment of the sums decerned for, or if he cannot be found, consigned with the clerk. If the effects are not sold, they are delivered over at the appraised value to the creditor for the amount of his debt and expenses, the officer must make a report in the form of Schedule G, annexed to the Act, *ib* § 20.

Ordinary Court.

After a charge has expired, the debtor's effects may be poinded. The forms are regulated chiefly by 1 and 2 Vict c 114, §§ 23 to 30. Any other creditor who exhibits and delivers to the officer a warrant to poind, may be conjoined in the poinding On the effects being poinded, the officer causes them to be appraised by two valuators, and leaves a schedule, specifying the poinded effects and value, with the debtor. Within eight days after the day of poinding, (unless cause be shewn why it could not be done within that period), the officer must report the execution thereof to the Sheriff. On the execution being reported, the Sheriff, if necessary, gives orders for the security of the moveables, and if they be of a perishable nature, for the immediate disposal thereof, under such precautions as he sees fit; and if not so disposed of, and if no lawful cause be shewn to the contrary, he grants warrant to sell them by public roup at such time and at such place, with such public notice of sale as appears to him most expedient, at the sight of a judge of the roup to be named by him. The sale cannot take place sooner than eight, nor later than twenty days after the publication of the notice Copy of the warrant of sale is served on the debtor (and also on the possessor of the poinded effects, if a different person from the debtor), at least six days before the date of the sale, except in the case of perishable effects. The effects are offered for sale at not less than their appraised value, and in case of no offer, the same or such part as, according to their appraised value, is sufficient to pay the poinding creditor, are delivered to him, and lie at his risk, subject to the claims of other creditors to be ranked as by law competent. The judge of the roup must within eight days report to the Sheriff the sale or delivery, and lodge roup-rolls and account in the Sheriff-clerk's hands, and the free proceeds are paid to the poinding creditor to the extent of his debt and expenses, but subject to the claims of other creditors to be ranked, if by law competent. The poinder or any other creditor may purchase at the poinding of the ground; 1 and 2 Vict. c. 113, § 23-30.

We have already given at page 101, the style of a summons of maills and duties, which is for the purpose of getting a decree against tenants personally for the rents due by them to the proprietor. A poinding of the ground may be raised by a heritable creditor or other person infeft, for the purpose of attaching all moveable property and effects situated on the subjects, but in the case of tenants, their property can be attached only to the extent of the rents due by them respectively.

———— Sheriff, &c (as on p. 80) Whereas it is shewn to me by *A. B.* pursuer, against *C. D* proprietor of the subjects after mentioned, and *E F.* and *G. H.* his tenants therein, in terms of the conclusions under-written. Therefore my sentence and decreet ought to be given and pronounced against the said defenders, charging officers of Court, jointly and severally, to pass, and in Her Majesty's name and authority and mine, to search for, seek, fence, arrest, apprise, compel, poind, and distrain, all and sundry the said defenders, their readiest moveable goods, gear, corns, cattle, horse, sheep, inside plenishing, and others whatsoever poindable or distrainable, being, or that shall happen to be, upon the grounds, of All and Whole (*describe the subjects*), all as particularly bounded and described in the bond and disposition in security after mentioned, and lying in the parish of   , and county of Lanark, but in so far as relates to the said *E. F.* and *G. H.* to the amount of the rents, only which may be due and payable by them respectively, and to make payment thereof to the pursuer to the amount of the principal sum of L 750 sterling, contained in a bond and disposition in security, granted by the defender in favour of the pursuer, dated the 15th, and recorded in the Particular Register of Sasines for the shire of Lanark, the 17th day of May 1852, liquidate penalty and termly failures, with interest of the said principal sum from the term of Martinmas 1852, and in time coming during the not-redemption, the terms of payment being first come and bygone, and to see the pursuer satisfied and paid of the same, and the said *C. D* and the other defenders, in the event of their app   to oppose the conclusions hereof, ought to be decerned to make pay   of the expenses of process.———— And my will is, &c.

Such a summons may also proceed at the instance of a party having right by assignation or otherwise to the bond. In that case, the following words would be added, after mention of the bond ————

To which bond and disposition in security, sums of money, subjects, and others therein contained, the pursuer has acquired right, and now stands duly vested therein, conform to, &c.

Poor-Law Act (*Proceedings under*).

By the Poor-Law Act 8 and 9 Vict. c. 83, § 73, the Sheriff is constituted judge betwixt a pauper and the parish and combination, to whom he has applied, and by whom he has been refused relief, as to whether he is legally entitled to relief, but not as to the amount of the relief. An appeal on the question of amount lies to the Board of Supervision The form of procedure under the said section of the statute is prescribed by A S 12th February 1846, to which we refer. It contains particular directions as to the forms which are not interfered with by the recent statute 16 and 17 Vict. c. 80. The party may apply either by himself or by an agent. If by an agent, he is entitled to have his case conducted as if he were on the Poor's-Roll. If the Sheriff, on the petitioner's statement, thinks that he is legally entitled to relief, an order is made on the inspector, or other officer, to lodge a statement why the application for relief was refused. This may be answered, and a record made up; but while the question is discussing, the Sheriff may make an order on the inspector, or other officer, for relief in the meantime being afforded to the applicant.

Poor's-Roll.

The mode of obtaining admission to the Poor's-Roll is prescribed by the Act of Sederunt 1839. §§ 134-6.

The Procurators of Court annually appoint one or more of their number to act gratis as procurators for the poor. The appointment must be approved of by the Sheriff.

The party applying must, in the first place, obtain a certificate signed by the minister of the parish, or by the heritor on whose lands the pauper resides, or by two elders, bearing that it consists with their personal knowledge that the person prosecuting, or who means to bring the action, is not possessed of funds for paying the expense thereof. § 135.

The following is the form of a

Petition for Admission to the Poor's-Roll

Unto the Sheriff, &c   (As on page 84).

The petitioner, *A B*, humbly sheweth,

That the petitioner has raised (or is about to raise) an action against the said
   C. D. (here the nature of the action must be set forth).

That the petitioner, from his (or her) poverty, is unable to defray the expenses of the said action, and herewith produces a certificate by (as the case may be)

> May it therefore please your Lordship to remit this petition to the procurators for the poor, and upon the report of their opinion, that the petitioner has a *probabilis causa litigandi*, remit to one of the procurators for the poor to attend to and conduct the pursuer's case.
> According to Justice, &c.
>
> (Signed)   *A. B.*

The Sheriff, if satisfied with the certificate, pronounces an interlocutor, remitting to the procurators for the poor. They intimate the petition to the other party, and, after hearing both parties, and inquiring into the case, report their opinion to the Sheriff. A. S § 1, 35. The Sheriff, on considering the report, either refuses the petition or remits to one of the procurators for the poor to conduct the case. The pauper is not liable in payment of any of the dues of Court or fees to the procurator, or to the officer, except actual outlay, unless expenses shall be awarded and recovered under the process. No person except the procurators for the poor may conduct any such case. A. S. § 135. The paupers in the cause have the word "Poor" prefixed to the pauper's name. It is in the power of the Sheriff, at any time when he sees cause, to deprive a party of the benefit of the Poor's-Roll A. S. § 135. It is also in the power of the Sheriff, on cause shewn, to relieve the procurator for the poor from paying the expenses of witnesses. A. S. § 136. It has been held that, if an agent gets decree for, but does not recover, expenses from the other party, he might get payment of these out of funds becoming due to his client; Taylor, 11th March 1841.

Relief.

The following is the form of a Summons of Relief:—

At the instance of an Heir subsidiarie liable against the Heir primarily liable.

————, Sheriff, &c. (as on p. 80).—Whereas it is shewn to me by *A B.*, heir of conquest, served and decerned to the deceased *E. F.*, pursuer, against *C. D.*, executor of the said deceased *E. F.*, decerned and confirmed by the Commissary of Edinburgh, in terms of the conclusions under written. Therefore the defender ought to be decerned to free and relieve the pursuer of the following sums of money, paid by the pursuer to the persons after-named: viz. to *G H.*, the principal sum of L.74 sterling, contained in a bill granted in his favour by the deceased, dated the 22d day of September 1852, and payable three months after date, with 5s. of expenses incurred thereon,— amounting together to the sum of L.74, 5s , paid by the pursuer on the day of   last (here mention any other payments), and for that purpose the defender ought to be decerned to make payment to the pursuer of the sum of L.   , being the total amount of the said respective sums paid by him as aforesaid, with the legal interest of the said respective sums, from the dates when the same were paid by the pursuer as aforesaid, and till payment, with expenses of process.—And my will, &c.

At the instance of a Cautioner against a Principal

————, Sheriff, &c. (as on p. 80). Therefore the defender ought to be decerned to pay to the pursuer the sum of L.1068 sterling, being the amount of principal, interest, and expenses paid by him on the 3d day of November last to *E F* (design), under a bond in favour of the said *E. F.*, for the sum of L 1000 sterling, interest and penalty, dated the 3d day of January 1853, granted to him by the pursuer and defender as joint obligants, but in which bond the pursuer truly acted as cautioner for the defender by becoming bound, at his request and for his behoof, and upon an undertaking by him to relieve the pursuer of all sums he might pay under, or in consequence of, his foresaid obligation, with interest of the said L.1068 sterling from the said 3d day of November last, and expenses of process.—And my will is, &c.

Removing and Irritancy
At a Superior's instance.

A superior may, under § 32 of the recent statute, when the property does not exceed L.25 of yearly value, and when his vassal has run in arrear of his feu-duty for two years, raise an action before the Sheriff concluding for removing; the warrant in which, when executed, has the effect of a decree of irritancy *ob non solutum canonem.* The section prescribes what must be set forth in the action. The summons will therefore, to some extent, differ from the form in the schedule attached to the statute. The following may be the form of the

Summons

————, Sheriff, (as on p. 80.) Shewn to me by *A. B.* (design him), against *C. D.* (design him), that the said *C. D.* is vassal of the pursuer in all and whole, &c., conform to (*here state the title by which the relation of superior and vassal subsists*). That the feu duty payable by the defender to the pursuer is L.   sterling, annually payable at the usual terms of Martinmas and Whitsunday. That the said subjects do not, in yearly value, exceed the sum of L 25 sterling. That the feu-duty for the said subjects payable at the terms of (*here state them, observing that two years' arrear is necessary to found the action*) has run into arrear, and has not been paid. THEREFORE the defender, and all others having, or pretending to have, right or possession from or under him, ought to be decerned to flit and remove from the said subjects and others, and that summarily, and leave the same void and redd, that the pursuer, and others authorised by him, may enter thereto, and possess the same in time coming; and my warrant ought to be granted to that effect, and the defender ought to be decerned to pay the expenses of process. —And my will is, &c.

The above summons is served on the usual *induciæ,* and similar procedure takes place as in any other ordinary action.

The statute declares that, if the defendant shall fail to appear, or if it shall be proved to the Sheriff by such evidence as he may require, that the subject is of the value, and that the feu-duty is in arrear as aforesaid, he shall grant warrant in terms of the conclusions of the summons § 32.

It is remarked by Sheriff Barclay, that the mode of ascertaining the yearly value is not provided for, excepting that it is to be to the satisfaction of the Judge, and that assessment for taxes may afford the evidence.

If warrant is granted in the above action, it cannot be executed till the first term of Martinmas or Whitsunday which shall first occur four months after the same is issued by the Sheriff. § 32. And such warrant, so executed, shall have the effect, in relation to the said possession, of a decree of irritancy *ob non solutum canonem.* § 32.

It is provided that it shall be competent to the vassals, at any time before such warrant is executed, to purge the irritancy incurred by payment of the arrears pursued for, with the expenses incurred by the superior in such proceedings. § 32.

It is also provided, that it shall be competent to the vassal, at any time within one year from the date of such removal, to raise an action of declarator in the Court of Session for vindication of such subject on any ground proceeding on challenge of the title of the superior, which shall not be called in question before the Sheriff, except on grounds instantly verified by the titles of the superior. § 32.

Removing at Landlord's Instance.

The recent statute contains some very important enactments in favour of landlords on the subject of removing.

Removing may now, under certain circumstances, take place without the necessity of any procedure in court.

The old law of removing was founded on the Act 1555, c 39, and the Act of Sederunt 14th December 1756. We refer, for a full history of this subject, to Sheriff Hunter's Law of Landlord and Tenant, which is a repertory of all that is important and valuable on that extensive branch of the law.—See second edition, vol. ii. p 39, *et seq*. By the above A. S., where the tenant's lease contains an obligation to remove, and a clause of registration so as to authorise horning, the landlord is empowered, forty days before the term of Whitsunday at or preceding the expiry of the tack, to charge the tenant to remove; and thereupon the tenant may be ejected within six days after the term of removal specified in the tack; but where the lease contains no obligation to remove, the Act of Sederunt authorises an action of removing before the Judge Ordinary, which must be called in court forty days before the term of Whitsunday of the year in which the removal is to take place; and if decree follow on this action, the tenant may be ejected, but he may lodge defences on finding caution for violent profits, and in that case a record will be made up.

The recent statute provides that, in place of the summons being necessarily called forty days before the term of Whitsunday, it is made competent at any time, provided there be an interval of at least forty days between the date of *the execution* of the summons and the term of removal, or where there is a separate ish as regards land and houses or otherwise, between the date of the execution of the summons and the ish which is first in date. § 29. The following is the form of a

Summons of Removing.

———— Sheriff, &c (as on p 80).—Shewn to me by *A B.* (design) heritable proprietor of the subjects and others after mentioned, conform to (here state landlord's ensine) against *C D.* (design) tenant of the pursuer in the subjects after specified, conform to tack between the pursuer and defender, dated the day of   herewith produced, in terms of the conclusions under-written· Therefore the said *C. D.* defender, ought, in terms of the Act of Sederunt, dated 14th December 1756, to be decerned to flit and remove, himself, his family, subtenants, cottars, and dependents, with their goods and gear, from All and Whole, &c and that at the term of Whitsunday next (or as the case may be) in terms of the said tack, and to leave the said premises void and redd, that the pursuer and others authorised by him may enter thereto and possess the same, and the said defender ought to be decerned to pay to the pursuer the expenses of process.—And my will is, &c.

This summons being executed at least forty days before the ish, will, when decree is obtained, be equally effectual to found process of ejection as the decree of removing under the old form.

Another kind of removing was introduced by 1 and 2 Vict., cap. 119. By that Act, section 8, where houses or other heritable subjects are let for any shorter period than a year, at a rent of which the rate shall not exceed L.30 per annum, it is competent to the pursuer to remove the tenant by form of the summary complaint attached to that statute, Schedule A. See App. to this Volume, p 10.

A removing and irritancy at the instance of a landlord against his tenant, in leases of longer endurance than twenty-one years, is made competent by the recent statute, § 32. This clause is that which makes removing and irritancy competent to a superior against his vassal in subjects not exceeding the yearly value of L 25 It closes with these words :—" Provided also that in leases for a longer endurance than twenty-one years, the landlord shall have the like remedies against his tenant in case of non-payment of rent *mutatis mutandis* that are hereby given to the superior against his vassal."

This clause does not specially bear that the subject of the lease shall not exceed L.25 in yearly value, but it appears to us that it is so intended from the words of the statute, " *the like remedies* " It is declared in the statute that the summons in the case of the superior shall set forth that the subject is of the value (namely, L 25), which implies that a similar statement shall be made in any summons at a landlord's instance

If a landlord has recourse to the action of removing and irritancy here mentioned, the following will be the style of the

Summons of Removing and Irritancy at the instance of a Landlord

————Sheriff, &c.—(as on p 80)—Shewn to me by *A. B.* (design him) heritable proprietor of the lands of   and others, against *C. D.* (design him) defender, that by lease, dated the   day of entered into betwixt the pursuer and defender, the pursuer let to the defender, and his heirs and assignees (as the case may be) All and Whole, &c. and that for the term of (state the number of years, observing that they must exceed twenty-one years from and after Whitsunday 1830, at they yearly rent of L.   , payable (state terms of payment). That the said subjects do not in yearly value exceed the sum of L 25 sterling That the rents payable at the terms of (here state them, observing that two years arrear is necessary to found the action) respectively have run into arrear, and have not been paid Therefore the said defender, his family, subtenants, cottars, and dependents, with their goods and gear, ought to be removed and ejected from the said premises, and the same left void and redd, that the pursuer and others authorised by him may enter thereto and possess the same in time coming, and my warrant ought to be granted to that effect.—— My will is, &c.

Removing by an Officer of Court.

By section 30 of the recent statute it is declared that " a probative lease specifying a term of endurance, or an extract thereof from the books of any court of record, shall have the effect of an extract-decree of removing at the instance of the granter, or the party in right of the granter, against the party in possession, whether he be the lessee named therein or not, decerning for removal and ejection at the expiration of the term or terms of endurance specified in such lease." § 30.

In order to eject under this constructive decree, the landlord must place the lease or extract thereof, with his written authority, in the hands of a Sheriff-officer of the county, or a messenger-at-arms, and cause him to give the following notice to the party in possession :—

Notice to Remove.

(Place and date)

You are required to remove from the farm of (insert name by which usually known) at the term of   next as to the houses and grass, and at the separation of the crop from the ground as to the arable land (*or as the case may be*) in terms of your lease thereof, dated

JOHN ROBSON, Sheriff-Officer.

(Or)   Messenger-at-Arms.

Addressed *C. D* (design him.)

This notice must either be delivered to the party in possession, or left at his ordinary dwelling-house, or transmitted to his known address through the post-office previous to the commencement of forty days before the expiration of the term of endurance in the lease, or where there is a separate ish as to lands and houses or otherwise, forty days before that ish which is first in date § 30.

The officer endorses on the lease or extract a certificate that such notice had been given in the form of Schedule J, which is declared sufficient evidence that such notice has been given § 30

Or an acknowledgment to that effect endorsed thereon by the party in possession, or by his known agent on his behalf, is also declared sufficient evidence that such notice has been given. § 30.

As already stated, this is equal to a decreet of removing on which ejectment by the officer or messenger may follow.

It is declared, however, that no removal or ejectment by virtue of the enactment shall be competent after six weeks have elapsed from the expiration of the term of endurance specified in the lease, or where the lease has a separate ish as regards land and houses or otherwise, after six weeks have elapsed from that ish which is last in date

The same procedure in every respect is competent to follow on a letter of removal by any tenant in possession of any lands or heritages, whether granted at the date of entering upon his lease, or at any other time. If the letter is dated more than six weeks before the term of removal, or the ish first in date specified in such letter of removal, the above procedure may take place,—the letter and notice having the same force and effect as an extract-decree of removing. § 31.

The following is the statutory form of the

Letter of Removal

Sir,   (Place and date)

I am to remove from the farm of (insert name by which usually known) at the term of   as to the houses and grass, and at the separation of the crop from the ground as to the arable land (or as the case may be) —I am your obedient servant,

(Address.)   (Signed by the tenant.)

If this letter is not holograph of the granter of it, it must be attested by one witness thus —— " L. M. witness."

It is farther declared that nothing contained in the Act shall be construed to prevent any proceedings under the above enactments from being brought under suspension in common form. § 30.

The following is the form of a Summons

For Repetition of Money paid through Mistake.

————, Sheriff, &c (as on p 80) Decerned to repeat and pay back to the pursuer the sum of L 50, which was paid by the pursuer to the defender on the 1st day of January 1853, on the erroneous supposition that the defender was the holder of a promissory-note, dated 1st December 1852, and granted by the pursuer to *C* for the said sum

For Repetition of the Price of an Unsound Horse.

————, Sheriff, &c (as on p. 80). Decerned to repeat and pay back to the pursuer the sum of L 50, being the sum paid by the pursuer to the defender as the price of a horse bought by the pursuer from him, on or about the 10th day of October last, and which horse turned out to be unsound, and of which the pursuer refused to take delivery.

Sequestration,
In Small Debt Court.

The summons of sequestration in the Small Debt Court was, by the form in the Schedule B of the Act, limited to the case of rent past due It is by the recent statute, extended to cases for rent *currente termino*, or in security, § 28. The requisite alteration, as applicable to such cases, will be made by the Sheriff-clerks who issue these summonses.

The officer, when he executes the warrant contained in the summons, gets the effects appraised by two persons, who may also be witnesses to the sequestration An inventory or list of the effects, with the appraisement, is given to or left for the tenant, who shall be cited to compear. 1 Vict c. 41, § 5.

An execution of the citation and sequestration, with the appraisement of the effects, must be returned to the clerk within three days. Ib § 5.

On hearing the application in the same way as in other causes, the Sheriff shall dispose of the cause as is just, and may either recal the sequestration in whole or in part, or pronounce decree for the rent found due, and grant warrant for the sale of the sequestrated effects, on the premises, or at such other place, and on such notice, as he shall, by general or special regulation, direct. Ib § 5.

Failing such directions, the sale shall be carried into effect in the manner directed for the sale of poinded and sequestrated effects. Ib. § 5. See *Poinding and Sale.*

In the Ordinary Court.

The following is the form of a petition for sequestration in urban subjects.

Petition for Sequestration.

Unto the Sheriff of the county of

A B. [design]

v.

C. D. [design]

The petitioner, *A. B*, humbly sheweth ;

That the petitioner, who is proprietor of, &c. let to the respondent that house situated in No   Street, for one year, from and after the term of

Q

Whitsunday last, at the yearly rent of L 80 sterling, payable in equal moieties at the terms of Martinmas and Whitsunday. That the sum of L 40, being the half-year's rent due at the term of Martinmas last, is resting-owing to the petitioner.

> May it therefore please your Lordship to grant warrant for service upon the respondent, and meantime to sequestrate the whole furniture and other effects belonging to the respondent, within the said premises, for payment of the said rent due at Martinmas last, and in security of the rent to become due at Whitsunday next, and to grant warrant to take an inventory thereof, and thereafter to roup so much thereof as will satisfy and pay the said rents, with expenses of sequestration and sale, the term of Whitsunday being always first come and bygone before rouping for that half-year's rent , and in the event of any balance remaining unpaid, to decern therefor against the respondent, with expenses.
>
> According to Justice, &c.

If the lease is an agricultural one, the sequestration craved is of the crop of the year for which the rent is due or current, and the alteration in the prayer will be corresponding, and in place of the words furniture and other effects, there will be inserted the words " crop, stocking, farm-implements and effects, horses, cattle and bestial of whatever description."

It has also been the practice in agricultural sequestrations to crave, when necessary, the appointment of a judicial manager to take charge of the farm and lands, until the time for sale arrives

We may observe that in the schedule E of the statute, the form of an incidental petition to sell sequestrated effects is given. There may be occasions in which such petition is necessary; but we conceive that the prayer of the original petition, in the full terms above given, remains competent.

The following may be the form of the Sheriff's interlocutor :—

Edinburgh,　　　　　　1853.

The Sheriff-substitute appoints the respondent to compear within the Sheriff Court-House, at　　　　　　　on the　　　　　　　day of
at eleven o'clock forenoon, to be heard in defence, and appoints a copy of the foregoing petition and of the deliverance to be served on the said defender forty-eight hours previously. Meantime sequestrates and grants warrant to inventory as prayed for.

The Sheriff-clerk will then take up the inventory according to the form at present in use, and the petition, with a copy of the Sheriff's deliverance, will be served by the officer, who will return his execution; the subsequent procedure will resemble that in any other summary petition.

Recal of Sequestration,
In the Small Debt Court.

The sequestration may be recalled either on payment to the pursuer of the rent claimed, with expenses, or consignment thereof in the hands of the clerk of Court, with L.2 to cover expenses.

In case of payment, evidence is produced to the clerk thereof, and he must write on the back of the summons or warrant, and sign the words "payment made," and in case of consignation, the clerk, in like manner, writes and signs the words "consignation made," and the same is intimated by an officer of Court to the sequestrating creditor

In either of these cases the sequestration is *ipso facto* loosed, without any intervention of the Judge. 1 Vict. c. 41, § 5.

In the Ordinary Court.

There are no provisions in the recent Sheriff Court Statute bearing directly on the recal of the sequestration in the Ordinary Court. It may of course be recalled by the Sheriff in the course of the proceedings, if he see fit; or, if necessary, an incidental petition may be presented

Breach of Sequestration.

In the event of breach of sequestration being committed, a petition is competent, with the concurrence of the procurator fiscal. The style and procedure will resemble that which we have already given in the case of breach of Interdict, *voce Interdict*

Service of Heirs.

The service of heirs formerly proceeded on brieves from Chancery, directed to the Sheriff or other judges; but a new form of procedure was introduced in 1847 by the statute 10 and 11 Vict c. 47, by which, and by the relative Act of Sederunt of 14th July 1847, the forms of procedure are minutely pointed out. We therefore refer to this statute and A. S., giving only a summary of the leading points.

The procedure is by petition, which is either to the Sheriff of Chancery or to the Sheriff of a county,—namely, in case of special service, the Sheriff of the county where the lands are situated; and in general service, the Sheriff of the county where the deceased had his domicile. In all cases it may, in the option of the petitioner, be presented to the Sheriff of Chancery; and it must be so presented, in case of petition for special service where the lands lie in different counties, or in case of general service, where the deceased had no domicile in Scotland at the time of his death.

The following is the form of a

Service in Special.

PETITION *by an Heir of Conquest for Special Service to the Sheriff of the county where the lands are situated.*

Unto the Honourable the Sheriff of the county of Lanark, the Petition of *A B*, residing in Bath Street, Glasgow;

Humbly Sheweth,

That the late *C. D.*, leather-merchant in Glasgow, died on or about the 1st day of September 1853, vest and seised in All and Whole the lands of Thistlebank (here describe them from the titles) lying in the parish of and county of Lanark, conform to disposition by   in his favour, dated the 1st day of June 1846, and to instrument of sasine following thereon, recorded in the particular Register of Sasines at   the 6th day of June 1846

That the petitioner is the immediate elder brother and nearest and lawful heir of conquest in special of the said *C. D*, in the lands and others foresaid

May it therefore please your Lordship to serve the petitioner nearest and lawful heir in special of the said deceased *C. D*, in the lands and others above described.

According to Justice, &c.

(Signed)   *A. B.*

(or)   ROBERT BAIRD,

Mandatory for the Petitioner.

The petition signed by the petitioner, or by a party having his written mandate, is lodged with the titles and inventory thereof with the Sheriff-clerk. The Sheriff-clerk prepares an abstract of it for publication, A. S. § 1. This abstract is transmitted to the Sheriff-clerk of Chancery for publication in the Record of Edictal Citations, A. S. § 2. The Sheriff-clerk of the county must also publish the abstract by affixing a copy on the doors of the Court-house, or in some conspicuous places of the Court, or of the office of the Sheriff-clerk, as the Sheriff may direct. § 7

If the deceased died in Scotland, no evidence can be led nor decree pronounced thereon by the Sheriff until the lapse of 15 days from the date of the latest publication, and in the case of petition to the Sheriff of Chancery, where the deceased died abroad, 30 days.

After the lapse of this period the Sheriff holds a Court, intimation being made to the petitioner's agent. At this Court the Sheriff may receive all such evidence, documentary and parole, as according to the law and practice heretofore existing might competently be laid before the jury summoned under the brieve of inquest, and parole evidence must be " taken down in writing, according to the existing practice in the Sheriff Courts in Scotland." § 10. We do not think that the new form of taking evidence by the Sheriff's notes applies to the case of services.

If, after the expiration of the *induciæ* of publication, the petitioner's agent wishes to have his evidence ready, so as to get the service passed on the Court-day, he may have it taken before the Provost or any of the Bailies of any city or royal burgh, who can act as commissioner without special appointment, or before any commissioner whom the Sheriff may appoint, § 10. A full and complete inventory of the documents produced must be made out, and must be certified by the Sheriff or Commissioner. § 10.

The Sheriff, without the aid of a jury, on considering the evidence, pronounces judgment, either serving or dismissing the petition, in whole or in part, and such judgment has the legal effect of the verdict of the jury, according to previous law and practice. § 10.

The proceedings are then transmitted by the Sheriff-clerk to Chancery, original documents or extracts of recorded writs produced, having been previously, on application, returned to the agent who produced them. The judgment is recorded in Chancery, and extract transmitted to the Sheriff-clerk of the county, to be delivered to the party or his agent. The recorded proceedings are at all times patent in the Chancery Office, and certified copies may be had § 12.

The decree of service is equivalent to a retour according to previous law and practice, and any extract thereof equal to the extract of such retour § 13. It has also the effect of a disposition from the deceased to his heirs § 21.

The recorded and extracted decree is challengeable only by reduction.

Where the service is as heir of provision in special, or heir of tailzie and provision, a corresponding change is made in the above form of the petition. All real burdens, restrictions, or qualifications, as well as all entail fetters, may be either inserted in the petition or referred to in the petition as set forth in the recorded deed of entail, or in any instrument of sasine duly registered.

Service in General

A service in general may be embraced in a petition for a service in special, the requisite addition to this effect being made in the peti ion. If a service in general only is required, the following is the form of a

Petition for General Service.

Unto the Honourable the Sheriff of Lanarkshire,

The Petition of *A B* residing in Bath Street, Glasgow;

Humbly sheweth,

That the late *C. D.* leather-merchant in Glasgow, died on or about the 1st day of September 1853, and had, at the time of his death, his ordinary or principal domicile in the county of Lanark.

That the petitioner is the immediate elder and only surviving brother, and nearest lawful heir in general to the said *C. D.*

May it therefore please your Lordship to serve the petitioner nearest and lawful heir in general to the said *C. D.*

According to Justice, &c

(Signed)   *A. B*

(or)   Robert Baird,

Mandatory for the Petitioner.

The procedure generally is the same as that in a special service. Publication is made both edictally at Edinburgh, and in the county of the domicile of the deceased. The only requisite evidence is that of propinquity.

Cases of Disputed Succession

Where it is apprehended by an heir that any other party intends to present a petition to be served, he may lodge a caveat in the manner provided by section 8. All objections in opposing a service are presented in writing, and disposed of in a summary manner by the Sheriff, without prejudice to his allowing parties to be heard viva voce thereon. A competing petition, or competing petitions, may be presented, and in that case the Sheriff may sist procedure in the first petition, conjoin the petitions, take evidence, pronounce judgment, and dispose of the matter of expenses. § 11.

Either of the parties, any time before the proof is begun to be taken, may advocate to the Court of Session, with a view to jury trial; and the procedure is like that of advocations under section 40 of the Judicature Act, § 17. The Court remit to the Sheriff to pronounce judgment. The Sheriff's judgment in favour of either party may also be advocated within fifteen days from its date, on caution, and the procedure is, as in cases of advocation of final judgments. § 18   The Court of Session may either take additional evidence, or remit to the Sheriff to take the same, or try an issue, and thereafter remit to the Sheriff to pronounce decree. § 18

A party, whose petition has without opposition been refused, may present another

Service by Limitation

A special service does not infer a general representation either active or passive. § 23.   A party petitioning for general service may have the benefit of a passive representation limited to the extent or value of the lands and other heritages described in a specification to be attached to the petition. § 25.

Servitude.

The Sheriff before whom any action or proceeding connected with a servitude may be brought, is the Sheriff of the territory within which the property or servitude is situated; 1 and 2 Vict. c 119, § 15   If the defender, or any of the defenders, if more than one, resides beyond the jurisdiction, he is cited by indorsation of the Sheriff-clerk of the county in which he resides.

The following will be the style of a

Summons of Declarator as to Mosses.

———— Sheriff, &c. (as on page 80). Shewn to me by *A B.* (*design*) against *C D.* (*design*), in terms of the conclusions underwritten   Therefore it ought to be found and declared, that the pursuer, as proprietor of the lands of   has a right of servitude jointly with the defender and   over the mosses in the lands of   , for the use and behoof of their respective properties, but to that extent only , and that the defender has no right to cast peats in said mosses for sale, or for the use of any other person or persons than those residing in his own lands of   , and the said defender, and his tenants, and other possessors of his lands, ought to be decerned to desist and cease from casting, winning, and carrying away peats or other fuel from the said mosses, for the purpose of selling or gifting the same to the inhabitants of the village of   , or other person or persons whatsoever . And the said *C. D.* should also be decerned to pay to the pursuer the expenses of process.   And my will is, &c.

We need not give any other styles as to servitudes.   In most cases where a party is interfered with in the exercise thereof, a petition for interdict will serve the purpose.

Suspension.

After the 1st of November next, two kinds of suspension will be competent in the Sheriff Court.   One of these is made competent by the recent Statute, § 26, in the case of a small debt decree for any sum exceeding L 8, 6s. 8d., if such decree shall have been put to execution by imprisonment, It is declared " the party so imprisoned shall be entitled to bring such decree under review of the Sheriff by way of suspension and liberation, and such suspension and liberation shall proceed in the form provided for summary petitions by this act § 26.

It seems to us that the following is a proper form of a

Petition for Suspension and Liberation

Unto the Sheriff of the County of

A. B (design)

v.

C. D (design.)

The petitioner A B. humbly sheweth,

That a decree pronounced in your Lordship's Small Debt Court, at the instance of the said A. B. against the petitioner, for the sum of L.10, 15s , and 6d. of expenses, dated the   day of   , has been put to execution by imprisonment of the petitioner in the prison of on the   day of   last, where he now is.

May it therefore please your Lordship to suspend the said decree, whole grounds, and warrants thereof, and all following thereon, and to grant warrant for liberation of the petitioner, and to find the respondent liable in expenses.

According to Justice, &c

It does not appear to us necessary that this petition should contain any statement of the grounds on which it is presented After service and meeting of the Sheriff with the petitioner's agent, and the respondent or his agent, a condescendence, if necessary, will be ordered We have little doubt of the Sheriff's power to minute the statement for the petitioner, as well as for the respondent at that meeting. At the same time we conceive that there would be no incompetency, in a case requiring so much despatch, in the petitioner annexing to his petition, before its presentment, a statement of the facts and pleas on which the prayer for suspension and liberation is founded. It will be observed that the statute makes no provision either for caution or consignation, but it is doubtless competent to the Sheriff, after meeting with parties, to order liberation, on such caution or consignation, if he sees fit.

Suspension of a Charge on a Decree of Registration or Horning for payment of a sum not exceeding L 25, exclusive of Interest and Expenses.

This kind of suspension was made competent to the Sheriff, by 1 and 2 Vict. c. 119, § 19. The form is by petition to the Sheriff Court of the petitioner's domicile, and must be presented on caution. On caution being found in the hands of the clerk of Court for the debt, interest, and expenses, to be incurred in the Sheriff Court, the Sheriff has power to sist execution, and to order intimation of the petition, and answers to be given in thereto ; and thereafter to proceed with the further disposal and decision of the cause in like manner as in summary causes in such Court, and to suspend the charge and diligence so far as regards the petitioner.

According to the present forms there is annexed to the petition of suspension a statement of facts and pleas ; and we conceive that the recent statute does not abrogate such form of procedure The petition of suspension and liberation may be as follows:

Unto the Sheriff of the county of

C D. *(design)*

v.

A B. *(design)*,

The petitioner humbly sheweth,

That the petitioner has been charged by virtue of a decree of your Lordship, contained in an extract registered protest, registered on your Lordship's books on the   day of   proceeding on a bill for L 20 sterling, dated the 2d day of September last, drawn by the said *A B* upon and accepted by the petitioner, payable three months after date, MOST WRONGOUSLY AND UNJUSTLY, as will appear to your Lordship from the annexed statement of facts and pleas in law The petitioner has found sufficient caution in the hands of the clerk of court for the sum charged for, and interest and expenses, conform to certificate under the clerk's hands herewith produced.

May it therefore please your Lordship to sist execution of the said charge, and to order intimation of this petition, and thereafter to suspend the said charge, whole grounds and warrants thereof, and all that has followed or is competent to follow thereon, and find the petitioner entitled to expenses

According to Justice, &c.

(Annex a Statement of Facts and Pleas.)

If the respondent resides in a different county, the warrant of service may be endorsed by the clerk of such county. § 19.

Transference.

If a defender die pending an action, his heir in heritage could not be called until the lapse of the *annus deliberandi* It is presumed that the privilege of transferring an action after the lapse of a year, where the defender's death has taken place, is not taken away by the 15th section of the recent Statute That saving clause, with respect to actions in which no procedure has been taken for three months, is, "that nothing herein contained shall apply to cases in which the right under such action has been acquired by a third party, by death or otherwise, within such period of six months" This, however, applies to the case of a pursuer, for in the case of a defender there generally is no right under the action acquired by a third party.

The following is the form of the summons of transference :—

——— Sheriff, &c. (as on p. 80) WHEREAS it is shewn to me by *A. B.* (design) pursuer, against *E. F* (design), only son and representative of *C. D.* (design) defender, in terms of the conclusions underwritten Therefore to the effect the pursuer, who is pursuer of an action or process, the summons of which is dated the 2d day of November 1853, brought by him before me against the said now deceased *C D.*, which is now depending before me, and in which the last interlocutor, dated the   day of   , is as follows (here quote it), may have have the same transferred, and such action and execution therein against the said *E. F.* as he would have had against his said deceased father, were he still in life.—AND MY WILL IS, &c.

As formerly explained, now that an action stands *eo ipso* dismissed, if either of the parties shall not take any proceedings therein for the space of three months continuously, there can be room for an action of wakening only in cases in which the right under such action has been acquired by a third party, by death or otherwise, within the period of six months from the date of no proceeding having been taken in the action; 16 and 17 Vict. c. 80, § 15.

In such a case, the following may be the style of a

Summons of Wakening

———— Sheriff, &c. (as on p. 80.) WHEREAS it is shewn to me by *L M.* (design), only son and representative of the deceased *A. B* or executor decerned and confirmed to the deceased *A. B.* (or assignee of *A B*, conform to, &c) against *C. D.* (design) defender, in terms of the conclusions underwritten: Therefore an ordinary action instituted at the instance of the said *A. B* against the said *C. D.* on the   day of   , before me; and in which the last interlocutor, dated the   day of   , is as follows, (*here quote it*) Ought and Should be wakened, to the effect the pursuer may have such action and execution against the said defender, as he would have had before the said process was allowed to fall asleep.—AND MY WILL IS, &c.

An action may be wakened of consent of parties, without the necessity of this summons. It would, however, not appear competent to parties, even of consent, to revive an action which the Statute, § 15, declares as standing dismissed by failure to proceed.

PRINTED BY STEVENSON AND COMPANY, 89 THISTLE STREET.

APPENDIX.

ANNO PRIMO & SECUNDO

VICTORIÆ REGINÆ.

CAP CXIX

An Act to regulate the Constitution, Jurisdiction, and Forms of Process of Sheriff Courts in Scotland, [16th August 1838]

I. WHEREAS the office of sheriff and the Sheriff Courts in *Scotland* have been found to be of great utility, by affording in all ordinary cases a cheap and speedy administration of justice · And whereas it is expedient to regulate the constitution and enlarge the jurisdiction of Sheriff Courts, and to amend the forms of proceedings therein Be it therefore enacted by the Queen's most excellent Majesty, by and with the advice and consent of the lords spiritual and temporal, and commons, in this present Parliament assembled, and by the authority of the same, That so much of an Act passed in the twentieth year of the reign of his *So much of* Majesty King *George* the Second, for taking away and abolishing the heritable *the Act of* jurisdictions in *Scotland*, and for certain other purposes, as enacts that every *20 G 2 as* sheriff depute and stewart depute shall be and reside personally within his county, *requires* shire, or stewartry during the space of four months at least in the year, and also *of Sheriffs* so much of the said Act as enacts a penalty upon being convicted of not so resid- *in their* ing, shall be and the same is hereby repealed ; and that all laws, statutes, acts of *counties* sederunt, and usages shall be and the same are hereby repealed in so far as they are *repealed.* inconsistent or at variance with the provisions of this Act Provided always, that the same shall be in force in all other respects whatsoever.

II. Provided always, and be it enacted, That every sheriff-depute shall attend *Sheriff de-* personally within his sheriffdom upon all necessary and proper occasions, and *pute to* shall, unless prevented by indisposition or other necessary cause of absence arising *hold Courts* from his official duties, hold at least four ordinary Courts within his sheriffdom for the *in his she-* exercise of his ordinary civil or criminal jurisdiction during each period between *riffdom,* the first day of *December* and the twelfth day of *May* ensuing, and other four such *and to at-* Courts during each period between the first day of *June* and the twelfth day of *tend Court* *November* ensuing, except in the sheriffdom of *Orkney* and *Zetland*, wherein the *of Session* sheriff depute shall hold at least eight such Courts during each period between the first day of *December* and the twelfth day of *November* ensuing, four such Courts being held in *Orkney* and four in *Zetland*, and each sheriff shall, fourteen days previously, announce the periods of holding such Courts by a notice put up in the

a

Sheriff Court rooms, and shall, within ten days after the twelfth day of *November* annually, make a return to her Majesty's principal secretary of state for the home department of the number of Courts held by him, and causes disposed of as aforesaid, from the first day of *December* preceding, stating the cause of absence in case he shall not have held Courts as herein provided, and every person who shall be hereafter appointed to the office of sheriff-depute shall be an advocate of three years' standing at least, and shall have been at the time of his appointment in practice before and in habitual attendance upon the Court of Session or acting as a sheriff substitute; and after such appointment every such sheriff, with the exception of the sheriffs of the counties of *Edinburgh* and *Lanark*, shall be in habitual attendance upon the said Court of Session during the sittings thereof; and if any such sheriff, excepting as aforesaid, shall not hold Court within his sheriffdom, or shall not attend the Court of Session as before provided, it shall be competent for her Majesty's advocate to present a summary petition and complaint to the Court of Session complaining of such sheriff not holding Courts or of such non-attendance, and the same being thereupon duly investigated and established upon a summary trial before the said Court, such sheriff shall be admonished for the first offence, and for the second shall be deprived of his office.

As to the removal of sheriff substitutes.

III And be it enacted, That no sheriff substitute receiving salary shall hereafter be removable from his office by the present or any future sheriff unless with the consent of the Lord President and Lord Justice-Clerk for the time being expressed in writing.

Sheriff substitutes to continue to hold office on the death of deputes

IV. And be it enacted, That on the death, resignation, or removal of any sheriff depute, his substitute or substitutes shall continue to hold his or their offices, and to exercise all the jurisdictions, powers, and authorities thereto belonging, without the necessity of any new appointment or commission from the succeeding sheriff; Provided always, that appeals may be taken in causes decided by such sheriff substitute to the sheriff to be appointed, which shall be laid before such sheriff when he shall enter upon his office

Sheriff substitutes to reside within their sheriffdoms

V. And be it enacted, That every person holding the office of sheriff substitute, and receiving salary on that account, shall reside personally within his jurisdiction, and shall not be absent therefrom more than six weeks in any year, nor for more than two weeks at any one time, nor so as to interfere with the regular sittings of his Court, without the special consent in writing of the sheriff of such county for the time being, who shall be bound, in the event of his giving such consent, either to attend personally during the absence of such substitute, or to appoint another fit person as substitute to act in his stead, and it shall not hereafter be lawful for any sheriff substitute so receiving salary to act as agent either in legal, banking, or other business, or as conveyancer, factor, or chamberlain, except for the crown, or to be appointed to any office, except such office as shall be by Statute attached to the office of sheriff substitute.

Superannuation allowances to sheriff substitutes

VI. And be it enacted, That Her Majesty, and her heirs and successors, may grant an annuity, payable in like manner as salaries to sheriff substitutes, to any person who has held, now holds, or may hereafter hold, the office of sheriff substitute, according to the proportions and with reference to the amount of their salaries and the periods of their services as herein-after mentioned, if from old age or any permanent infirmity such person has been or shall hereafter be disabled from the due exercise of his office: Provided always, that such annuity shall not exceed one-third of the salary payable to such person in case the period of his service shall have been not less than ten years, and shall not exceed two-thirds of such salary in case the period of service shall have been not less than fifteen years, and shall not exceed three-fourths of such salary in case the period of service shall have been not less than twenty years or upwards: Provided also, that no such annuity shall be granted unless such sheriff substitute shall have duly fulfilled the duties of his office during one of the periods before-mentioned, and is from old age or permanent infirmity disabled from the due exercise of his office, which facts shall be certified by the Lord President, the Lord Justice-Clerk, and the Lord Advocate for the time being, as having been established to their satisfaction by proper evidence.

VII And whereas by the death of *Duncan Mathieson*, Esquire, advocate, late sheriff substitute of *Leith*, the office of sheriff substitute of *Leith* has become vacant, be it enacted, That the said office of sheriff substitute of *Leith*, as heretofore constituted, shall cease and determine, any thing in any Act of Parliament to the contrary notwithstanding. *Office of sheriff substitute of Leith to cease.*

VIII And whereas it is expedient to diminish the expense and delay with which the process of removing from houses and other heritable subjects, of the rent hereinafter provided, let for any shorter period than a year, in *Scotland*, is attended, be it enacted, That where houses or other heritable subjects in *Scotland* are let for any shorter period than a year, at a rent of which the rate shall not exceed thirty pounds *per annum*, it shall be competent for any person, authorized by law to pursue a removing therefrom, to present a summary complaint to the sheriff of the territory, who shall order it to be served, and the defender to appear on such day as he may in each case think proper, in the form or to the effect of schedule (A.) annexed to this Act *Summary complaint for removing from premises let for less than a year.*

IX. And be it enacted, That if the defender shall fail to appear after being duly cited, the sheriff shall proceed to determine the cause in the same manner as if the defender had been personally present. Provided always, that where the decree shall have been pronounced in absence, and shall not have been carried into execution, the defender may present a petition to the sheriff for a further hearing of the cause, with evidence of intimation thereof having been made to the opposite party written thereon, and the sheriff, if he shall see cause, and upon payment by the defender to the complainer of such expenses as the sheriff may judge reasonable, may recall his decree, and proceed to hear and determine the cause as on the original complaint without delay, and provided also, that where decree shall be pronounced in absence, the sheriff may give such order for preservation of the goods and effects of the defender as he may deem proper. *Defender may repone against decree in absence.*

X And be it enacted, That the complaint or copy thereof served on the defender shall be a sufficient warrant to any sheriff officer to cite witnesses or havers for either party to appear on the day of trial, and give evidence in such summary cases of removing; and the fees allowed to the clerk or officers of court on such complaint and proceedings shall be the same as those allowed on summonses and similar proceedings in small debt causes in Sheriff Courts in *Scotland* under an act passed during the last session of Parliament, intituled "*An Act for the more effectual Recovery of Small Debts in Sheriff Courts, and for regulating the Establishment of Circuit Courts for the Trial of Small Debt Causes by the Sheriffs in Scotland*" Provided always, that the travelling expenses of officers and their assistants under the said recited Act, and this Act shall not be allowed for more than the distance from the residence of the officer employed to the place of execution or service, in case such distance shall be less than from the court house to such place, and the sheriff shall have power to modify such expenses in case the officer residing nearest to the place of execution or service shall not be employed; and provided also, that such travelling expenses shall not be allowed against an opposite party for a greater distance than twelve miles. *Warrant to cite witnesses, and provision as to fees. 7 W 4, & 1 Vict. c. 41.*

XI. And be it enacted, That the citation and farther procedure in such summary removings shall, in so far as not provided for by this Act, be the same as those established by the said recited Act for the trial of small debt causes in Sheriff Courts; and where decree of removing is pronounced it shall be in the form *Citation and farther procedure in removings to be* the same as provided for small debt causes Judgments to be final.

or to the effect of the said schedule (A) and shall have the full force of a decreet of removing and warrant of ejection ; and the judgments to be pronounced in such summary actions of removing shall be final, and not subject to review, either in the Circuit Court of Justiciary or in the Court of Session.

Sheriff may adjourn the cause.

XII And be it enacted, That the sheriff may, of consent of parties, or where the ends of justice require it, adjourn the further hearing of or procedure in any summary process of removing raised under the authority of this Act, and he may likewise order written answers to be given in to the complaint ; and all such orders shall be final, without being subject to appeal or advocation . Provided always, that the sheriff shall in all such cases where the defences cannot be instantly verified, ordain the defender to find caution for violent profits

Where defender has found caution he may give in written answers to complaint

XIII. And be it further enacted, That in all cases where the defender has found caution he shall be allowed to give in written answers to the complaint , and in all cases where written answers shall be ordered such cases shall thereafter be conducted, as nearly as may be, according to the forms in use in ordinary processes of removing, and the judgment of the sheriff therein shall be subject to review in common form

Members of college of justice not exempt

XIV. And be it enacted, that no person shall be exempt from the jurisdiction of the sheriff in any process of removing raised under the authority of this Act, on account of privilege, or being a member of the College of Justice or otherwise.

Sheriffs jurisdiction extended in questions of nuisance and servitude.

XV. And be it enacted, That the jurisdiction, power, and authority of sheriffs of *Scotland* shall be and the same are hereby extended to all actions or proceedings relative to questions of nuisance or damages arising from the alleged undue exercise of the right of property, and also to questions touching either the constitution or the exercise of real or prædial servitudes ; and all parties against whom such actions or proceedings may be brought shall be amenable to the jurisdiction of the sheriff of the territory within which such property or servitude shall be situated.

Transmission book to be kept by sheriff clerks.

XVI. And be it enacted, That the sheriff clerk of every Sheriff Court shall keep a book in which he shall enter in a tabular form, in columns, in the form of schedule (B.) hereto annexed, every cause transmitted to the sheriff or sheriff substitute in order to be advised, specifying in separate columns, ordinary and summary causes, the sheriff to whom the same has been transmitted, the date of such transmission, the date of the cause being received by the sheriff and returned advised, and any remarks which the sheriff may enter or direct to be entered in such book relative to any such cause , and an inventory of the process shall be kept by the clerk, in which the borrowing and returning of processes shall be entered , and no process shall be given up by the clerk without a receipt upon such inventory.

Additional Court days to be appointed to dispose of arrears of business.

XVII And be it enacted, That in case there shall be an arrear of business undisposed of by the sheriff in any Sheriff Court, it shall be the duty of the sheriff from time to time to appoint additional court days, whether in time of session or vacation, for the purpose of disposing of such arrear.

Sheriffs may repone against decrees in absence.

XVIII. And be it enacted, That where decree in absence in any civil cause shall have been pronounced or extracted in any Sheriff Court other than in causes in the Small Debt Court, or in processes of removing raised under the authority of this Act, a petition may be presented to the Sheriff Court in which such decree was pronounced to be reponed against the said decree, and any letters of horning or charge following thereon, where the same shall not have been implemented in whole or in part, and on consignation in the hands of the clerk of court of the expenses incurred, as the same may be modified on taxation, the said sheriff shall repone the defender, and revive the action or proceeding in which such decree had been pronounced, as if decree had not been pronounced or extracted, and shall have power to award to the pursuer such part of the expenses consigned as he may judge reasonable ; and the sheriff shall pronounce such order for intimation to and appearance of the opposite party as may be just , and such order may be executed against a person in any other county as well as in the county where such order is issued, the same being previously indorsed by the sheriff clerk of such other county, who is hereby required to make and date such indorsation ; and such order being so made and executed, all further orders and interlocutors in the cause shall be sufficient and effectual.

XIX And be it enacted, That where a charge shall be given on a decree of registration proceeding on a bond, bill, contract, or other form of obligation, registered in any Sheriff Court books, or in the books of Council and Session, or any others competent, or on letters of horning following on such decree, for payment of any sum of money not exceeding the sum of twenty-five pounds of principal, exclusive of interest and expenses, any person so charged may apply by petition to the Sheriff Court of his domicile for suspension of the said charge and diligence, on caution ; and on sufficient caution being found in the hands of the clerk of Court for the sum charged for, and interest and expenses to be incurred in the Sheriff Court, the sheriff shall have power to sist execution against the petitioner, and to order intimation of the petition of suspension, and answers to be given in thereto, and thereafter to proceed with the further disposal and decision of the cause in like manner as in summary causes in such Court, and to suspend the charge and diligence so far as regards the petitioner , provided that the said order for intimation and answers as aforesaid may be made and carried into execution against any person, in any other county, as well as in the county where such order is issued, in manner and to the effect herein-before provided.

Suspensions competent in Sheriff Courts of charges for sums under 25l.

XX. And be it enacted, That if any petition of suspension as aforesaid shall be presented in any Sheriff Court, and a preliminary objection be made to the competency of such petition, or to the regularity thereof, an appeal against the judgment of the sheriff substitute repelling or sustaining such objection may be taken in common form to the sheriff, whose judgment thereon shall be final, and not subject to review, either in the Circuit Court of Justiciary or in the Court of Session.

Sheriffs judgment on preliminary objection to suspension final.

XXI And whereas by an Act passed in the first year of the reign of His late Majesty King *William* the Fourth, intituled " *An Act for uniting the Benefits of Jury Trial in Civil Causes with the ordinary Jurisdiction of the Court of Session, and for making certain other Alterations and Reductions in the Judicial Establishments of* Scotland," it is enacted, that the sheriffs of *Scotland* shall within their respective sheriffdoms, including the navigable rivers, ports, harbours, creeks, shores, and anchoring grounds in or adjoining such sheriffdoms, hold and exercise original jurisdiction in all maritime causes and proceedings, civil and criminal, including such as may apply to persons residing furth of *Scotland*, of the same nature as that heretofore held and exercised by the High Court of Admiralty And whereas doubts have arisen regarding the extent of such jurisdiction, and it is expedient that such doubts should be removed ; be it therefore enacted and declared, That the said recited Act shall be construed and held to mean that the powers and jurisdictions formerly competent to the High Court of Admiralty of *Scotland* in all maritime causes and proceedings, civil and criminal, shall be competent to the said sheriffs and their substitutes, provided the defender shall, upon any legal ground of jurisdiction, be amenable to the jurisdiction of the sheriff before whom such cause or proceeding may be raised ; and provided also, that it shall not be competent to the Sheriff to try any crime committed on the seas which it would not be competent for that judge to try if the crime had been committed on land.

Sheriffs' jurisdiction in maritime causes under 1 W. 4. c. 69, explained.

XXII. And be it enacted, That in maritime causes or proceedings raised or

Caution judicatum

solvi not required in maritime causes in Sheriff Courts.

brought before any Sheriff Court in *Scotland*, caution judicatum solvi, or de damnis et impensis shall not be required in any such cause or proceeding from any party who shall be domiciled in *Scotland*, any law or practice to the contrary notwithstanding, unless the judge shall require it on special grounds, to be stated in the interlocutor requiring the same, or a note annexed thereto.

Summonses, &c. in Sheriff Courts to be served in presence of one witness.

XXIII And be it enacted, That summonses, petitions, complaints, charges, arrestments, and other proceedings in Sheriff Courts, excepting poindings, shall be deemed to be duly served and executed, provided the same shall be served or executed by the usual officer of the law in such courts in presence of one person, who shall witness such service or execution, and both of whom shall attest the execution of the same by their subscriptions in common form.

Citation of parties, witnesses, and havers

XXIV. And whereas it is expedient to authorize citation to Sheriff Courts of persons in *Scotland* without the necessity of having recourse to letters of supplement from the Court of Session; be it enacted, That it shall be competent to cite all persons within *Scotland*, as parties in any civil or criminal action or proceeding in any Sheriff Court, who may be amenable to the jurisdiction of such court, in respect of such action or proceeding by the warrant of such Sheriff Court; and it shall also be competent to cite witnesses and havers within *Scotland* in any civil or criminal action or proceeding in any such courts by the warrant of such courts, and all such warrants shall have the same force and effect in any other sheriffdom as in that in which they were originally issued, the same being first endorsed by the sheriff clerk of such other sheriffdom, who is hereby required to make and date such endorsation, and such citation duly made shall be deemed to be due and regular citation, and if any witness or haver duly cited shall fail to appear, it shall be competent to any party for whom such witness or haver is cited to apply for a new warrant to compel his attendance at such court, at such reasonable time as may be fixed, which warrant shall require such witness or haver to attend as aforesaid, under a penalty not exceeding forty shillings, unless a reasonable excuse be offered and sustained, and every such penalty shall be paid to the party applying for the new warrant as aforesaid, and shall be recovered in the same manner as penalties under the before-recited Act for the more effectual recovery of small debts in the Sheriff Courts, or under any Act by which the same shall have been or may be repealed, altered, or amended, without prejudice always to letters of second diligence for compelling witnesses and havers to attend as at present competent, and it shall be competent to execute and carry into effect such letters of second diligence in any other sheriffdom, the same being endorsed by the sheriff clerk of that sheriffdom, as before provided. Provided always, That nothing in this Act contained shall affect the competency of applying for and obtaining letters of supplement in common form for the purpose of citing such parties, witnesses, or havers; and provided also, That it shall be no objection to any witness or haver that he has appeared without citation.

Sheriffs' criminal warrants may be executed out of the county.

XXV. And be it enacted, That any criminal warrant granted by any sheriff against any person charged with having committed a crime or offence within the jurisdiction of the said sheriff, and also any warrant granted by a sheriff against a person as being in *meditatione fugæ*, shall be sufficient for the apprehension of the said person within any other county, and for conveying and disposing of the said person in terms of the warrant, without the necessity of its being backed or endorsed by any other magistrate: Provided always, That the said warrant shall be executed against the person mentioned therein, either by a messenger-at-arms, or by an officer of the Court where the same was issued.

Sheriff of two counties may hold Commissary Court in either.

XXVI. And whereas by an Act passed in the Fourth year of the reign of His Majesty King *George* the Fourth, intituled "*An Act for the Regulation of the Court of the Commissaries of Edinburgh, and for altering and regulating the Jurisdiction of Inferior Commissaries in Scotland*," it is provided, That where two counties shall be under the jurisdiction of one sheriff, such two counties shall constitute one Commissariat; be it enacted and declared, That when two counties shall be under the jurisdiction of one sheriff as aforesaid, it shall nevertheless be lawful for such sheriff, if he shall think proper, to hold Commissary Courts in both of such counties in manner and to the effect provided by the said recited Act.

XXVII And whereas it is expedient to remedy the inconvenience of summoning jurors to attend in Sheriff Courts from distant parts of the county; be it enacted, That except in the counties of *Haddington, Linlithgow, Peebles, Selkirk, Kinross, Clackmannan, Nairn,* and *Cromarty,* it shall no longer be necessary to summon persons to attend at any Sheriff Court to serve as jurors in any criminal cause who shall reside beyond such distances from the Court House, at which the jurors shall be summoned to attend, as may from time to time be fixed by the several sheriffs of the several counties, with the approbation of Her Majesty's principal secretary of state for the home department, and upon such limits being fixed the sheriff clerks of the several counties, except as aforesaid, shall make up and correct in manner provided by law, lists of persons qualified to serve as jurors resident within such limits from each Court House at which the sheriff or his substitute holds Courts, which jurors are or may be summoned to attend. Provided always, That in *Orkney* and *Zetland* the jurors shall be summoned from the main land of each district respectively, and that the attendance of jurors at Sheriff Courts shall not exempt them from attendance at Circuit Courts of Justiciary in their ordinary course of rotation as heretofore, and provided also, That magistrates of royal burghs and towns, entitled to return or to contribute in returning members to serve in Parliament, and keepers of lighthouses and their assistants, shall be freed and exempted from being returned and from serving upon juries.

Sheriffs' juries may be summoned from list of jurors residing within certain distance of Court to which they are summoned.

XXVIII And whereas it is expedient that the office of sheriff clerk should be regulated, and that a uniform rate of fees should be established in the several Sheriff Courts in *Scotland;* be it enacted, That the table of fees contained in schedule (C) hereto annexed, and to be contained in any additional table which may be framed in terms hereof, and no others, shall be exacted and received by all sheriff clerks to be hereafter appointed, subject to such addition thereto or alteration thereof as may be made by the Lord High Treasurer of the United Kingdom of *Great Britain* and *Ireland,* or by the commissioners of Her Majesty's Treasury, or any three of them, a copy of such alteration being always notified two months in the *Edinburgh Gazette* before being made effectual, and being also laid before both Houses of Parliament within one month after the making thereof, or, if Parliament shall not be then sitting, within fourteen days after the next meeting thereof; and the said Lord High Treasurer or Commissioners shall fix the salary which any future sheriff clerk shall receive, and which shall be payable and paid by or out of the fees and emoluments in civil and criminal proceedings exigible, and received by such sheriff clerks respectively; and any surplus of such fees and emoluments, after satisfying such salaries, shall be applied towards defraying the expenses attending the establishment of the Sheriff Court and Sheriff Small Debt Circuit Courts within the county in which such fees and emoluments shall be collected, in such manner and subject to such regulations for ascertaining the amount of such surplus and accounting for the same as the said Lord High Treasurer or Commissioners, or any three of them, shall direct; and where in any of the smaller counties the fees and emoluments which shall hereafter be received under the provisions of this Act may be insufficient for the maintenance of a person duly qualified to execute the duties of a sheriff clerk, it shall be lawful to the said Lord High Treasurer or Commissioners, or any three of them, to direct that a salary shall be payable to such sheriff clerk, in addition to the said fees, of such amount as they shall think necessary; and no person who shall hereafter be appointed to the office of sheriff clerk, or who shall acquire right to any fees or emoluments in any Sheriff Court, in virtue of the provisions of this Act, from and after the passing of the same, shall acquire a vested right to the fees or emoluments of such

Emoluments of future sheriff clerks to be regulated.

office, or shall be entitled to any compensation in consequence of the subsequent abolition of such office or fees, or of any alteration in the constitution of such office, or in the amount of such fees, or in the mode of paying such sheriff clerk or officer, either by such fees or such salary as may hereafter be determined : Provided always, that it shall be lawful for the said Commissioners, or any three of them, by agreement with any existing sheriff clerk, to establish the table of fees hereby fixed or to be fixed under the authority of this Act in any Sheriff Courts, and to award to such sheriff clerk such compensation by way of additional salary as they may think fit; and all such salaries to sheriff clerks shall be payable out of the funds from which the salaries of sheriffs are payable · Provided always, that every sheriff clerk shall keep an account stating in columns the amount of the different fees drawn by such clerk under this Act, and the sources thereof, and shall annually, at the beginning of each year, render such account to the said Commissioner of Her Majesty's Treasury in such manner as they shall direct.

Existing sheriff clerks and officers not to acquire vested right to increased fees. XXIX. And be it enacted, That no existing sheriff clerk or other officer of any Sheriff Court, shall acquire a vested right to any increased amount of fees or emoluments which may be drawn by them from and after the passing of this Act, or shall be entitled to prefer any claim to compensation in consequence of being prevented from drawing or being deprived of such increased amount of fees or emoluments, or of any alteration either in the mode of levying or disposing of the same.

Citations, &c in Zetland. XXX And be it enacted, That hereafter all proclamations, denunciations, edictal citations, and other public notices made at the market cross of the burgh of *Lerwick* in *Zetland* shall be equally valid as if the same had been made as heretofore at the gate of the castle of *Scalloway*.

Power of Court of Session to make regulations by Acts of Sederunt, &c. not to be affected. XXXI. And be it enacted, That nothing herein contained shall in any way abridge or affect the power vested in the Court of Session to make and establish rules and regulations by Acts of Sederunt, as authorized by an Act passed in the sixth year of His Majesty King *George* the Fourth, intituled "*An Act for the better regulation of the Sheriff and Stewart and Burgh Courts in* Scotland ," and the said Court shall so frame such Acts of Sederunt as may be best calculated to carry into effect the purposes of this Act, and also of an Act passed in the sixth and seventh years of the reign of His late Majesty, intituled " *An Act for regulating the process of cessio bonorum in the Court of Session, and for extending the jurisdiction of Sheriffs in* Scotland *to such causes*, " and also, if necessary, to alter or amend the table of fees for practitioners in Sheriff Courts, and adapt the same to the forms of process ; and the Court of Session shall also from time to time make further orders and regulations to amend the forms and preserve uniformity in the proceedings and fees in all Sheriff Courts, the said Court taking into consideration the reports laid before Parliament by the Commissioners appointed under the sign manual of His late Majesty King *William* the Fourth, dated the sixth day of *June* One thousand eight hundred and thirty-three, and the sixteenth day of *August* One thousand eight hundred and thirty-four, and the said Court shall also by Act or Acts of Sederunt from time to time adapt and apply to Sheriff Courts any alterations and amendments which may be made in the forms of proceedings in the Court of Session, so as to make them uniform in as far as it may be expedient so to do, and the said Court may meet for the aforesaid purposes during vacation as well as during Session, and may alter and amend such regulations from time to time ; and all Acts of Sederunt so passed by the Court of Session shall, in terms of the said recited Act of His Majesty King *George* the Fourth, apply to and receive effect in the Courts of the Royal Burghs in *Scotland* as well as in the Sheriff Courts : Provided always, that within fourteen days from the commencement of every future session of Parliament there shall be transmitted to both Houses of Parliament copies of all such Acts of Sederunt.

XXXII And be it enacted, That in order the better to carry into effect the purposes of the said recited Act and of this Act, and to preserve uniformity in the proceedings of Sheriff Courts, the several sheriffs of the several sheriffdoms shall meet together in *Edinburgh* in the first week of the first winter session of the said Court after the passing of this Act, and at the like period every three years thereafter, and adjourn such meetings from time to time as they shall see cause, and at such meetings they shall consider how far uniformity of proceedings exists in Sheriff Courts, and any propositions which may be laid before them, or which they may deem proper to submit to the said court for attaining that object; and on or before the first day of *January* next ensuing after each such meeting, the said sheriffs shall submit to the court any regulations which they may propose should be enacted by Act of Sederunt, and the same shall be printed and sent to the different Sheriff Courts, to be exhibited there for the space of fourteen days, and the said sheriff shall, on or before the twelfth day of *March* next ensuing, prepare and cause to be printed for the consideration of the court a revised draft, and on the meeting of the court in the summer session next ensuing the court shall take such draft into consideration, and pass an Act of Sederunt on or before the twelfth day of *July* following, in such terms as they shall think fit: Provided always, that nothing herein contained shall prevent the said sheriffs from meeting for the purposes aforesaid and submitting propositions as aforesaid to the said court at any other times, or the said court from passing any Act or Acts of Sederunt under the powers herein-before given at any other times, as such sheriffs or such court respectively shall think proper, and provided also that the necessary expenses of such meetings of sheriffs and of preparing and printing such propositions shall be allowed in the annual accounts in Exchequer of such one of the said sheriffs as may from time to time be appointed by them to be their convener, in the like manner as other ordinary expenses of sheriffs are allowed

Sheriffs to meet periodically, and to submit propositions to the Court.

XXXIII. And be it enacted, That it shall be lawful for all agents duly qualified to practise before the Court of Session, to practise as agents in all Sheriff Courts in all actions or proceedings to which the jurisdiction of the sheriffs is extended by this Act, and which could not have been competently brought before the Sheriff Courts prior to the passing hereof Provided always, that they shall not be entitled to payment of any other or higher fees than those legally exigible by other agents before these courts; and provided also, that all such agents in practising in Sheriff Courts shall be subject to such orders and regulations as the Court of Session shall make by Act or Acts of Sederunt in manner herein-before provided.

Agents qualified to practise before Court of Session may practise in Sheriff Courts.

XXXIV. And be it enacted, That in all cases in this Act the word "person" shall extend to a partnership, or body politic, corporate, or collegiate, as well as to an individual, and every word importing the singular number only shall extend and be applied to several persons or things as well as one person or thing, and every word importing the plural number shall extend and be applied to one person or thing as well as several persons or things; and every word importing the masculine gender only shall extend and be applied to a female as well as a male Provided always, that those words and expressions occuring in this clause to which more than one meaning is attached shall not have the different meanings given to them by this clause in those cases in which there is any thing in the subject or context repugnant to such construction.

Meaning of words in this Act.

XXXV. And be it enacted, That the whole provisions of this Act, unless where otherwise herein specially provided, shall commence and take effect from and after the Thirty-first Day of *December* One thousand eight hundred and thirty-eight.

Commencement of Act.

XXXVI. And be it enacted, That this Act may be amended or repealed by any act to be passed during the present Session of Parliament.

Act may be amended.

SCHEDULES referred to in the foregoing Act.

***

SCHEDULE (A)

No. 1

Form of Summary Complaint

Unto the Honourable the sheriff of the county of
COMPLAINS A. B. [*name and design the Complainer*] against C. D [*name and design the Defender*], that the complainer [*or his author, as the Case may be,*] let to the said defender [*or his author, as the Case may be*], a dwelling house, garden, and pertinents [*or other subjects, as the case may be*], situate in
for the period from   to   ,
that the said defender is bound to remove from the said subjects at the date last mentioned, and it is necessary to obtain decree of removing against him, [*or, as the case may be,* refuses or delays to remove therefrom, although the period of his lease has expired]: Therefore decreet ought to be granted for removing and ejecting the said defender, his family, sub-tenants, cottars, and dependants, with their goods and gear, furth and from the said subjects, [*here insert the date at which the removal or ejection is sought for, as the case may be,*] that the complainer or others in his right may then enter to and possess the same. [*If expenses are sought, add,* and the said defender ought to be found liable in expense of process and dues of extract.]

[*Signature of the Party or Agent*

***

No. 2.

Form of Warrant thereon.

The sheriff grants warrant to cite the said defender to compear personally before him at the court-house [*or elsewhere, as the case may be,*] upon the [*insert the day of the month and hour, if need be,*] to answer the foregoing complaint, under certification of being held as confessed; ordains such citation to be made at least [*state the period which the Sheriff may fix to intervene betwixt the citation and diet of compearance,*] previous to the said diet of compearance, and grants warrant to cite witnesses for both parties to appear, time and place foresaid, to give evidence in the said matter, under the pains of law.   Given under the hand of the clerk of Court at   the
day of

                                                         Sheriff-Clerk.

***

No. 3.

Form of Citation for Defender.

C. D., defender above designed, you are hereby summoned to appear and answer before the sheriff in the matter complained of, and that at [*here specify time and place*], under certification of being held as confessed
This notice is served upon the   day of
                                                         by me,
                                                         Sheriff-Officer.

No. 4.

Form of Execution of Citation.

Upon the   day of   I duly summoned the above-designed *C D*, defender, to appear and answer before the sheriff in the matter, and at the time and place, and under the certification above set forth. This I did by delivering a copy of the above complaint, with a citation thereto annexed, to the said defender personally [*or otherwise, as the case may be*]

Sheriff-Officer.

No. 5

Form of Decreet and Warrant of Ejection.

At   the   day of   the which day the sheriff [in absence of the defender, or having heard parties, *as the case may be*] decerns and grants warrant for removing and ejecting the said *C D*, defender, and others mentioned in the complaint, from the subjects therein specified, such ejection not being sooner than [*here insert the time appointed for removal, and whether after a charge on such induciæ as may be deemed proper, or instantly*] finds the said defender liable in expenses [*or otherwise, as the case may be*], and decerns.

[Sheriff's Signature]

Note.—The whole of the above to be in the same paper.

SCHEDULE (B.)

Transmission Book to be kept by Sheriff Clerks.

Names of Cause, [as *A* versus *B*., or *A*., Petitioner, &c.]		Date of Transmission to Sheriff Substitute.	If Proof led, state whether before Sheriff or Substitute or Commissioner, and its Duration.	Date of Case being returned and advised.	Date of Transmission to Sheriff.	Date of Cause being returned and advised	REMARKS *
Ordinary Causes	Summary Causes.						

* *Note*—Where cases have been longer than ten days unadvised after transmission to the sheriff, the reason to be stated in this column.

Also the names of any commissioners to whom remits have been made to take proofs.

SCHEDULE (C.)

TABLE of FEES in CIVIL BUSINESS for the SHERIFF CLERKS OF SCOTLAND.

	In Cases of L.12, and under			Above L.12		
	£	s	d.	£	s	d.
Libel, summons, or claim to found an action,	0	0	9	0	1	3
When more defenders than one are sued for a separate debt or prestation, the above fees to be paid on one of the debts or prestations highest in amount, and a third of the above fees to be paid for each of the other debts or prestations, according to the amount of the claim against each defender or set of defenders.						
Certifying copy of libel, in terms of Act of Sederunt for Sheriff Courts, c. 18, s 4,	0	0	6	0	0	6
Summary petition, or complaint (except petition of sequestration), and deliverance thereon,	0	1	0	0	1	6
Defence, answer, or first paper for each defender or set of defenders, or compearer, or set of compearers, in any action,	0	0	6	0	1	0
Each paper or pleading, for either party, subsequent to the first step, including objections and answers in a proof when stated in separate papers,	0	0	3	0	0	6
Appeal to the Sheriff Depute,	0	0	6	0	0	6
Receiving and marking each set of productions, except the productions lodged with the first paper for each party, for which no charge is to be made,	0	0	3	0	0	3
Extracting each decreet in absence, in the abridged form,	0	1	0	0	1	6
When a decreet is extracted against more defenders than one sued for a separate debt or prestation, the above fee of extract to be paid on one of the debts or prestations highest in amount, and a third of the above fee for extract to be paid on each of the others, according to the amount of the claim against such defender or set of defenders						
Extracting each decree in foro, in the abridged form,	0	2	0	0	2	6
If the decree, whether in absence or in foro, shall exceed one sheet, for writing each succeeding sheet,	0	0	6	0	0	6
Recording abridged decreets, per sheet,	0	0	6	0	0	6
Indorsing decrees or warrants, and dating and recording such indorsation,	0	1	0	0	1	0
Protestations for not insisting,	0	0	6	0	0	9
Extract thereof,	0	0	6	0	0	9
Acts and commissions, first sheet,	0	0	6	0	0	9
Subsequent sheets, each,	0	0	6	0	0	6
If the proof be taken on the interlocutor allowing it, without extracting an Act and Commission, there will be paid by each party leading proof,	0	0	6	0	0	9
Diligence or precept for citing parties incidentally, witnesses or havers,	0	0	6	0	0	9
Second diligence,	0	0	6	0	0	9
Each deposition or declaration,	0	0	0	0	0	0
Writing each sheet thereof, after the first, when the sheriff clerk acts as writing clerk,	0	0	6	0	0	6
The sheriff clerk or his depute, when acting as commissioner in taking a proof, deposition of party, or declaration, will be allowed the following fees, viz.						
In causes not exceeding 8l, each hour,	0	1	3			
Above 8l., and not exceeding 25l, each hour,	0	2	0			
Above 25l, each hour,	0	2	6			
As also his clerk's fee for writing, at the rate of 4d. per sheet.						

	In Cases of L. 12, and under			Above L. 12.		
	£	s.	d.	£	s.	d.
Sequestration of a tenant's effects, or of joint tenants in one possession ; viz.						
Warrant of sequestration, and service, . .	0	1	3	0	1	6
Taking the inventory, when taken by the clerk, if the rent to be secured be 12*l* or under—						
Clerk and witnesses, . . .	0	2	6			
When the rent is above 12*l*. and does not exceed 25*l*.—						
Clerk and witnesses, . . .	..	...		0	3	9
When the rent is above 25*l*. and does not exceed 50*l*.—						
Clerk and witnesses, . . .				0	5	0
When the rent is above 50*l* —						
Clerk and witnesses, . . .	...	...		0	6	3
Writing out inventory and schedule, per sheet of each in any of the above cases, . . .				0	0	6
If the clerk and witnesses are necessarily employed more than two hours in taking the inventory, or travelling for that purpose, he will be allowed, in addition to the above fees for every hour after the first two,						
Clerk and witnesses, . .	0	0	9	0	0	9
But under these charges for the hours after the first two, the clerk not to have in one day for himself and witnesses more than 5*s*.						
Warrant of sale, ...	0	0	6	0	1	0
Extract thereof, per sheet, when required, .	0	0	6	0	1	0
Intimating sale to Tax Office, . . .	0	0	6	0	0	6
The clerk, when he executes any warrant to roup, and collects the proceeds, will be held liable for the amount of the roup roll, and will be allowed for his trouble and risk, including auctioneer's fees, as follows—						
When the amount of the roup roll is 8*l*. or under, he will be allowed 3*s*. 9*d*.						
When the amount of the roup roll is above 8*l*. and does not exceed 100*l*, he will be allowed at the rate of 2½ per cent.						
When the amount of the roup roll exceeds 100*l* but does not exceed 1000*l*, he will be allowed 2½ per cent. for the first 100*l*., and for every additional 100*l* or part of 100*l* 1½ per cent. And when the amount exceeds 1000*l*., he will allowed the above rates for the first 1000*l*, and one per cent. for each additional 100*l* and part of 100*l*.						
The above poundage to cover all charges for trouble in relation to the sale, and for collecting the proceeds, drawing advertisements and articles of roup, but the clerk will be allowed all his necessary disbursements or expenses, such as advertising, paying crier, travelling charges, &c. He will also, when the proceeds are above 20*l*., be allowed 3*s*. 9*d*. for an assistant clerk.						
If roup be stopped after time of sale is fixed, .	0	1	3	0	1	3
Receiving the report of sale, and note of the sum arising from it, and marking the same, . .	0	0	6	0	1	0
Allowing inspection of the same, . .	0	0	6	0	0	6
In sales under other warrants of the sheriff, including poindings, the same fees to be paid as in sales under sequestrations						
At intimating caption to compel return of a process, including dues of caption, if issued, . .	0	0	6	0	0	6
Enrolling a cause, to be paid by the party requiring enrolment, ...	0	0	6	0	0	6
When any cause at avizandum is enrolled by order of the sheriff, the above fee to be paid by the parties equally.						

	In Cases of L.12, and under			Above L.12.		
	£	s.	d	£	s.	d.
At borrowing a process, or part of a process, the clerk being for this fee bound to compare the process, both when borrowed and returned, and to mark the return,	0	0	6	0	0	6
Attending at judicial inspections or visitations, when required by the sheriff or either of the parties, sealing up repositories, or executing any other order or warrant of the sheriff, not otherwise provided for in this table—						
First hour employed, . . .	0	2	0	0	2	6
Every other, . . .	0	1	3	0	2	0
Besides necessary outlays.						
Auditing accounts of expenses when remit made to the Clerk—						
In decrees in absence, . . .	0	0	6	0	0	6
In litigated cases, when the amount of the account rendered is under 5l, . .	0	1	9	0	1	9
When 5l and under 10l, . .	0	2	6	0	2	6
When 10l and under 20l., . .	0	3	6	0	3	6
When 20l and under 40l., . .	0	5	0	0	5	0
When 40l. and under 60l., . .	0	6	0	0	6	0
When 60l. and under 80l., . .	0	7	6	0	7	6
When 80l and upwards, . .	0	10	6	0	10	6
Caveat, ...	0	0	6	0	0	6
Precepts or warrants of arrestment, when contained in the summons, . .	0	0	3	0	0	3
When not contained in the summons, . .	0	0	9	0	1	0
At loosing an arrestment in either case, . .	0	0	9	0	1	0
Each bond of caution and relative certificate, .	0	2	6	0	3	9
Edict or summons of curatory, or for giving up inventories, ...	0	1	3	0	1	3
Calling in Court, receiving and entering the nomination of curators,	0	2	6	0	2	6
Docqueting and signing tutorial or curatorial inventories, per sheet of each duplicate, . .	0	0	3	0	0	3
Extract Acts of curatory, or upon production of inventories—						
First sheet, ...	0	2	6	0	2	6
Every other sheet, ...	0	1	3	0	1	3
Second extracts, per sheet, . .	0	1	3	0	1	3
Production of a bill of advocation, and marking the same, including trouble of transmitting the process when necessary, .				0	2	6
Transmitting extracted processes, in consequence of a warrant from the Court of Session or the sheriff,	0	0	9	0	1	3
Appeal against a decree or sentence of the sheriff to the Court of Justiciary or Circuit Court, or answers thereto,	0	1	0	0	1	3
Searching for a process in which no procedure has taken place for a year, if search does not exceed five years, and no extract ordered, . .	0	0	6	0	1	0
Each additional year after the first five in which the search is made, . .	0	0	3	0	0	3
For each consignation of money in the clerk's hands, if under 10l, . .	0	1	3	0	1	3
And an additional fee for the amount above 10l. at the rate of 5s on each 100l consigned.						
On the lodging of a bank receipt when money ordered to be consigned is lodged in a bank instead of being consigned,	0	1	3	0	1	3
The fees in these three last articles not to be chargeable on proceeds of roups or sales conducted by the clerks.						
Each warrant to uplift consigned money, .	0	1	3	0	1	3
Full extract, or second extract, or authenticated copy of a process or part of a process, or other procedure or paper, when required by a party, and furnished by the clerk, per sheet, . . .	0	0	6	0	0	9

Note.—In all cases where the conclusions are ad factum præstandum, or not entirely pecuniary, the highest class to be the rate of charge, but fees on papers in summonses of removal or ejection to be charged according to the rent of the subject from which the defender is summoned to remove or to be ejected.

	£	s.	d.
Recording hornings, inhibitions, interdictions, lawburrows, with their executions, discharges, and other writings recorded in the registers of hornings and inhibitions, per sheet,	0	0	10
First or subsequent extracts thereof, when required, per sheet,	0	0	9
Recording bonds, tacks, dispositions, and other writings in the register of deeds and probative writs, per sheet,	0	0	9
First extracts of such deeds or writings, when required, per sheet,	0	0	6
Subsequent extracts, per sheet,	0	0	9
Recording protests on bills, including extract,	0	1	3
Subsequent extracts,	0	0	9
Recording accounts, states, and the like, per sheet of figures,	0	1	0
Extract thereof, per sheet,	0	0	9
Inspection of records of entailed vouchers,	0	0	6
Searching the record of hornings or inhibitions, including minute-book, each year or part of a year,	0	0	3
In all not exceeding,	0	3	9
Searching for deeds recorded for the first year, or part of the year specified	0	0	6
every additional year,	0	0	3
Certificate of search, if required,	0	1	8
Inspection of records when a party or his agent makes the search, each record-book and corresponding minute-book,	0	1	3
Examinations under the Bankrupt Act, when the sheriff clerk acts as clerk to the examination, each diet,	0	3	9
Writing declarations or oaths therein, per sheet,	0	0	6

SERVICES.

General Service—

	£	s.	d.
Procuring the brieve executed, and intimation to agent,	0	1	9
Attending in Court at service, framing and recording the minutes, and instrument money,	0	3	6
Fees of the service,	0	10	0
Engrossing the retour,	0	2	6

Special Service, or Service as Heir of Provision—

	£	s.	d.
Procuring the brieve executed, and intimation to agent,	0	1	9
Attending in Court at service, framing the minutes, and recording, first sheet,	0	3	0
Each other,	0	1	0
Framing the retour, first sheet,	0	7	6
Each other sheet,	0	5	0
Engrossing the retour, each sheet,	0	1	0
Extracts from the record of service, when required, each sheet,	0	1	0

Infeftments—

	£	s.	d.
Drawing instrument of sasine on chancery Precepts, first sheet, } 250 words per sheet,	0	7	6
Each subsequent sheet,	0	5	0
Extending the same, first sheet,	0	1	6
Each subsequent sheet,	0	1	0
Besides the stamped vellum or parchment.			
And that the clerk receive for taking infeftment thereon, when the rent of the property does not exceed 100*l.* per annum,	0	10	6
100*l.* and not exceeding 200*l.*,	1	1	0
200*l.* and not exceeding 500*l.*,	1	11	6
500*l.* and not exceeding 1000*l.*,	2	2	0
And for every additional 1000*l.*,	0	10	6
But not to exceed in all,	5	5	0
And if the distance exceed three miles, each additional mile, until it exceeds ten miles,	0	2	6
But under this charge not to receive more per day than	1	1	0
Besides travelling charges			
Extracts of minutes of procedure of freeholder meetings, when required, per sheet,	0	1	3
Each person taking the oaths to Government, when the oaths are not administered at a county meeting,	0	1	0
Certificate thereof, when required,	0	1	6
Qualifying a peer to vote at an election,	1	1	0
Extract of the fiars, each year,	0	0	9

	£	s	d.
Receiving such precept from the Court of Session, making up list of jury, and instructing officer to summon, and making return,	0	2	6
Receiving countermand of trial, and instructing officer,	0	2	6
Writing and booking each necessary letter,	0	1	3
Each duplicate and copy,	0	0	6

Fees for Public Business payable in Exchequer—

	£	s	d.
For the principal precept of intimation of election of a member of Parliament, besides expense of printing,	0	10	6
Writings relative to elections of members of Parliament (exclusive of the precept), to summoning the Commissioners of Supply for laying on the Land Tax, and to other public business payable in the Exchequer, each sheet,	0	1	0
When consisting of more than one sheet, each additional sheet,	0	1	6
Superintending the execution of chancery precepts, and returning the execution, for each precept,	0	0	6
Superintending the publication of royal proclamations or writs, each,	0	5	0
Warrant to summon jury and witnesses for striking the fiars and making list, and instructing officer to summon them,	0	10	0
Attendance at striking the fiars, and writing the evidence and procedure, and recording the verdict,	1	11	6
To the sheriff clerk for instructing the persons employed in taking up the lists of jurors, receiving the returns, and engrossing the lists in the jury books, for each 100 names, exclusive of printing,	0	5	0
To the district clerk, or other person having local knowledge, for attending and assisting the sheriff at revising lists, at the rate of 21s. per day, including travelling charges and postages.			

N.B.—The sheet of writings to be computed at three hundred words, when not otherwise specified ; but if the writing does not contain three hundred words, to be charged as one sheet ; and if after finding the sheet or sheets which any such writings shall comprise, calculated at the rate aforesaid, any number of words less than three hundred words shall remain, such fewer words shall be charged as a sheet. Although the fees for recording hornings, inhibitions, deeds, and other writings in the registers of hornings and inhibitions, and of deeds and probative writs, are to be paid for at certain rates for every sheet, yet it is understood that the clerks are to frame those records so as to contain in each sheet the number of words prescribed by the regulations of the Lord Clerk Register.

The fees in the above table to be paid, though the duty be performed by the clerk depute or by an assistant clerk, and to be exclusive of postages and outlays.

The fees in criminal and any other business to be subject to the regulation of the Lord High Treasurer, or Commissioners of Her Majesty's Treasury, or any three of them, from and after the passing of this Act.

ACT OF SEDERUNT

FOR REGULATING THE

FORM OF PROCESS IN SHERIFF COURTS.

PREPARED IN TERMS OF THE ACT OF 1st & 2d VICT. c 119, § 32.

EDINBURGH, *10th July* 1839.

The Lords of Council and Session, taking into consideration an Act passed in the first and second year of the reign of Her present Majesty Queen Victoria, cap. 119, intituled An Act to regulate the Constitution, Jurisdiction, and Forms of Process of Sheriff Courts in Scotland; together with the reports laid before Parliament by the Commissioners appointed under the sign-manual of His late Majesty King William the Fourth, dated 6th June 1833, and 16th August 1834; and considering that it was provided by the said statute (§ 32), that the sheriffs of Scotland should meet from time to time, from and after the first week of the winter session commencing in November 1838, and should submit to this Court, on or before the first day of January 1839, such propositions as they should think ought to be enacted by Act of Sederunt for the regulation of Sheriff Courts; which propositions were to be sent to the Sheriff Courts, to be exhibited there for the time therein mentioned; after which the said sheriffs were directed to prepare a revised draft of the said propositions for the consideration of this Court, on or before the 12th day of March 1839; and this Court was authorized and empowered, on due consideration of the said draft, to pass an Act of Sederunt in such terms as the Court should think fit · And the whole of these proceedings having been followed out in the manner prescribed by the statute, as appears from the reports of the sheriffs hereto annexed, and the Lords having maturely considered the said draft and revised draft, and the suggestions by the sheriffs, and by the procurators in their Courts, and others, in relation thereto, Do HEREBY ENACT AND DECLARE,

That the following form of process in civil causes before the Sheriff Courts shall be established and observed from and after the commencement of the winter session of the Sheriff Courts next following the date of this Act;

And that, with regard to all actions at present in any Sheriff Court, or which may be brought into Court prior to that time, the form of process hereby established shall be observed, in so far as is consistent with justice and the convenience of parties.

PART I.

OF ORDINARY CIVIL ACTIONS.

CHAP. I.

DIETS AND SESSIONS OF COURT

1. Each Sheriff Court, except those held at a place where an ordinary sheriff substitute does not reside, shall sit for the despatch of ordinary business at least one day in every week during the summer and winter sessions; such day to be fixed by the sheriff in each county by a regulation of Court.

2. The winter session shall commence, at the latest, on the 15th of October, or first ordinary court-day thereafter, and shall continue until the 4th day of April inclusive, excepting during the Christmas recess, which must not be longer than three weeks. The summer session shall commence on the first court-day after the 15th of May, and continue until the last court-day in July.

3. It shall be competent for each sheriff to extend the duration of the sessions by a regulation of Court, and, in particular, to appoint court-days during the vacations. And in case there shall be any arrear of business undisposed of by the sheriff, it shall be his duty, from time to time, to appoint additional court-days, whether in time of session or vacation, for the purpose of disposing of such arrear

1st and 2d Vict. c. 119, § 17.

4. During the vacations, summary applications shall be received, and interlocutors in summary cases shall be dated and entered in the Court-book, or Diet-book, as in time of session.

5 The sheriff of each county shall, before the termination of each session, appoint at least two court-days during each vacation, the first towards the middle, the last towards the end of the vacation, for the despatch of all ordinary business, including the calling of new causes; and papers appointed to be put into process on these days must be lodged with the sheriff clerk, before the hour of meeting of the Court.

6. For seven days after each of these days, and after the last court-day of each session, it shall be competent to sign interlocutors in ordinary causes.

7. The reclaiming days shall run during the vacation.

CHAP. II.

FORM OF THE SUMMONS.

8. All defenders shall be cited upon a summons, signed on each page by the clerk, fully libelled, and having the name of the pursuer's procurator marked on the back

9. Not more than six defenders, on separate grounds of action, shall be included in one libel, except in actions of multiplepoinding, maills and duties, poinding of the ground, and forthcoming.

10. The summons must contain a concise and accurate statement of the facts, and must also set forth, in explicit terms, the nature, extent, and grounds of the complaint, or cause of action, and the conclusions deduced therefrom;—where an account is founded on, it shall be sufficient to refer to it by the first and last dates. The summons must bear *a partibus* for calling,—the sums concluded for

must be marked in figures on the margin ,—the true date of signing must be filled up , and the clerk is discharged from calling any summons that is not marked, and signed as directed.

11. No libel shall be amended after citation is given thereon, except by authority of the sheriff.

12. Every libel or summons may also contain a warrant for arresting the defender's effects and debts, on the dependence.

CHAP. III.

EXECUTION OF THE SUMMONS.

13. The officer who executes the summons, shall deliver to the defender, if he find him, personally,—or if he do not find him, shall leave at his dwelling-place,— a full copy of the summons to the will, with a copy of citation, in presence of one witness   When a libel is amended in absence of the defender, a copy of the amendment must be served upon him in the same manner, and on the same *induciæ*, as the original libel.   If there be more defenders than one, each shall be served with a copy of the libel, or of such part thereof as concerns himself   In actions of poinding the ground, mails and duties. and forthcoming, the tenants and arrestees shall be served with short copies of citation, and the proprietor and common debtor with a full copy of the libel to the will   All copies of summonses served shall be signed on each page by the officer.

14. Edicts for choosing curators, summonses for curators giving up inventories, multiplepoindings, transferences, transumpts, wakenings, and cognitions, may be executed by delivering a copy of citation before one witness, containing the names and designations of the pursuer and defender, and bearing the extent and special grounds of the pursuer's claim, without any copy of the summons.

15. All executions or returns shall be signed by the officer and the witness who was present at the execution, and shall specify whether the citation was given to the defender personally or otherwise ; and if otherwise, shall specify particularly the mode of citation.

16. If any defender amenable to the jurisdiction of the sheriff in whose Court the summons is raised, be not resident within that sheriffdom, he may be cited by warrant of the said sheriff, provided the same be endorsed by the sheriff clerk of the sheriffdom within which the defender resides. *1st and 2d Vict c.119, § 24.*

17 Where an officer returns an irregular or defective execution, he shall be liable to the party who employed him in damages, which it shall be in the power of the sheriff to award summarily in the course of the process; and such officer may also be punished as the sheriff shall think the case merits.

18. If the officer executes the warrant of arrestment, contained in the summons, by arresting the defender's effects, he must forthwith return an execution of arrestment to the clerk.

19. The name of the pursuer's procurator shall be marked on the back of the copy of the libel, and on the citation left for the defender.

CHAP. IV.

DIET OF COMPEARANCE.

20. All summonses shall contain a warrant for citing the defender to compear on the seventh day next after the date of citation, if a court-day, or, if not, on the first court-day thereafter (except in the cases after mentioned), with continuation of days ; and the citation shall be conform to such warrant.

NOTE.—It is recommended that a note of the days of the week on which the ordinary courts are held should be printed or written at the foot of all copies of citations.

21. In the case of libels or edicts for choosing curators, and of summonses for giving up inventories, the defenders shall be cited to appear on the tenth day after the date of citation, if a court-day, or, if not, on the first court-day thereafter, with continuation of days.

22. When the defender is a minor, his tutors and curators shall be called edictally upon the same *induciæ* as the principal defender.

CHAP. V.

CALLING OF THE CAUSE, AND NON-COMPEARANCE OF THE DEFENDER.

23. The summons may be called upon the day to which the defender has been cited, namely, the seventh day, if a court-day, or upon the first court-day thereafter, and the pursuer, at the calling, must, along with his summons, produce the deeds, accounts, and other writings on which he founds, so far as the same are in his custody, or within his power, or state where he believes them to be, in which case the sheriff may grant him a diligence for recovering them.

24. If the defender be absent at the calling of the cause, the sheriff may either hold him as confessed and decern, or allow such competent proof in support of the libel, as the pursuer or his procurator shall require, or the sheriff may deem necessary; but before proceeding in the proof, it must be shewn to the sheriff, or commissioner taking the proof, that regular notice of the appointment *See § 115, infra.* for proof has been given to the defender. And the defender shall not be reponed against the decree in absence, or interlocutor allowing the proof, unless he shall apply to have the decree or interlocutor recalled, as hereinafter directed, by a petition, accompanied with defences prepared in terms of Chapter VII. § § 32 and 33, and shall consign in the hands of the clerk of court the ex-*1st and 2d Vict c 119, § 18.* penses incurred, as modified on taxation; and the sheriff shall have power to award to the pursuer such part of the expenses consigned, as he may judge reasonable.

CHAP. VI.

PROTESTATION BY THE DEFENDER FOR NOT INSISTING.

25. Upon the day of compearance, or any subsequent court-day, during the currency of the summons, if the defender produce the copy thereof given to him, and if the pursuer fail to appear and insist, the defender may crave protestation for not insisting, which the sheriff shall admit, and modify the protestation money, according to circumstances, so as to indemnify the defender for his trouble and expenses, besides the dues of extract.

26. No protestation shall be extracted till the expiry of seven free days after the day on which the same was granted, excepting in cases where arrestments have been used, when the protestation may be extracted and given out on the lapse of forty-eight hours. The protestation, when extracted, may contain a precept of poinding and arrestment for recovery of the protestation money, and the dues of extract.

27. If protestation be not extracted, the pursuer shall be allowed to call and insist in his action without a new citation, upon paying over to the defender or his procurator, or, in his absence after due intimation—or refusal to accept, consigning in the sheriff clerk's hands, for the defender's use, the sum awarded in name of protestation money, except the expense of extract.

28. In case the protestation be extracted, the instance shall fall, and the defender shall not be obliged to answer, except upon a new summons, and citation on the ordinary *induciæ*.

CHAP VII.

PROCEDURE WHEN APPEARANCE IS MADE FOR BOTH PARTIES

29. The defender or his procurator, if prepared, may give in his defences to the libel at the calling of the cause; but if he crave to see the libel, in order to state his defences, the defences shall be lodged on or before the seventh day thereafter, and if such seventh day be a court-day, before the hour of meeting of the court; with power to the sheriff to appoint an earlier or a later day, when, from the nature of the case, he may see cause to do so.

30. A procurator appearing for a defender, must produce, along with his defences, either a written mandate for the defender, or the copy of citation given to the defender.

31. When there are more defenders than one, appearing by different procurators, the procurator for the pursuer shall make out a copy or copies of the summons, or an excerpt or excerpts thereof, applicable to the case of each defender or set of defenders appearing by one procurator, which shall be signed and certified by the clerk of court, and given out for stating defences, and the clerk shall retain the original summons; and in all the future procedure the process shall be given out to the procurators for the defenders respectively, according to their order in the summons, who shall each be allowed to see the same for such time as the sheriff shall think proper.

32. Upon the day appointed the defender shall give in all his defences, both dilatory and peremptory.

He shall in the *first* part of his defences meet, in their order, the statements of fact in the summons, by admitting or denying the same, either absolutely or with qualifications, but without argument, and with such explanations in point of fact, applicable to each averment, as are necessary to make his answers intelligible; and shall also set forth articulately, without argument, the facts on which he may found a separate substantive plea in law; and, in the *second* part of his defences, he shall subjoin, under distinct heads, a summary of all the defences or pleas in law which he is to maintain, with such argument as he may think fit.

33. Along with his defences, the defender must produce the deeds or writings on which he founds, so far as the same are in his custody, or within his power; and if they are not within his custody or power, he shall state where he believes them to be, and crave a diligence for recovering them.

34 In actions of removing, and in summary applications for ejection, the defender shall come prepared with a cautioner for violent profits, at giving in his defences or answers, unless he instantly verify a defence excluding the action

35. The defences, when given in, shall be seen, and replies lodged on or before the seventh day thereafter, and if such seventh day be a court-day, before the sitting of the court, with power to the sheriff to appoint a later or an earlier day, if he see cause. If, however, the parties are ready to close the record upon the summons and defences alone, or on these papers, along with a minute by the pursuer, written on the summons, and simply admitting or denying the statements in the defences, it shall not be necessary to lodge replies, and it shall be competent for the sheriff to close the record accordingly in manner hereinafter directed.

36. In the *first* part of the replies, the pursuer shall commence by setting forth articulately, and in substantive propositions, without argument, the whole facts on which he founds, which facts must be comprehended under the general statement in the summons; and he shall then meet, in their order, articulately and without argument, the statements of fact in the defences, by admitting or denying the same, either absolutely or with qualifications, and with such explanations in point of fact, applicable to each averment, as are necessary to make his answers intelligible: and, in the *second* part of the replies, he shall subjoin, under distinct heads, a summary of the pleas in law which he is to maintain, with such argument as he may think fit.

37. When the replies are given in, the sheriff shall proceed to advise the pleadings; and it shall be in his power, if he see cause, to allow the defences to be amended, in which case he shall particularly specify, in his interlocutor or note, the points on which amendments are required, and such amendments, whether consisting of answers to the pursuer's statements, or to his pleas in law, shall be strictly confined to the points so specified, and shall be made on, or subjoined to the original defences, with reference to their proper heads, and in the same form and manner in all respects as is herein-before prescribed for preparing defences.

38. If dilatory defences have been stated, they shall be immediately disposed of by the sheriff, unless he thinks that, either from their being connected with the merits, or on any other ground, they should be reserved till a future stage of the cause

39. No reclaiming petition against any judgment repelling the dilatory defences shall be allowed; but if the judgment has been pronounced by the sheriff-substitute, the defender may appeal to the sheriff.

40. If the sheriff sustain the dilatory defences, or any of them, he shall at the same time determine the matter of expenses; but if he repel the dilatory defences, the cause shall then proceed in its due course of preparation.

41. If it shall appear to the sheriff, after the dilatory defences (if any have been proposed) are disposed of, that the grounds of action on the merits, as set forth in the summons, are in terms not sufficiently positive and clear, or that the conclusions are not regularly or clearly deduced, he may either dismiss the action, decerning for expenses if he shall see cause, and reserving to the pursuer the right to bring a new action, if otherwise competent; or he may allow an amendment of the libel, and give interim decree against the pursuer for the expenses incurred by the incorrect form of the summons; and the amendments as approved shall be written on the original summons, and authenticated by the subscription of the clerk.

42. If the defences or replies be not prepared in the manner herein-before directed, the sheriff may order the same to be withdrawn, and correct defences or replies, as the case may be, to be given in; and he may give interim decree against the party in fault for the expenses thus occasioned.

43. If it shall appear to the sheriff that the summons, defences, and replies, set forth fully the facts respectively founded on, and sufficiently bring out the merits of the cause, he shall require the parties within a time to be specified, to state whether they are willing to hold their said pleadings as containing their full and final statement of facts; and if they agree so to do, they shall, within the said time, set forth their assent to that effect in a note subjoined to their respective pleadings, or written on the interlocutor sheet, or minutes of process, and subscribed by them, or their respective procurators, and the sheriff shall then close the record, by writing the words " record closed," and dating and subscribing the same.

44. If the parties do not, within the time specified, state whether they are willing to hold their said pleadings as containing their full and final statement of facts, the sheriff shall be entitled to close the record in the same manner, and to the same effect, as if the parties had expressly agreed.

45. If either of the parties shall state that he does not agree to hold the summons, defences, and replies, as sufficiently setting forth the facts respectively founded on, or if it shall appear to the sheriff that the record cannot properly be closed without alterations on or additions to these pleadings, he shall ordain the parties, or their procurators, to attend him on such day as he shall appoint, for the purpose of adjusting the record, intimating at the same time by a note, or in such manner as he may think proper, the points to which he wishes their attention to be directed. At this meeting, or at any adjournment thereof which the sheriff may think reasonable, the parties, or their procurators, may propose any alterations on, or additions to, the defences or replies; which alterations or additions shall be written by them on the original defences or replies, in such mode and form as the sheriff shall allow And if the sheriff shall then be of opinion that

the record may be closed, and the parties, or their procurators, are willing to close it, they shall set forth their assent to that effect in a note subjoined to their respective pleadings, or written on the interlocutor sheet, or minutes of process, and subscribed by them or their respective procurators ; and the sheriff shall then close the record, by writing the words " record closed," and dating and subscribing the same.

All alterations or additions made on the margin of the record at any period before it is closed, shall be authenticated by the initials of the sheriff.

46. If the parties fail to attend the meeting so appointed, or if any party be absent, and the party present shall consent to close the record, it shall be competent for the sheriff to do so, in the same manner, and to the same effect, as if both parties had expressly agreed ; or otherwise to appoint a new meeting for adjusting and closing the record, with certification.

47. If at the meeting it shall appear to the sheriff, that, from the intricacy of the case, or any other cause, the record cannot properly be closed, or if both parties shall decline to close, the sheriff shall order a condescendence (from either of the parties) and answers, within such time as he may think proper.

48. If one party shall be willing to close, while the other declines to do so, the sheriff shall have power to close the record if he deems it expedient, but in the event of his allowing a condescendence, in consequence of such declinature, when he would otherwise think it unnecessary, he shall find the party so declining liable in such part of the previous expenses, as he may think reasonable, for which he shall grant interim decree ; and he shall then order a condescendence and answers ; and it shall not be competent for the clerk to receive the paper of the party who so declined to close, until certified that the said expenses have been paid.

49. In the condescendence, the party shall, without argument, in substantive propositions, and under distinct heads or articles, set forth the whole facts and circumstances pertinent to his case, which he avers and offers to prove, and shall state, at the end of each article, the specific mode of proof.

50. In the answers, the respondent shall articulately, and without argument, admit or deny, either absolutely or with qualifications, each separate averment in the condescendence, setting forth in his admission or denial such explanations in point of fact as are necessary to make his answer intelligible. If the respondent, besides his answers to the averments in the condescendence, has to aver any facts or circumstances pertinent to the case on which he founds a separate substantive plea, he shall set them forth without argument, in substantive propositions, and under distinct heads or articles, and shall state at the end of each article, the specific mode of proof.

51. The parties shall subjoin to their condescendence or answers a note of the whole pleas in law on which they respectively found. They shall also produce therewith all writings in their custody, or within their power, not already produced, on which they mean to found ; but when books of business are founded on, excerpts therefrom may be produced in the first instance, the books themselves being produced in the course of the proof if required. If the writings are not in their custody or power, they shall take a diligence for their recovery, or report any diligence previously granted.

52. If the answers contain a separate statement of facts, the condescender shall be entitled to subjoin to his condescendence articulate answers thereto, with any plea or pleas in law which may thence arise ; but otherwise he shall not be entitled to make any alteration on his condescendence until the parties meet before the sheriff, as hereinafter provided.

53. If the sheriff think that any of the parties has either stated in the condescendences or answers, allegations which ought to have been brought forward in the previous pleadings, or has improperly withheld writings, or other documents, which ought to have been previously produced, he may find the party in fault liable in the whole, or such part of the expenses, previously incurred by the other party, as may appear proper, and give interim decree therefor.

54. As soon as the condescendence and answers, prepared in the manner

before directed, are lodged, the sheriff shall order the parties, or their procurators, to attend him on such day as he shall appoint, for the purpose of adjusting and closing the record, intimating, if necessary, at the same time by a note, or in such manner as he may think proper, the points to which he wishes their attention to be directed. At this meeting, the parties or their procurators, may propose any alterations on, or additions to, the condescendence and answers; which alterations or additions shall be written by them on the original condescendence and answers, in such mode and form as the sheriff shall allow, after which, or if the parties or any of them be absent, it shall be competent for the sheriff to close the record, whether the parties are willing or not, by writing the words "record closed," and dating and subscribing the same, and all alterations or additions made on the margin of the record before closing, shall be authenticated as herein before directed.

55. If, in the summons, defences, and replies, or in the condescendence and answers, a statement of fact, within the opposite party's knowledge, be averred by one party and not denied by the other, the latter shall be held as confessed.

56. When the record has been closed in any of the modes above mentioned, no new averments of fact, amendment of the libel, or new ground of defence, or productions within the power of the party, shall be allowed or received, under the exception of *res noviter veniens ad notitiam*, or of facts emerging since the record was closed.

57. When the sheriff shall see cause, he may order written pleadings on the relevancy of the allegations in the record.

58. It shall be competent to either party, before final judgment in a cause, to apply, either by motion in Court, or by a short note without argument, for leave to lodge a statement of any matter of fact or document *noviter veniens ad notitiam*, or emerging since the record was closed. The sheriff shall thereupon appoint the said party, within a time to be specified, to give in a condescendence, stating, in the first place, the facts which he alleges to have newly come to his knowledge, or to have emerged since the record was closed; and secondly and *separatim*, setting forth the circumstances under which they have only recently come to his knowledge, or emerged; and shall, if he see cause, appoint the other party, within a specified time, to answer the latter part of the said condescendence. And upon the said answers being given in, the sheriff shall, either upon proof or otherwise, determine whether or not the said matter, as *res noviter veniens ad notitiam*, or as having emerged since the record was closed, ought to be added to the record, and shall pronounce an interlocutor accordingly, at the same time determining, or specially reserving, the point of expenses: And in case he shall be of opinion that the said facts ought to be added to the record, he shall appoint the opposite party to answer the first part of the said condescendence; and the sheriff shall thereafter of new close the record upon these additional papers.

59 The sheriff shall, by a special order, fix the time within which each paper shall be lodged, except in so far as herein before or after provided, and the clerk shall not receive them after the time so fixed, except by consent of the opposite agent, written thereon and subscribed by him. Nor shall the time for so lodging papers be in any case prorogated, except by the sheriff, on cause shewn, and on payment of an amand, or of the whole or part of the expenses previously incurred, if the sheriff shall think proper. If the party shall fail to lodge any paper ordered within the time originally fixed, or afterwards prorogated, the sheriff may close the record, and either give judgment,—allow a proof,—or otherwise dispose of the cause as he shall think fit.

60. When it shall appear to the sheriff that all the facts requisite to the decision of the cause are ascertained so as to render any proof unnecessary, he may proceed to decide the cause, without farther argument, or he may order memorials, or minutes of debate, if he see cause.

61. It shall be competent to the pursuer, before any interlocutor of absolvitor is pronounced, to enter on the record an abandonment of the cause, on paying full expenses to the defender, and to bring a new action, if otherwise competent.

62. In pronouncing judgment on the merits, the sheriff shall also determine the matter of expenses, in so far as not already settled

63 All pleadings shall be subscribed by the party himself (he being answerable as to their being in regular form, and containing nothing improper or disrespectful to the Court), or by a procurator of Court, or other person legally authorized to act, and shall state the name and designation of the person by whom they are drawn, otherwise they shall not be received

64 No petition, memorial, minute, note, protest, or written pleading, other than those which are expressly allowed by the present regulations, shall, without previous permission by the sheriff, be received by the clerk.

65 It shall be the duty of the sheriff to enforce, in the strictest manner, the present regulations, by ordering peremptorily all such pleadings as are not in terms thereof, to be withdrawn, and also, if necessary, by imposing amands, or awarding to the opposite party expenses to such an extent as may seem expedient and proper.

CHAP VIII.

APPOINTMENTS ON PARTIES TO CONFESS OR DENY, AND JUDICIAL EXAMINATION OF PARTIES.

66. When the record shall have been closed, or at such earlier stage of the cause as to the sheriff shall seem proper, he may order both parties, or either of them, between and a certain day, by a writing under their hands, to confess or deny facts specified by the sheriff, or to attend personally for examination, and answer such interrogatories as the sheriff or commissioner shall think proper, and if the party fail to comply with such order within the time assigned, he shall be held as confessed, to such extent as the sheriff may think just, and decree may thereupon be pronounced, reserving to the sheriff to repone him upon cause shewn, and on payment of such amand or expenses, as the sheriff may think proper.

67. All such examinations shall take place in presence of the sheriff, but when he cannot attend, or in cases of special emergency, he may appoint a commissioner.

CHAP. IX.

PROOF AND CIRCUMDUCTION

68. If the facts are not sufficiently ascertained, the sheriff shall allow a proof of such facts averred in the record as he may deem necessary, and it shall be the duty of the sheriff or his substitute to take the proof; but when this cannot be done without interfering with more important duties, which cannot be delegated, a remit may be made to a commissioner.

69 When the sheriff considers it necessary to grant act and commission, the clerk shall only extract so much of the process as relates to the points on which the proof is to be taken, but it shall not be necessary to take out such extract, if the proof is to be taken within the county. The commissioner, if the proof is to be taken within Scotland, shall either be the clerk of court, his acting depute, a practitioner before any court of law of at least three years' standing, a justice of the peace, or other magistrate.

70. If the mean of proof be by writings alleged to be in the other party's hands, a day shall be assigned to that party for producing them, or to depone thereanent, as in an exhibition, or a diligence may be granted against him as a haver; and in case he shall fail to exhibit or depone on the day appointed, he shall be held as confessed upon the point offered to be proved by such writings

71. When the mean of proof is by writings not in the party's hands, or by witnesses, a day shall be assigned for recovery of such writs, or for proving by

witnesses, and diligence shall be granted to that effect, to be reported against the day assigned   (*Vide infra* § 126 *as to cases where the claim exceeds* L 40.)

72. Witnesses and havers, residing in another sheriffdom, must be cited in the terms, and under the provisions, of 1st and 2d Vict. c. 119, § 24.

73. The evidence of any witness about to leave Scotland, or whose testimony is in danger of being lost on account of extreme old age, or dangerous sickness, may, upon application, in a depending process, be taken to he *in retentis*. The party, if required by the sheriff, must instruct the fact alleged as the cause of the application. In case of old age, a certificate to that purpose must in general be exhibited ; and in case of sickness, the certificate of a physician or surgeon, or of the minister of the parish, must always be produced. If such proof is applied for before the record is closed, the party shall specify in the application the fact or facts on which the witnesses are to be examined.

74. It shall be in the power of the sheriff or commissioner taking the proof, to order to witnesses such expenses as shall seem just, to be paid by the party adducing them, or his procurator. The dues of oaths must be paid by the party requiring them

75. If havers or witnesses within the county, who have been cited on *induciæ* of not less than forty-eight hours, do not appear upon the day to which they are cited, and if no satisfactory reason be assigned for their non-attendance, second diligence shall be granted at the party's instance for apprehending and imprisoning them, until they find caution, under such penalty as may be fixed by the sheriff, to appear at the subsequent diets of proof when required , and which diligence shall always be reported on the day assigned for that purpose, either along with the witnesses, or with an execution by an officer, bearing that they have been searched for and could not be found. The sheriff, when taking a proof himself, or on report of the commissioner, shall decide whether witnesses not appearing on the day to which they were first cited should be entitled to expenses, or should be liable in the expense of second diligence, and execution thereof, or fined for their contumacy. See on this subject 1st and 2d Vict c 119, § 24.

76. Before proceeding in any proof, the diet for which has been fixed in absence of either party or his procurator, it must, if required, be shewn to the sheriff, or commissioner taking the proof, that notice of the appointment to prove has been made to that party or his procurator, in terms of the interlocutor allowing the proof , and the sheriff or commissioner, in taking a proof or declaration, or an oath of party on reference, may, notwithstanding the absence of one of the parties or his procurator, proceed with the proof.

77. Such incidental debates as arise during the examination of a party, or in the course of a proof, shall be considered as closed, by a short written statement of the grounds of objection, with answers thereto unless otherwise appointed by the sheriff ; and these objections and answers, as also any further debate thus allowed, shall be taken down on separate papers referred to, and not engrossed in the proof, unless otherwise ordered by the sheriff or commissioner. No reclaiming petition shall be competent against any judgment pronounced in the course of taking a proof; but all such judgments shall be subject to review by appeal to the sheriff-substitute or sheriff, without prejudice to the right of further appeal from the judgment of the sheriff-substitute to the sheriff, as in other cases When the sheriff or commissioner repels an objection to a witness, or to an interrogatory, it shall be his duty to proceed with the examination, and in all other cases, it shall be competent to him to do so ; and he shall have power, in any case, to order the proof, subject to such objection, to be sealed up if he shall see cause. All questions arising in the course of a proof may be disposed of in time of vacation.

78. When a witness is brought forward by one party, he shall be subject, at the same diet, to examination in chief by the adverse party, and to cross-examination by both parties, the adverse party paying his proportion of the expense of such examination.

79. When the proof is by oath of party, a day shall be assigned for his appearing and deponing. Such oath shall be taken by the sheriff, but if he can-

not attend, or in any case of special emergency, he may appoint a commissioner. If the party fail to appear upon the day assigned, and if no satisfactory reason be given for his absence, and the sheriff do not see cause to prorogate the diet, the term shall be circumduced against him, and he shall be held as confessed, and either decerned against, or avizandum made with the cause, as the nature of the case may require.

80. When any fact has been referred to oath of party, if, before emitting the oath, another mean of proof be demanded, it shall not be allowed, except upon the person who made the reference previously paying the expense which the other party has been put to by this change of procedure, as the same shall be modified by the sheriff.

81. Upon the day assigned for reporting the diligence or commission, the party who obtained it shall report the same   If he do not, the other party may crave circumduction, and the term shall be circumduced, unless sufficient cause for not reporting, be shewn to the sheriff, who may prorogate the term upon payment of part of the expenses, or without any such condition, as he may think proper. When a cause is at proof on commission, it shall not be put to the roll until the term for proving is expired, unless, from circumstances occurring in the course of the proof, it becomes necessary to enrol the cause, to have the sheriff's directions thereanent.

82. No party shall be reponed against a circumduction, or against a holding as confessed, except upon cause shewn to excuse his former failure, and upon payment of such sum as the sheriff shall modify for indemnifying the other party.

83. When a proof is reported, and an interlocutor pronounced thereon, no further proof shall be allowed, except upon very weighty reasons shewn, and upon payment to the other party of such a sum for expenses as the sheriff shall determine.   When such further proof is applied for, the facts, and the witnesses by whom they are to be proved, must be particularly condescended on in the Petition craving the additional proof

84. In all cases where the oath of party is required, the party by whom the reference or deference is made must either subscribe, along with his procurator, the paper in which the requisition is made, or sign a separate writing to that effect, to be produced along with the paper, or judicially adhere to the reference or deference in presence of the sheriff, or of the commissioner.

85. When proof, either by oath of party, or by witnesses, is concluded and reported, the sheriff shall proceed to advise the cause, unless he shall deem it necessary, either from the intricacy of the proof, or the importance of the cause, to appoint memorials or minutes of debate upon the proof or upon the whole cause.

86 These memorials or minutes shall not contain any quotation from the proof, or any of the writings in process, except when absolutely necessary, but reference may be made to the parole proof by the page, and by the letters of the alphabet (which for that purpose shall be put on the margin of the proof), and to the written evidence by the pages

CHAP. X.

OF STATEMENTS OF ACCOUNTS, AND REPORTS ON REMITS.

87. It shall be competent to the sheriff, when he sees cause, to order either or both parties to give in full and complete statements of accounts, and thereupon to order objections and answers, and afterwards he may allow the parties to revise those papers, by making alterations or additions on them in such mode or form as he shall direct, which alterations or additions shall be such only as are rendered necessary by new statements or arguments in the paper of the opposite party.

88. When the sheriff sees cause, he may, either before or after the record is closed, appoint visitations and inspections, or remit to accountants, auditors, inspectors, or other persons of skill, to report, and to prepare and lodge plans, where

necessary, and the reporters may afterwards be required to verify their reports upon oath.

89. The sheriff may allow objections to, or observations on, the report and answers, and thereafter may allow these papers to be revised, under the provisions contained in sect. 87.

90. The expense of these remits and reports shall, in the first instance, be paid by the parties' procurators jointly, unless the sheriff shall in particular cases see reason to order otherwise. But the expense of accountants' reports shall not be chargeable against the agent unless so arranged. The fees of auditing shall in the first instance be paid by the party whose account is taxed

CHAP. XI.

IMPROBATION OF WRITS AND EXECUTIONS

91. Improbation against executions of process, or against any writs founded on by either party, shall not be received unless proponed by the party who makes the challenge, or by his procurator specially authorized for that purpose by a written mandate, and upon consignation of a sum not exceeding five pounds, nor under ten shillings, as the sheriff shall modify, to be forfeited to the other party in case the proponer shall afterwards pass from or fail in his improbation, besides being liable in the expenses and damages which shall be awarded against him at the conclusion of the cause, and other legal consequences of failing in the improbation.

CHAP. XII

OATH OF CALUMNY

92. If at any time the oath of calumny be insisted for when the party from whom it is demanded is not present, it shall not be allowed, unless upon consignation of a sum not exceeding forty shillings, nor under five shillings, to be fixed by the sheriff, and if he see cause, to be forfeited to the other party, in case the oath is afterwards passed from, or is negative, besides payment of what shall be awarded by the sheriff as travelling charges, and other expenses, occasioned by the oath of calumny being insisted on.

CHAP. XIII.

RECLAIMING PETITIONS

93. Every reclaiming petition must recite, *verbatim*, the interlocutor reclaimed against, and bear upon the margin the true date of that interlocutor, and must be drawn in the terms specified in chap. ix. sect. 86.

94. In all cases, the interlocutor pronounced on advising a reclaiming petition, whether agreeing with, or varying from the interlocutor reclaimed against, shall be final, without prejudice to either party craving the judgment of the sheriff by appeal.

95. Reclaiming petitions, in ordinary actions, shall be lodged with the clerk, and marked on the back by him on or before the fourteenth day after the date of the interlocutor, excepting in actions of removing and aliment, in which actions, reclaiming petitions must be lodged on or before the seventh day after the date of the interlocutor. The clerk is enjoined not to receive any petition after the expiry of those days respectively. Answers to reclaiming petitions, if ordered, must be lodged within the same number of days as the petitions respectively, unless otherwise ordered by the sheriff.

96. When any party desirous of reclaiming against an interlocutor, is prevented by another party having borrowed the process, it shall be competent for him, within the reclaiming days, to present a *pro forma* petition, praying for leave to lodge an additional petition ; and upon a certificate thereon subscribed by the clerk, that the petitioner has been thus prevented, the sheriff may, if he see cause, allow such additional petition to be lodged within such period as he may think proper.

97. No new production shall be received, either with a reclaiming petition or the answers.

CHAP XIV.

APPEAL TO THE SHERIFF.

98. Parties thinking themselves aggrieved by any judgment of the sheriff-substitute, whether interlocutory or final, except in the cases otherwise provided, may, on or before the seventh day after the date of the interlocutor, apply for the opinion of the sheriff by appeal. But when the decree may be extracted in a shorter time, the appeal must be made within the days of extract. The appeal must be made by a motion in Court, or by a minute without argument, referring by date to the interlocutor appealed from, and craving the opinion of the sheriff on the whole or any part of such interlocutor. It shall be competent to the sheriff substitute to refuse to allow the appeal against any interlocutor, which, in his opinion, ought to be carried into immediate effect.

99. It shall be competent for the sheriff, when the case is before him on appeal, on any point, to open up the record *ex proprio motu*, if it shall appear to him not to have been properly made up

100 No reclaiming petition against the judgment of the sheriff, pronounced on appeal, shall be competent, whether such judgment affirm or alter the judgment of the sheriff-substitute.

CHAP. XV

OF ACTIONS OF WAKENING.

101. When a process is allowed to lie over for year and day, the party desirous to waken and insist in it, must raise a summons of wakening in the usual form, unless both parties or their procurators agree, by a written consent, to the cause being wakened.

CHAP. XVI.

MULTIPLEPOINDINGS.

102. When a multiplepoinding is raised in the name of the holder of a fund, by one of the claimants, it shall be served on the nominal pursuer, as well as upon the other claimants, and an execution of such service shall be returned along with the executions of citation.

103. When the person possessed of the fund *in medio* is the real pursuer, he shall state in his summons, or in a precise and articulate condescendence to be lodged at the calling. the amount, and particulars thereof, and also any claim or lien which he may think he has thereon, and when he is only the nominal pursuer, he shall, either at the first calling of the cause, or on or before the seventh day thereafter, and if such seventh day be a court-day, before the meeting of the Court, give in such a condescendence, or lodge objections as his defences against the summons served as a claim upon him ; otherwise he shall be held as confessed, or a condescendence of the fund *in medio* may be ordered from any of the claimants.

104. The claimants in a multiplepoinding shall state their respective claims in the form of condescendences, with the conclusions to be drawn from the facts so stated in the shape of notes of pleas, producing therewith their grounds of debt and other writings for instructing their claims ; and it shall be competent to the sheriff, if he see cause, to appoint the creditors to meet and choose a common agent, who shall prepare and lodge a state of the claims and preferences, putting his objections as therein stated to each or any of the claims in the form of answers to a condescendence, with a note of pleas ; and, *quoad ultra,* the duty and nature of his office shall be similar to that of a common agent in a process of ranking and division in the Court of Session , and if no common agent shall be appointed, the parties shall be required to revise their condescendences, each being allowed to state, in a note annexed to his condescendence, his objections to any other claim or claims, in the form of answers to a condescendence, with a note of pleas , and the sheriff, if he see cause, may order these several papers to be revised, and the case shall be proceeded with in a manner as nearly as possible approaching to that herein before directed in regard to ordinary actions.

CHAP. XVII.

EXPENSES.

105. The sum of expenses to be given in any decree, whether in absence or *in foro,* shall always be taxed before extract.

106 In all cases where a decree is given for expenses, the sheriff, if he see cause, may, upon the application of the procurator who conducted the suit, allow the decree for expenses to go out and be extracted in the name of such procurator.

107. Although a party has been found entitled to expenses generally, he shall not be allowed to include in his account, the expense of any particular part or branch of the litigation in which he has been unsuccessful, or which has been occasioned by his own fault.

108. Where expenses have been imposed on any party by an interlocutor pronounced during the progress of the cause, no claim for repetition thereof shall be competent at the end of the cause.

109. It shall be competent for either party, within forty-eight hours after an account has been taxed, to lodge a note of specific objections to such taxation, which the sheriff shall dispose of, with or without answers, as he shall see cause No reclaiming petition shall be competent against any interlocutor regarding the taxation or modification of accounts of expenses ; nor shall any appeal be competent against any such interlocutor, unless lodged within forty-eight hours from its date.

CHAP. XVIII.

SECTION II.

TAXATION OF PROCURATOR'S ACCOUNTS

110. In order to provide an easy method by which the accounts of practitioners, as between agent and client, may be checked and liquidated, it shall be competent either to the client or to the agent to present a summary application to the sheriff before whom any cause may depend, or may have depended, to get the account claimed by the agent audited and taxed such application shall be served on the

party, and on its being produced in Court, with a service of intimation of at least seven days, it shall be forthwith granted , and the said account shall thereupon be audited and taxed, and the parties shall have it in their power to state objections to the report, all in manner before provided.

111. The sum so ascertained as the amount of the account shall form the only charge against the client, and a precept or decree, on a charge of fifteen days, may issue therefor; provided always that the judgment of the sheriff shall be liable to review in common form.

112. The said application may be presented either during the dependence of a process, or after it is out of Court, by an extracted decree; but it shall not be competent where liability for payment of the account is disputed by the client, in which case the agent shall be bound to proceed by an ordinary action.

CHAP. XIX.

EXTRACTING THE DECREE, AND REPONING AGAINST DECREES IN ABSENCE.

113. Decrees may be extracted after the expiry of six free days from the day when the interlocutor is pronounced on the merits (forty-eight hours having also expired after the modification of expenses in litigated causes), except in those cases where extract shall be superseded by the sheriff, or where he shall find it expedient to allow extract immediately, or within a shorter time than six free days. But decrees of removing, other than those obtained under the provisions of 1st and 2d Vict c 119, §§ 8 to 14, may be extracted forty-eight hours after the interlocutor is signed.

114 When a party shall intimate in writing, to the clerk of Court, that he intends to advocate the cause, and shall therewith lodge a bond of caution for such expenses as have been incurred in the Sheriff Court, and as may be incurred in the Court of Session, fifteen days in the ordinary case, and thirty days in causes before the Courts of Orkney and Shetland, shall be allowed, after final judgment, to apply by note of advocation to the Court of Session, before extract shall be competent; but on the elapse of the foresaid terms respectively, if no note of advocation shall have been intimated to the clerk of Court, he may give out the extract, on the application of either party , it being competent, however, to intimate a sist or note of advocation at any time before the decree has been actually extracted.

115. Where decree in absence in any civil cause shall have been pronounced or extracted in any Sheriff Court, other than in causes in the Small Debt Court, or in processes of removing raised under authority of the Act 1st and 2d Vict. c. 119, 1st and 2d Vict. c. 119, § 18. a petition may be presented to the Sheriff Court in which such decree was pronounced, to be reponed against the said decree, and any letters of horning or charge following thereon, where the same shall not have been implemented in whole or in part, and, on consignation in the hands of the clerk of Court, of the expenses incurred, as the same may be modified on taxation, the sheriff shall repone the defender, and revive the action or proceeding in which such decree had been pronounced, as if decree had not been pronounced or extracted, and shall have power to award to the pursuer such part of the expenses consigned as he may judge reasonable; and the sheriff shall pronounce such order for intimation to and for appearance of the opposite party, as may be just; and such order may be executed against a person in any other county, as well as in the county where such order is issued, the same being previously indorsed by the sheriff clerk of such other county, who is hereby required to make and date such indorsation; and such order being so made and executed, all further orders and interlocutors in the cause shall be sufficient and effectual, and the cause shall be proceeded with in common form.

CHAP. XX.

SUSPENSION IN SHERIFF COURTS.

1st and 2d
Vict c
119, § 19.
116. Where a charge shall be given on a decree of registration proceeding on a bond, bill, contract, or other form of obligation, registered in any Sheriff Court books, or in the Books of Council and Session, or any others competent, or on letters of horning following on such decree, for payment of any sum of money not exceeding the sum of twenty-five pounds of principal, exclusive of interest and expenses, any person so charged may apply by petition to the Sheriff Court of his domicile for suspension of said charge and diligence, on caution ; and on sufficient caution being found in the hands of the clerk of Court for the sum charged for, and interest and expenses to be incurred in the Sheriff Court, the sheriff shall have power to sist execution against the petitioner, and to order intimation of the petition of suspension, and answers to be given in thereto, and thereafter to proceed with the further disposal and decision of the cause in like manner as in summary causes in such Court, and to suspend the charge and diligence so far as regards the petitioner ; provided that the said order for intimation and answers as aforesaid may be made and carried into execution against any person in any other county as well as in the county where such order is issued, in manner and to the effect hereinbefore provided. *Vide* § 16.

1st and 2d
Vict c
119, § 20
117. If any petition of suspension as aforesaid shall be presented in any Sheriff Court, and a preliminary objection be made to the competency of such petition, or to the regularity thereof, an appeal against the judgment of the sheriff-substitute repelling or sustaining such objection may be taken in common form to the sheriff, whose judgment thereon shall be final, and not subject to review either in the Circuit Court of Justiciary or in the Court of Session.

118. No reclaiming petition shall be competent against the judgment of the sheriff-substitute disposing of such objections.

CHAP XXI

ADVOCATIONS, SUSPENSIONS IN THE COURT OF SESSION, AND SISTS.

119. Any party who has given notice of his intention to advocate, and has lodged his bond of caution, in terms of § 114, may be allowed to see the process until it is competent to extract the decree.

120 The leave of the sheriff when required before advocating interlocutory sentences to the Court of Session, in terms of the Act 50th Geo III. c 112, § 36, must be obtained upon an application by petition. This petition must not contain any argument, but shall merely narrate the interlocutors to be advocated.

121. Where a person wishes to bring under review of the Court of Session any final judgment of a sheriff, upon finding juratory caution only for expenses, he shall apply by petition to the sheriff, praying that such caution may be received, which application shall be intimated to the opposite party or his agent

122. Before any such application shall be granted, the complainer shall be required to depone at a time and place to be previously intimated to the opposite party or his agent, in order that they may have an opportunity of cross-interrogating him, if they see fit, whether he have any lands in property or liferent, or bonds, bills, or contracts containing sums of money ; and in case he acknowledge the same, he shall condescend thereon, and depone that he has no other lands, bonds, bills, or contracts containing sums of money belonging to him.

123. The complainer shall also lodge with the sheriff clerk, 1. The bond of caution. 2. A full inventory of his subjects and effects of every kind. 3. An enactment subjoined to the inventory, bearing that he will not dilapidate any of his property, and that he will not dispose of the same, or uplift any of the debts

due to him, without consent of the respondent or his agent, or the authority of the sheriff (under pain of imprisonment, or being otherwise punished as being guilty of fraud,) till the advocation be discussed, and till there be an opportunity of doing diligence for any expenses that may ultimately be found due by him.

124. Farther, the complainer shall lodge in the hands of the said clerk the vouchers of any debts due to him, and the title-deeds of any heritable subject belonging to him, so far as the same may be in his possession, or within his power, and the complainer shall also grant a special disposition to the respondent (if so required) of any heritable subject he may be possessed of, and an assignation of all debts or other rights due to him for the respondent's farther security; the said disposition and assignation to be made out at the expense of the respondent, and by his agent, and the same, with the said vouchers and title-deeds, if so deposited, to remain in the hands of the said clerk, subject to the directions of the sheriff, till the advocation be discussed.

125. Upon all this being done to the satisfaction of the sheriff, he shall grant leave to advocate on juratory caution, and the sheriff clerk shall certify the same.

126. In all causes originating in the Sheriff Court, in which the claim is in amount above L.40, when an interlocutor is pronounced, allowing a proof (unless an interlocutor allowing a proof to lie *in retentis* or granting diligence for the recovery and production of papers), it shall not be competent to either of the parties to take any proof, except one allowed to lie *in retentis*, until after the expiry of 15 free days in the ordinary case, and 30 days in cases before the Courts of Orkney and Shetland, in order to give time for an advocation, in terms of the statute 6th Geo. IV. chap 120, sec 40; and unless the passing of a note of advocation shall be duly intimated within the said periods of 15 and 30 days respectively, the proof shall proceed, provided always, that by agreement of parties the proof may be taken without such delay.

127. When the certified notice of a note of advocation, under the hand of the depute or assistant clerk of Session, required by the Act 1st and 2d Vict. c. 86, § 1, has been received by the sheriff clerk, he shall mark the said notice, and furnish a certificate to the party producing the same, and all farther proceedings in the Sheriff Court shall then cease.

128. The said note of advocation and notice shall immediately be intimated to the adverse party by delivering to him, or his procurator, a copy of the same; and a certificate of intimation shall be endorsed on the said note by the advocator's agent. The process shall then be produced by the procurator whose receipt stands for it, in order that it may be transmitted by the clerk agreeably to the Act of Parliament 1st and 2d Vict c. 86, § 1, and the A. S. 17th January 1797, and minuted as having been sent, and failing his producing the process, the sheriff may grant caption for recovering it, and enforce such fine for non-compliance with this regulation, as to the sheriff shall seem reasonable.

129. If a remit on a note of suspension of a decree in absence be pronounced in terms of the Act of Sederunt, 11th August 1787, the charger's procurator shall be allowed to see the note, and remit thereon, and shall, within six days, return the same to the clerk of Court, with an account of the expense incurred in the first process, decree, and charge thereon, and also the expense incurred in the Bill-Chamber. These expenses shall be taxed and modified, and an order made on the suspender to pay or consign the same within eight days, and against this order no reclaiming petition or appeal shall be allowed. If the sum modified be not paid or consigned in eight days, the process shall be transmitted to the sheriff, who may allow the diligence to be put to further execution, and no petition shall be received against this last judgment, unless the petitioner consign with the petition the modified expenses.

130. In all advocations of interlocutors pronounced by sheriffs, it shall be competent for the sheriff to regulate, in the meantime, on the application of either party, all matters respecting interim possession, having due regard to the manner in which the interests of the parties may be affected in the final decision of the cause.

c

CHAP. XXII.

APPEALS TO THE CIRCUIT COURT OF JUSTICIARY.

131. In civil causes, appeals to the next Circuit Court, in terms of the Acts 20 Geo. II. c. 43, and 31 Geo. II. c. 42, 54 Geo. III. c 67, are competent only after a final judgment has been pronounced, and the matter of expenses has been disposed of, and where the subject matter in the suit does not exceed in value L 25 sterling.

132. The appeal may be taken in open Court, at the time of pronouncing the judgment, or within ten days thereafter, by both lodging the appeal in the clerk's hands, and serving the other party or his procurator in the cause with a copy thereof, and both the lodging and service must take place not only within ten days after the date of the judgment, but also fifteen days at least before the diet of the Circuit Court.

133. At the time of entering the appeal, or within the said ten days, the complainer must lodge, in the hands of the clerk, a bond, with a sufficient cautioner, for answering and abiding by the judgment of the Circuit Court, and for paying the costs, if any shall be by that Court awarded, and if no bond has been lodged, the clerk may give out the extract.

CHAP. XXIII.

THE POOR'S ROLL.

134. As parties, from poverty, are sometimes unable to pursue or defend any civil or criminal action, the procurators of Court shall annually appoint one or more of their number to act as procurators for the poor *gratis*, such appointment to be approved of by the sheriff.

135. Application for the benefit of the poor's roll shall be made by petition, along with which there shall be produced a certificate, signed by the minister of the parish, or by the heritor on whose lands the pauper resides, or by two elders, bearing, that it consists with their personal knowledge, that the person prosecuted, or who means to bring the action, is not possessed of funds for paying the expense thereof. This petition shall be remitted to the procurators for the poor, who shall intimate the petition to the other party; and after hearing both parties, or inquiring into the case, report their opinion specially to the sheriff whether the petitioner has a *probabilis causa litigandi*. On considering which report the sheriff shall either refuse the petition, or remit to one of the procurators for the poor, who shall attend to and conduct the cause to its final issue, though he cease to be one of the agents for the poor; and the pauper shall not be liable in payment of any of the dues of the Court, or fees to the procurator, or to the officer, except actual outlay, unless expenses shall be awarded and recovered in the process. No person, except the procurators for the poor, shall conduct any such case. It shall be in the power of the sheriff, at any time when he sees cause, to deprive a party of the benefit of the poor's roll.

136. It shall be in the power of the sheriff, on cause shewn, to relieve the procurator for the poor from paying the expenses of witnesses.

PART II.

OF SUMMARY APPLICATIONS, ARRESTMENTS, &c.

CHAP I

SUMMARY APPLICATIONS, HOW AND IN WHAT CASES TO BE ALLOWED.

137. In all cases which require extraordinary despatch, and where the interest of the party might suffer by abiding the ordinary *induciæ*, application by summary petition may be made to the sheriff, who, on considering the petition, may, if he see cause, order it to be served on the person complained of, and to be answered within such *induciæ* as the sheriff, in each case, may think proper. And the procedure, in such cases, shall not abide the ordinary course of the court-days, it being always competent to pronounce such *interim* order as the exigencies of the case require.

138 It shall be no objection to such application that it contains a conclusion for a claim of damage, or other claim arising out of the subject matter thereof; and it shall be competent for the sheriff to decern for such claim, as in an ordinary action.

139 The officer serving and intimating such petition shall give to the defender, or leave for him at his dwelling-place, in presence of one witness, a full copy of the petition and deliverance, with a citation and requisition, and return an execution subscribed by himself and the witness.

140. The petition must be prepared in all respects in terms of § 10, and the prayer thereof must set forth specifically, and in explicit terms, the remedy craved. The answer must be prepared in terms of § 32 and 33.

141. If answers are not lodged within the time appointed, the clerk, on production of the warrant, and a regular execution, shall certify that answers are not lodged, and thereon the sheriff shall grant the desire of the petition, or pronounce such other judgment as he shall see fit

142. When answers have been lodged, the process shall be given out to the pursuer, to reply within such number of days as were allowed for answering, unless the sheriff see cause to fix an earlier or later day. The replies must be prepared in terms of § 37.

143. In cases where the defender has lodged answers by the time appointed, but the petitioner has either failed to report the warrant and execution, or to reply within the time allowed, the process may be forced back by a caption, in order that the case may be laid before the sheriff; or, in the respondent's option, protestation may be granted, and the petition be dismissed, with expenses

144. Reclaiming petitions must be lodged on or before the seventh day after the date of the interlocutor; and the clerk is enjoined not to receive any petition after that day, and answers to reclaiming petitions, if ordered, must be lodged within the same number of days, unless otherwise ordered by the sheriff.

145. Summary cases shall proceed and be conducted in terms of the regulations, and subject to the compulsitors provided in the case of ordinary actions, in all particulars, except as above specified.

146. Decrees in summary cases may be extracted in terms of § § 113 and 114; but warrants to roup, and other such warrants requiring speedy execution, may be extracted immediately after being pronounced, unless otherwise ordered by the sheriff, or unless due intimation has been given of the intention to reclaim or advocate, it being competent to the sheriff to regulate, in the mean time, on the application of either party, all matters regarding interim possession, as in § 130.

CHAP. II.

ACTIONS OF REMOVING AND OF ALIMENT.

147. Actions of removing and of aliment, brought in the form of a summons, are to be entitled to the privileges of summary processes in every respect. See other regulations as to these cases in § § 34, 95, 113.

148. For regulations regarding removings from premises let for less than a year, and at rents not exceeding the rate of L.30 a-year, see 1st and 2d Vict. c. 119, § 8 to § 14.

149. No appeal to the sheriff shall be competent against judgments of the sheriff-substitute in cases of summary remo   g   der the said Act, except when they have been remitted to the ordinary r

CHAP. III

SEQUESTRATIONS FOR RENT.

150. When a petition for sequestration is presented, the sheriff may pronounce an interlocutor, sequestrating the crop, stocking, and effects, and grant warrant to take an inventory thereof, and ordain the petitio , and warrant to be served on the tenant. and him to give in answers thereto within such *induciæ* as to the sheriff shall seem proper. If no answers are lodged with the time assigned, the sheriff, on production of the executions of sequestration and service of the petition on the defender, may grant warrant of sale. Every warrant to sell sequestrated effects shall be carried into execution at the sight of the clerk of Court, or other person authorized by the sheriff; and in every case where a sale follows on such warrant, the sale shall be reported within fourteen days after the date of the roup, and the principal roup-rolls, or copies regularly certified, must, within the same period, be lodged in process, together with an account of the expenses incurred in the sequestration and sale, and also a state of the debt due by the defender, shewing the difference between the debt and the proceeds of the effects sold.

151. In petitions for sequestration, it shall be competent to conclude for payment of the rent, and decree may thereupon be pronounced for the same and expenses, or for such balance as may remain due after sequestration and sale, and under deduction of the expenses thereof, under the provisions of the foregoing section.

152. It shall be competent to the sheriff, on cause shewn, at any stage of the proceedings, to appoint a fit person to take charge of the sequestrated subjects, or to require caution from the tenant that they shall be afterwards made furthcoming.

CHAP. IV.

ARRESTMENTS.

153. The clerk is authorized to issue precepts of arrestment, upon there being produced to him a libelled summons not containing a warrant of arrestment, or a petition with pecuniary conclusions. The precept shall always set forth the ground

of application for the arrestment; and no blank warrant of arrestment shall be granted upon any pretence whatever.

154 If the pursuer shall use arrestment on a libelled summons, the same shall be effectual, provided the warrant of citation shall be executed against the defender within twenty days after the date of the execution of the arrestment, and the summons be called in Court within twenty days after the diet of compearance, or, when the expiry of the said period of twenty days falls within the vacation, provided the summons be called on the first court day thereafter, whether such court-day be one of those hereby authorized to be held in vacation (§ 3), or in the ensuing session ; and if the warrant of citation shall not be executed, and the summons called in manner above directed, the arrestment shall be null, without prejudice to the validity of any subsequent arrestment duly executed in virtue of the said warrant. *1st and 2d Vict. c. 114, § 17.*

155. Any warrant or precept of arrestment granted by any sheriff, whether contained in a libelled summons, or proceeding upon a depending action, or liquid document of debt, may lawfully be executed within the territory of any other sheriff, the same being first indorsed by the sheriff clerk of such sheriffdom, who is required to make and date such indorsation. *1st and 2d Vict. c. 114, § 19.*

156. For regulations regarding the recall or restriction of arrestments by the sheriff, see 1st and 2d Vict. c. 114, § 21.

CHAP. V.

MEMBERS OF COURT.

157. No person shall be permitted to practise as a procurator in any Sheriff Court, unless he be a writer to the Signet, or solicitor before the Supreme Courts, or have been admitted a procurator, and have practised as such before some Sheriff Court, or have served three years as an apprentice to a writer to the Signet, to a solicitor before the Supreme Courts, or to a procurator before any Sheriff Court in Scotland, or Court of Royal Burgh, or to a sheriff clerk,—be twenty-one years of age, and be regularly admitted by the sheriff, without prejudice to the legal rights of chartered bodies.

158. Any agent in the Court of Session proposing to practise before a Sheriff Court, in applications for the benefit of *cessio*, in terms of 6 and 7 Will. IV. c. 56, or in any proceeding not competent in a Sheriff Court before the passing of the 1st and 2d Vict. c. 119, shall produce to the clerk of Court sufficient evidence of his being duly qualified to practise as an agent before the Court of Session.

159. Procurators of Court and Agents qualified as above, and resident within the jurisdiction of the Court, shall alone be entitled to borrow any process, by themselves, or their clerks duly authorized, and for whom they shall be responsible, by the ordinary compulsitors of the law.

160. The sheriff clerk, or his depute, shall not act either directly or indirectly as a procurator.

PART III.

CHAP. I.

CONSISTORIAL AND MARITIME CAUSES.

161. The form of process in consistorial and maritime causes shall be the same, as nearly as possible, with that in ordinary actions before the Sheriff Court.

CHAP. II.

GENERAL REGULATIONS.

162. In all defended causes, the interlocutors of Court must be written on a separate sheet or sheets of paper, and not on the pleadings of the parties.

163. In every process there shall be an inventory to accompany it, in which every paper given in shall be entered, with its corresponding number, by the party who lodges it. The sheriff clerk shall mark all pleadings and productions (or when several productions are lodged at once, the inventory thereof), with the date of lodging the same, and shall also keep another inventory, in terms of 1st and 2d Vict. c. 119, § 16.

164 The sheriff clerk, or his depute, shall keep a transmission book, in the form of schedule (B) annexed to the Act 1st and 2d Vict. c. 119, and he shall besides insert therein two columns to shew the date of the sheriff's receiving each process and of his returning it advised, in terms of § 16 of the said Act.

165. The sheriff clerk shall take up a roll of motions on the enrolment of any of the parties, which shall be called on each court-day. And each sheriff shall make such regulations with reference to the roll, and to the Court-book or Diet-book, as are applicable to the circumstances of his county.

166. It is hereby declared that the term sheriff in the present Act of Sederunt, shall include sheriff substitute in all cases, except in such passages as relate to appeal from the sheriff-substitute to the sheriff, or where, from the context, it is obvious that *this* is not intended.

The Lords appoint this Act, and the Appendix thereto, to be inserted in the Books of Sederunt, and published in the usual manner.

C. HOPE, *I.P.D.*

APPENDIX to the foregoing Act of Sederunt.

REPORT OF THE SHERIFFS.

THE COMMITTEE on the FORMS of PROCESS appointed at the meeting of Sheriffs held on the 14th of November last, in terms of the Act of 1 and 2 Vict c. 119, sec. 32, beg to report, that they have repeatedly and very carefully revised the Act of Sederunt 1825, keeping in view the suggestions contained in the report of the law commission, and the communications which they have received ; and have prepared a draft of an amended Act of Sederunt, which they now submit to the Sheriffs. After the most serious consideration, they are of opinion that the alterations they recommend, and which embrace every thing that has occurred to them as useful, will tend to shorten and improve the procedure in Sheriff Courts

AD DUFF.	ROBERT THOMSON.
ANDW. MURRAY.	ADAM ANDERSON.
JOHN CAY.	GRAHAM SPEIRS.
JOHN TAIT.	

EDINBURGH, 11th Dec 1838.

EDINBURGH, 15th Dec. 1838.

AT an adjourned General Meeting of the Sheriffs,—*Present*, Messrs Duff, Horne, Boswell, Colquhoun, Dunlop, Bruce, Walker, L'Amy, Maconochie, Murray, Cay, Tait, Miller, Jardine, Thomson, Anderson, Speirs, Currie, Hunter, Shaw Stewart, and Monteith , and at an adjournment of the said meeting, on the 17th of December, the above report and relative draft of an Act of Sederunt were fully considered and approved of, subject to certain alterations. and the Sheriffs remitted to the former Committee to embody these alterations in the draft, and to take such measures as should appear to them to be expedient for fulfilling the objects of the Act 1 and 2 Vict. c. 119, sec. 32.

AD. DUFF, *Chairman.*
JOHN CAY, *Convener.*

EDINBURGH, 28th *February* 1839.

THE COMMITTEE have now to lay before the Sheriffs a revised draft of the Act of Sederunt regarding the Form of Process in Sheriff Courts In preparing it, they have had before them observations and suggestions from the Sheriffs-substitute of Selkirkshire, Aberdeenshire, Caithness-shire, Nairnshire, Perthshire, and Clackmananshire ; the Sheriff-substitute and Sheriff-clerk of Dumbartonshire , the Sheriff-clerk of Kinross-shire ; the Advocates in Aberdeenshire ; the Procurators in

f

Ayrshire, Caithness shire, Fifeshire, (Cupar District), Kincardineshire, Perthshire, and Forfarshire, (Dundee District.) They have given most careful attention to all their observations, and have adopted many of the suggestions, which they think valuable improvements. The revised draft has been so printed, as to point out where alterations have been made.

AD. DUFF.   ROBERT THOMSON.
A. BELL.   ADAM ANDERSON.
ANDW. MURRAY.   JOHN CAY, *Convener.*
JOHN TAIT.

———

EDINBURGH, *4th March* 1839.

AT an adjourned meeting of Sheriffs,—*Present,* Messrs Duff, L'Amy, Bruce, Thomson, Cay, Jardine, Currie, Hunter, Douglas, Murray, Anderson and Tait. The meeting having reconsidered the revised draft of an Act of Sederunt, regarding the Form of Process in the Sheriff Courts, with the proposed alterations and amendments, approve thereof, and authorize the Convener respectfully to submit the same to the Court, with the whole of the observations on the former draft which had been received.

AD. DUFF, *Chairman.*
JOHN CAY, *Convener.*

ANNO PRIMO

VICTORIÆ REGINÆ.

CAP. XLI.

An Act for the more effectual Recovery of Small Debts in the Sheriff Courts, and for regulating the Establishment of Circuit Courts, for the Trial of Small Debt Causes by the Sheriffs, in Scotland.—[12th July 1837.]

WHEREAS an Act was made in the tenth year of the reign of his Majesty King *George* the Fourth, intituled, *An Act for the more effectual Recovery of Small Debts, and for diminishing the expenses of Litigation in Causes of small amount, in the Sheriffs Courts in* Scotland, the provisions of which have been found beneficial, but experience has pointed out certain alterations by which its benefits will be extended and rendered more effectual ; and it is expedient that such alterations and the former provisions should be consolidated in one Act · Be it therefore enacted, by the Queen's most excellent Majesty, by and with the advice and consent of the Lords Spiritual and Temporal, and Commons, in this present Parliament assembled, and by the authority of the same, That the said recited Act shall be and the same is hereby repealed from and after the first day of *October* next, save and except as to such causes as shall have been commenced under the authority of the said recited Act before the said first day of *October* next, and shall be then depending, all which causes shall be carried to a conclusion according to the rules prescribed by the said Act, notwithstanding this Act, and this Act shall commence and take effect from and after the said first day of *October* next. *10 G. 4, c. 55. Recited Act repealed, except as to Causes commenced.*

II. And be it enacted, That it shall be lawful for any sheriff in *Scotland* within his county to hear, try, and determine in a summary way, as more particularly herein-after mentioned, all civil causes and all prosecutions for statutory penalties, as well as all maritime civil causes, and proceedings, that may be competently brought before him, wherein the debt, demand, or penalty in question shall not exceed the value of eight pounds six shillings and eightpence sterling, exclusive of expenses and fees of extract : Provided always, that the pursuer or prosecutor shall in all cases be held to have passed from and abandoned any remaining portion of any debt, demand, or penalty beyond the sum actually concluded for in any such cause or prosecution. *Sheriffs may hear and determine in a summary way. Causes for sums under 8l 6s. 8d. sterling.*

III. And be it enacted, That all such causes and prosecutions which the pursuers or prosecutors thereof shall choose to have heard and determined according to the summary mode hereby provided shall proceed, except as herein-after provided, upon summons or complaint, agreeably to the form in Schedule (A.) annexed to this Act, and containing warrant to arrest upon the depending action, stating shortly the origin of debt or ground of action, and concluding against the defender, *Providing forms of proceedings.*

which summons or complaint being signed by the sheriff clerk, shall be a sufficient warrant and authority to any sheriff's officer for summoning the defender to appear and answer at the time and place mentioned in such summons and complaint, not being sooner than upon the sixth day after such citation, and the same, or the copy thereof, served on the defender, shall also be a sufficient warrant for summoning such witnesses and havers as either party shall require ; and a copy of the said summons or complaint, with the citation annexed, and also a copy of the account, if any, shall be served at the same time by the sheriff's officer on the defender personally or at his dwelling-place, or in case of a company, at their ordinary place of business, and the officer summoning parties, witnesses, or havers, shall in all cases under this Act return an execution of citation, signed by him, or shall appear and give evidence on oath of such citation having been duly made ; and all such citations given by an officer alone without witnesses, and executions thereof subscribed by such officer, shall be good and effectual to all intents and purposes.

Causes of higher value than *8l 6s 8d* reduced to *8l 6s 8d.* may be remitted to the Small Debt roll.

IV. And be it enacted, That in any cause before the Sheriff's Ordinary Court, in which the debt, demand, or penalty in question shall not exceed the value of eight pounds six shillings and eightpence sterling. or shall have exceeded the value of eight pounds six shillings and eightpence sterling, but from interim decree or otherwise the value shall, previous to the closing of the record, be reduced so as not to exceed eight pounds six shillings and eightpence sterling, exclusive of expenses and fees of extract, it shall be competent to the sheriff, if he shall think proper, and with the consent of the pursuer, to remit such cause to such of his Small Debt Court rolls as may be proper, either of his own motion or upon the motion of any party in the cause Provided that if the pursuer shall not consent, the provisions of this Act as to the fees or expenses to be allowed in causes below the value of eight pounds six shillings and eightpence brought not according to the summary form herein provided, shall be applied to such causes subsequent to the proposition for remit, if the sheriff shall think proper so to modify the expenses Provided also, that when a case has been remitted by the sheriff-substitute from the ordinary Court to the Small Debt Court, an appeal shall be competent to the sheriff against such remit, but no reclaiming petition shall be allowed against such remit

Recovery of rents not exceeding *8l. 6s 8d*

V. And be it enacted, That it shall be competent for the sheriff in the Small Debt Courts, established or to be established under this Act, to hear, try, and determine, in the summary form hereby provided, applications by landlords or others having rights to the rents and hypothec for sequestration and sale of a tenant's effects for recovery of rent, provided the rent or balance of rent claimed shall not exceed eight pounds six shillings and eightpence sterling, and the summons and warrant of sequestration and procedure shall be agreeable to the forms directed in the Schedule (B) annexed to this Act, and the officer, when he executes the warrant, shall get the effects appraised by two persons, who may also be witnesses to the sequestration, and an inventory or list of the effects, with the appraisement, shall be given to or left for the tenant, who shall be cited in manner and to the effect aforesaid ; and an execution of the citation and sequestration, with the appraisement of the effects, shall be returned to the clerk within three days, and on hearing the application in manner provided by this Act relative to other causes, the sheriff shall dispose of the cause as shall be just, and may either recall the sequestration in whole or in part, or pronounce decree for the rent found due, and grant warrant for the sale of the sequestrated effects on the premises, or at such other place and on such notice as he shall by general or special regulation direct, and failing such directions the sale shall be carried into effect in the manner hereinafter directed for the sale of poinded and sequestrated effects ; and if after sequestration the tenant shall pay the rent claimed, with the expenses, to the pursuers, or consign the rent, with two pounds sterling to cover expenses, in the hands of the clerk of court, the sequestration shall *ipso facto* be recalled, in case of payment, on the clerk writing and signing on the back of the summons or warrant the words

" payment made," which, on evidence being produced to him of payment of the rents claimed, with expenses, he is hereby required to do, and in case of consignation, after the clerk shall in like manner have written and signed the words " consignation made," on the same being intimated by an officer of court to the sequestrating creditor.

VI. And be it enacted, That the pursuer of any civil cause, including maritime civil causes and proceedings, may use arrestment on the dependence of the action of any money, goods, or effects, to an amount or extent not exceeding the value of eight pounds six shillings and eightpence sterling, owing or belonging to such defender, in the hands of any third party, either within the county in which such warrant shall have been issued, or in any other county or counties Provided always, that before using such warrant in any other county it shall be presented to and indorsed by the sheriff clerk of such other county, who is hereby required to make such indorsement on payment of the fee herein-after mentioned Provided also, that any arrestment laid on under the authority of this Act shall, on the expiry of three months from the date thereof, cease and determine, without the necessity of a decree or warrant of loosing the same, unless such arrestment shall be renewed by a special warrant or order, duly intimated to the arrestee, in which case it shall subsist and be in force for the like time and under the like conditions as under the original warrant, or unless an action of forthcoming or multiplepoinding, in manner herein-after provided, shall have been raised before the expiry of the said period of three months, in which case the arrestment shall subsist and be in force until the termination of such action of forthcoming or multiplepoinding *Arrestment of goods of defender.*

VII. And be it enacted and declared, That wages of labourers and manufacturers shall, so far as necessary for their subsistence, be deemed alimentary, and, in like manner as servants' fees, and other alimentary funds, not liable to arrestment. *Wages not liable to arrestment.*

VIII. And be it enacted, That when any arrestment shall have been used on the dependence of any action, it shall be competent to the defender to have such arrestment loosed, on lodging with the sheriff clerk of the county in which such arrestment shall have been used, a bond or enactment of caution, by one or more good and sufficient cautioners, to the satisfaction of such sheriff clerk, agreeable to the form in Schedule (C.) annexed to this Act, or on consigning in the hands of such sheriff clerk the amount of the debt or demand, with five shillings for expenses in cases of actions for sums below five pounds, and ten shillings in cases of higher amount, or on producing to such sheriff clerk evidence of the defender having obtained decree of absolvitor in the action, or of his having paid the sums decerned for, or of his having consigned in the hands of the Clerk of the Court in which the action depended the sums decerned for, or the amount of the debt or demand, and expenses as aforesaid, when no decree has yet been pronounced , and a certificate in the form in the said schedule given by the sheriff clerk of the county in which such arrestment shall have been used of a bond or enactment of caution to the extent of the debt or demand, and expenses having been lodged with him, or of consignation, as above provided, having been made in his hands, shall operate as a warrant for loosing any arrestment used either in that or in any other county on the dependence of the same action, without any other caution being found or any other consignation being made by the defender. *For providing how arrestments may be loosed.*

IX. And be it enacted, That any person entitled to pursue an action of forthcoming where the sum or demand sought to be recovered under the forthcoming shall not exceed the value of eight pounds six shillings and eightpence sterling, exclusive of expenses and fees of extract, who shall choose to have the same heard and determined according to the summary mode provided by this Act, shall proceed by summons or complaint agreeably to the form in schedule (D.) annexed to this Act, concluding for payment of the sum for which arrestment has been used, *Rendering Arrestments effectual.*

or for delivery of the goods and effects arrested, which summons or complaint, being signed by the sheriff clerk of the county in which the arrestee resides, shall be a sufficient warrant and authority to any sheriff's officer for summoning the arrestee and the common debtor to appear and answer at a Sheriff Court of the county in which the arrestee resides, the same not being sooner than the sixth day after the date of citation, and also for summoning witnesses and havers for all parties ; and in the event of the common debtor not residing and not being found within the county in which such action of forthcoming shall be brought, he may be cited by any sheriff's officer in any other county on the said warrant, the same being first presented to and indorsed by the sheriff clerk of such other county, who is hereby required to indorse the same on payment of the fee herein-after mentioned, to appear at a Sheriff Court in the county in which the arrestee resides, the same not being sooner in such case than on the twelfth day after the date of citation : Provided always, that the arrestee and the common debtor shall be cited to appear on the same court day, and that a copy of the said summons or complaint, with the citation annexed thereto, shall be duly served by the officer, all in the same manner as herein before provided in other causes and prosecutions under authority of this Act, but always allowing to a party cited to appear in the Sheriff Court of a different county from that in which the citation shall be given double the time required by this Act to be allowed to a party cited to appear in the Sheriff Court of the county within which the citation shall be given   Provided also, that the pursuer of such action of forthcoming shall not by such action be held to have restricted the amount of the debt due by the common debtor

Actions of Multiple-poinding.

X. And be it enacted, That where any person shall hold a fund or subject which shall not exceed the value of eight pounds six shillings and eightpence, which shall be claimed by more than one party, under arrestments or otherwise, it shall be competent to raise a summons of multiplepoinding in the Small Debt Court, established or to be established under this act, to the jurisdiction of which the holder of the fund or subject shall be amenable, which summons and procedure thereon shall be agreeable to the form in schedule (E.) annexed to this Act, and the claimants and common debtors, and also the holder of the fund or subject, if the process be raised in his name by any other party interested, shall be cited in manner directed to be followed in actions of forthcoming raised under this Act, and it shall be competent to the Sheriff, when he shall see cause, to order such further intimation or publication of the multiplepoinding as he may think proper, by advertisement in any newspaper or otherwise ; but no judgment preferring any party to the fund or subject in medio shall be pronounced at the first calling of the cause, or until due intimation has been given, such as may appear satisfactory to the sheriff, in order that all parties may have an opportunity of lodging their claims on the fund or subject in medio, and such claims shall be prepared agreeably to the form in schedule (E); and the sheriff shall hear, try, and determine the cause as nearly as may be in the summary form provided by this Act.

Counter Claims.

XI. And be it enacted, That where any defender intends to plead any counter account or claim against the debt, demand, or penalty pursued for, the defender shall serve a copy of such counter account or claim by an officer on the pursuer, in the form set forth in schedule (A.) hereunto annexed, or to the like effect, at least, one free day before the day of appearance, otherwise the same shall not be heard or allowed to be pleaded, except with the pursuer's consent, but action shall be reserved for the same.

Compelling Attend-ance of Witnesses

XII. And be it enacted, That every officer to whom any warrant as aforesaid for citing witnesses and havers shall be intrusted shall cite such witnesses or havers as any party shall require , and all such warrants shall have the same force and effect in any other county as in the county where they are originally issued, the same being first presented to and indorsed by the sheriff clerk of such other county, who is hereby required to indorse the same on payment of the fee hereinafter mentioned; and if any witness or haver, duly cited on a citation of at least forty-eight hours, shall fail to appear, he shall forfeit and pay a penalty not exceeding forty shillings, unless a reasonable excuse be offered and sustained; and every such penalty shall be paid to the party citing the witness or haver, and shall be recovered in the same manner as other penalties under this Act, without prejudice always to letters of second diligence for compelling witnesses and havers to attend, as at present competent, and it shall be competent to the sheriff of any county where a witness or haver resides who has failed to comply with the citations originally issued to grant letters of second diligence for compelling the attendance of such witnesses or havers, and it shall be no objection to any witness that such witness has appeared without citation or without having been regularly cited.

XIII. And be it enacted, That when the parties shall appear the sheriff shall hear them *viva voce*, and examine witnesses or havers upon oath, and may also examine the parties and may put them or any of them upon oath, in case of oath in supplement being required or of a reference being made, and if he should see cause may remit to persons of skill to report, or to any person competent to take and report in writing the evidence of witnesses or havers who may be unable to attend upon special cause shown, and such cause shall in all cases be entered in the book of causes kept by the sheriff clerk, due notice of the examination being given to both parties, and thereupon the sheriff may pronounce judgment, and the decree stating the amount of the expenses (if any) found due to any party, (which may include personal charges, if the sheriff think fit,) and containing warrant for arrestment, and for poinding and imprisonment when competent, shall be annexed to the summons or complaint, and on the same paper with it, agreeably to the form in schedule (A) annexed to this Act, or to the like effect, which decree and warrant, being signed by the clerk, shall be a sufficient authority for instant arrestment, and also for poinding and sale and imprisonment, where competent, after the elapse of ten free days from the date of the decree, if the party against whom it shall have been given was personally present when it was pronounced, but if he was not so present poinding and sale and imprisonment shall only proceed after a charge of ten free days, by serving a copy of the complaint and decree on the party personally or at his dwelling-place, and if any decree shall not be enforced by poinding or imprisonment within a year from the date thereof, or from a charge for payment given thereon, such decree shall not be enforced without a new charge duly given as aforesaid.

Hearing and Judgment

Arrestment.

XIV. And be it enacted, That no procurators, solicitors, nor any persons practising the law, shall be allowed to appear or plead for any party without leave of the Court upon special cause shown, and such leave, and the cause thereof, shall in all cases be entered in the book of causes kept by the sheriff clerk, nor shall any of the pleadings be reduced to writing or be entered upon any record, unless with leave of the Court first had and obtained, in consequence of any difficulty in point of law or special circumstances of any particular case. Provided always, that when the sheriff shall order any such pleadings to be reduced to writing, every case in which such order shall be made shall thenceforth be conducted according to the ordinary forms and proceedings in civil causes and in prosecutions for statutory penalties, and shall be disposed of in all respects as if this Act had not been passed.

Procurators, &c not to appear, or plead, nor pleadings to be reduced to writing, without leave of Court.

XV. And be it enacted, That any defender who has been duly cited, failing to appear personally or by one of his family, or by such person as the sheriff shall allow, such person not being an officer of Court, shall be held confessed, and the other party shall obtain decree against him; and in like manner if the pursuer or prosecutor shall fail to appear personally or by one of his family, or by such person as the sheriff shall allow, such person not being an officer of Court, the defender shall obtain decree of absolvitor, unless in either case a sufficient excuse for delay shall be stated, on which account, or on account of the absence of witnesses, or any other good reason, it shall at all times be competent for the sheriff to

Parties not appearing or not having sufficient excuse to be held confessed.

adjourn any case to the next or any other Court day, and to ordain the parties and witnesses then to attend.

Hearing in cases of decree in absence.

XVI. And be it enacted, That where a decree has been pronounced in absence of a defender, it shall be competent for him, upon consigning the expenses decerned for, and the further sum of ten shillings to meet further expenses, in the hands of the clerk, at any time before a charge is given, or in the event of a charge being given before implement of the decree has followed thereon, provided in the latter case the period from the date of the charge does not exceed three months, to obtain from the clerk a warrant signed by him sisting execution till the next Court day, or to any subsequent Court day to which the same may be adjourned, and containing authority for citing the other party, and witnesses and havers for both parties; and the clerk shall be bound to certify to the sheriff on the next Court day every such application for hearing and sist granted; and such warrant, being duly served upon the other party personally or at his dwelling place, in the manner provided in other cases by this Act, shall be an authority for hearing the cause; and in like manner, where absolvitor has passed in absence of the pursuer or prosecutor, it shall be competent for him, at any time within one calendar month thereafter, upon consigning in the hands of the clerk the sum awarded by the sheriff in his decree of absolvitor as the expenses for the defender and his witnesses, with the further sum of five shillings to meet further expenses, to obtain a warrant, signed by the clerk, for citing the defender and witnesses for both parties, which warrant, being duly served upon the defender in the manner provided in other cases by this Act, shall be an authority for hearing the cause as hereby provided in the case of a hearing at the instance of the defender, the said sum of expenses awarded by the sheriff, and consigned as aforesaid, being in every case paid over to the other party, unless the contrary shall be specially ordered by the Court; and all such warrants for hearing shall be in force, and may be served by any sheriff officer in any county, without indorsation or other authority than this Act.

Book of causes, &c to be kept.

XVII. And be it enacted, That the sheriff clerk shall keep a book, wherein shall be entered all causes conducted under the authority of this Act, setting forth the names and designations of the parties, and whether present or absent at the calling of the cause, the nature and amount of the claim and date of giving it in, the mode of citation, the leave and cause of procurators' appearance, the several deliverances or interlocutors, and the final decree, with the date thereof, which book shall be signed each Court day by the sheriff, and the said entries by the clerk shall be according to the form in schedule (F.) annexed to this Act, or with such addition as the sheriff shall appoint; and the sheriff clerk shall also keep a book or books containing a register or registers of all indorsations of decrees and warrants issued in other counties, and of all warrants for arrestment on the dependence, and of all loosings of arrestment, and of all reports of poindings or sequestrations and sales of goods and effects, which registers shall be open and patent at office hours to all concerned, without fee; and the sheriff clerk shall cause a copy of the roll of causes to be tried on each Court day to be exhibited to the public on a patent part of the Court house at least one hour before the time of meeting of such Court, and which shall continue there during the time the Court shall be sitting; and the sheriff clerk, or an officer of Court, shall audibly call the causes in such roll in their order.

Power to direct payment by instalments.

XVIII. And be it enacted, That the sheriff may, if he think proper, direct the sum or sums found due to be paid by instalments weekly, monthly, or quarterly, according to the circumstances of the party found liable, and under such conditions or qualifications as he shall think fit to annex.

Decrees may be enforced in any other county.

XIX. And be it enacted, That any decree obtained under this Act may be enforced where competent against the person or effects of any party in any other county as well as in the county where the decree is issued: Provided always, that such decree, or an extract thereof, shall be first produced to and indorsed by the sheriff clerk of such other county, who is hereby required to make such indorsement on payment of the fee herein-after mentioned

XX. And be it enacted, That the sequestration or poinding and sale shall be carried into effect by the officer in a summary way, by getting the effects sequestrated or poinded duly apprised by two persons, who may also be witnesses to the sequestration or poinding, and leaving an inventory or list thereof for the party whose effects are sequestrated or poinded, and not sooner than forty-eight hours thereafter carrying such effects to the nearest town or village, or, in case the sequestration or poinding shall take place in a town or village, to the cross or most public place thereof, and selling the same to the highest bidder by public roup between the hours of eleven forenoon and three afternoon at the cross or such most public place, on previous notice of at least two hours by the crier, but reserving to the sheriff, by such general regulation or special order in any particular case as he shall think fit, to appoint a different hour or place for the sale or a longer or different kind of notice to be given of the time of selling; and in sequestrations and poindings the overplus of the price, if there shall be any, after payment of the sums decerned for, and the expenses, if expenses are awarded, including what is allowed by this Act for sequestration or poinding and sale, shall be returned to the owner or consigned with the sheriff clerk if the owner cannot be found; or if the effects are not sold the same shall be delivered over at the appraised value to the creditor to the amount of the sum decerned for and expenses, if awarded, and the allowances for sequestration or poinding and sale, and a report of the proceedings in the sequestration or poinding and sale and proceeds, or of the delivery of the effects, shall in every case be made by the officer to the sheriff clerk within eight days thereafter, agreeably to the form in schedule (G.) annexed to this Act, or to the like effect, and where the sheriff shall order a sale of goods or effects arrested, the same course of proceeding shall be adopted as is above directed in the case of poinding and sale; and no officer to whom the enforcement of decrees or warrants in cases falling under this Act may be committed shall be liable to any penalty, fine, or punishment for selling goods or effects under authority of such decrees or warrants by public auction, although such officer may not be licensed as an auctioneer, anything in any Act or Acts to the contrary notwithstanding; and if any person shall secrete or carry off or intromit with any poinded or sequestrated effects *in fraudem* of the poinding creditors or of the landlord's hypothec, such person shall be liable to summary punishment by fine or imprisonment, as for contempt of Court, either at the instance of the private party, with or without the concurrence of the procurator fiscal, or at the instance of the procurator fiscal, or *ex proprio motu* of the sheriff, besides being liable otherwise as accords of law

Appraisement and sale of poinded and sequestrated effects.

XXI. And be it enacted, That in all charges and arrestments and executions of charges and arrestments, under this Act, one witness shall be sufficient, any law or practice to the contrary heretofore notwithstanding.

One witness sufficient.

XXII. And be it enacted, That all actions of damages for compensation for loss or injury by the Act or Acts of any unlawful, riotous, or tumultuous assembly in *Scotland*, or of any person engaged in or making part thereof, authorized to be brought by an Act passed in the third year of the reign of His Majesty King *George* the Fourth, where the sum concluded for does not exceed Eight pounds six shillings and eightpence sterling, as also all actions for recovery of assessments by virtue of an Act passed in the ninth year of His said Majesty's reign, intituled *An Act for the Preservation of the Salmon Fisheries in Scotland*, may be heard and determined in the summary way provided by this Act, and this notwithstanding the amount of such assessments, shall exceed eight pounds six shillings and eightpence sterling.

Actions for damages by riot under 3 G. 4. c. 33, and for recovery of assessments authorized by 9 G. 4, c 39, may be determined by this Act.

XXIII. And whereas by an Act passed in the twentieth year of the reign

Sheriffs to hold Circuit

Courts for Small Debt causes of His Majesty, King *George* the Second, for taking away and abolishing the heritable jurisdictions in *Scotland*, it is provided that sheriffs may hold itinerant courts at such times and places within their respective jurisdictions as they shall judge expedient, or as shall be directed or ordered by His Majesty, his heirs and successors, and by the said recited Act of the tenth year of the reign of His Majesty King *George* the Fourth, provision is made for the necessary accommodation for holding Courts for the purposes of the said Act, which the sheriff should judge it expedient to hold at other than the usual places for holding the same. And whereas it is expedient to make better provision for holding itinerant or circuit courts for the purposes of this Act; be it enacted, That the several sheriffs of the several sheriffdoms in *Scotland* shall, in addition to their ordinary small debt courts, by themselves or their substitutes, hold circuit courts, for the purposes of this act at such of the places within each sheriffdom set forth in the schedule (H) annexed to this act, and for such number of times within each place in each year, not exceeding the number of times mentioned in the said schedule (H) as shall be directed by warrant under Her Majesty's sign manual, and to be published in the *London Gazette*, at such times as they shall deem best and most convenient to fix for the general business of the county, if there shall be any cause at such places at such times to try, but as nearly as may be at equal intervals between each court, except as hereinafter provided, and shall remain at each such place until the causes ready to be heard shall be disposed of; and each sheriff clerk, or a depute appointed by him, is hereby required to attend at such places and times within his sheriffdom, and to find the necessary accommodation for holding all such courts, on his own charges and expenses, in respect of the fees allowed by this Act. Provided always, that no sheriff clerk shall acquire a vested right to any increased amount of fees or emoluments to be drawn under this act, or shall be entitled to compensation in consequence of being deprived of such increased amount of fees or emoluments, or of any future regulation thereof by any Act to be hereafter passed.

Sheriffs empowered to change places and times. XXIV. And be it enacted, That the several sheriffs of the several sheriffdoms, with the consent and approbation of one of Her Majesty's Principal Secretaries of State, may from time to time change the places or number of times at which such circuit courts shall be directed to be held as aforesaid, or discontinue the same or any of them in any sheriffdom in which such circuit courts or any of them may be found unnecessary or inexpedient, or direct any two of such courts held in islands or other places where it may be deemed expedient to be held at short intervals from each other, or direct circuit courts to be held at such places in any sheriffdom, although not mentioned in the said schedule (H.), or in such additional places in counties mentioned in the said schedule, as may seem necessary and proper; and all such additional circuit courts shall be held in terms of the provisions and directions of this Act.

Sheriff clerks to appoint deputes, and to give notices. XXV. And be it enacted, That the sheriff clerk of each sheriffdom shall attend personally, or appoint a depute to act at each of the places at which courts may be directed to be held in terms of this act, and such depute shall, in the absence of the principal clerk, attend at and during the holding of such circuit courts, and shall thereat perform all the duties by this act required to be performed by the sheriff clerk, and if such depute shall not be resident in such place, the sheriff clerk may also appoint a proper person resident in such place, or in its immediate vicinity, to issue the summonses or complaints which may be applied for and issued under the provisions of this Act, and the principal clerk shall give or cause to be given due intimation of the name, description, and residence of each person so appointed depute clerk, and of the person appointed to issue summonses and complaints as aforesaid, by notice in the form set forth in schedule (L) hereunto annexed, and which notice, being signed by the sheriff clerk shall, without being stamped, be a sufficient commission to such sheriff clerk depute, and such notice, or a copy thereof, shall be affixed on or near the doors of the church of the parish within which such court is to be held, and also, if he shall see cause, by advertisement in the newspaper or newspapers of the greatest reputed circulation in the neighbourhood, and notice shall in like manner be given by the sheriff clerk, in the form of schedule (K.) hereunto annexed, of the times at which such circuit courts shall be fixed to be held Provided always, that no person who shall act as depute clerk for the purposes of this act, and for no other purposes, shall be thereby disqualified from acting as a procurator before any court, except the Small Debt Court in which he shall act as aforesaid, or from being registered or from voting under any Act or Acts of Parliament relative to the election of Members of Parliament or of Magistrates of Burghs.

XXVI. And be it enacted, That each sheriff shall, three months before holding any circuit court in terms of this Act, by a minute entered in the sederunt book of his Court, and published in such manner as he may think proper, and of which a printed copy shall be publicly affixed at all times on the walls of every sheriff court room within his sheriffdom, apportion the parishes or parts of parishes which shall, for the purposes of this act, be within the jurisdiction of any small debt court, to be held within his sheriffdom as aforesaid, and thereafter from time to time alter such apportionment as the circumstances may require, and such alterations shall be published as aforesaid for at least three months before the same shall take effect, and all causes shall be brought before the ordinary small debt court, or any circuit small debt court within the jurisdiction of which the defender shall reside, or to the jurisdiction of which he shall be amenable : Provided always, that if there shall be more defenders than one in one cause of action who shall be amenable to the jurisdiction of different courts, or if from any other cause the sheriff shall be satisfied that such course shall be expedient for the ends of justice, it shall be competent to the sheriff, upon summary application in writing made by or for any pursuer, lodged with the sheriff clerk or upon verbal application made by or for any pursuer in open court, to order a summons or complaint to be issued, and the cause to be brought before his ordinary small debt court, or before any of his circuit small debt courts, as shall appear most convenient ; and such summons or complaint shall be issued accordingly on the sheriff writing and subscribing thereon the name of the court before which the same is to be heard.

Actions to be brought in the place of defender's domicile.

XXVII. And be it enacted, That the sheriff may, where the ends of justice and the convenience of the parties require it, adjourn and remove the further hearing of or procedure in any sequestration, multiplepoinding, or any other cause, from his ordinary small debt court to any of his circuit small debt courts, and from any of his circuit small debt courts to his ordinary or any other circuit small debt court, or to any diet of his ordinary court, to be there dealt with according to the provisions of this Act, or to any other time or place specially appointed for the purpose ; and such order of adjournment and removal shall be held due notice to the parties of such adjournment and removal being made unless further notice shall be ordered.

Sheriff may adjourn causes to any of his other Small Debt Courts.

XXVIII. And whereas in the upper district of *Morayshire* which borders on the river *Spey*, there is no place in which circuit courts can be conveniently held, but such court could be conveniently held in the village of *Grantown*, situated in a detached part of the county of *Inverness*, in the immediate vicinity of the said district of *Morayshire*, be it therefore enacted, That in case it shall be directed by one of Her Majesty's principal secretaries of state that a circuit court should be established in terms of this Act for the upper district of *Morayshire*, it shall be competent to the sheriff of *Morayshire*, or his substitutes, to grant warrants and to hold courts for the trial of all causes competent under this Act, and to pronounce judgment therein, within the said village of *Grantown*, in the same way and to the same effect in all respects as if such courts were held and warrants were granted and judgments pronounced within the said county of *Moray* ; and it shall also be competent to the sheriff clerk and officers of *Morayshire* to issue summonses and

Sheriff of Moray may hold Courts at Grantown.

perform other duties authorized by this Act within the village of *Grantown* in like manner as within the county of *Moray*.

Sheriff and Sheriff clerk's expenses at Circuit Courts.

XXIX. And be it enacted, That an account of the travelling and other charges incurred by the sheriff and sheriff clerks in going to, living at, and returning from the places where such circuit courts shall be held as aforesaid shall be rendered annually in Exchequer with the other charges of the sheriffs, and such accounts being there audited shall be allowed to an amount for the sheriff not exceeding five pounds, and for the sheriff clerk not exceeding one pound ten shillings for each court, and paid out of the public revenue of *Scotland* as the charges of the sheriffs are in use to be paid.

Decree not subject to review, except as hereby provided.

XXX. And be it enacted, that no decree given by any sheriff in any cause or prosecution decided under the authority of this Act shall be subject to reduction, advocation, suspension, or appeal, or any other form of review, or stay of execution, other than provided by this Act, either on account of any omission or irregularity or informality in the citation or proceedings, or on the merits, or on any ground or reason whatever.

Form of review provided.

XXXI. And be it enacted, That it shall be competent to any person conceiving himself aggrieved by any decree given by any sheriff in any cause or prosecution raised under the authority of this Act, to bring the case by appeal before the next Circuit Court of Justiciary, or, where there are no circuit courts, before the High Court of Justiciary at *Edinburgh*, in the manner, and by and under the rules, limitations, conditions, and restrictions contained in the before-recited Act, passed in the twentieth year of the reign of His Majesty King *George* the Second for taking away and abolishing the heritable jurisdictions in *Scotland*, except in so far as altered by this Act: Provided always, that such appeal shall be competent only when founded on the ground of corruption or malice and oppression on the part of the sheriff, or on such deviations in point of form from the statutory enactments as the court shall think took place wilfully, or have prevented substantial justice from having been done, or on incompetency, including defect of jurisdiction of the sheriff; provided also, that such appeals shall be heard and determined in open court, and that it shall be competent to the court to correct such deviation in point of form, or to remit the cause to the sheriff with instructions or for re-hearing generally, and it shall not be competent to produce or found upon any document as evidence on the merits of the original cause which was not produced to the sheriff when the case is heard, and to which his signature or initials have not been then affixed, which he is only to do if required, nor to found upon nor refer to the testimony of any witness not examined before the sheriff, and whose name is not written by him when the case is heard upon the record copy of the summons, which he is to do when specially required to that effect · Provided further, that no sist or stay of the process and decree, and no certificate of appeal shall be issued by the sheriff clerk, except upon consignation of the whole sum, if any, decerned for by the decree and expenses, if any, and security found for the whole expenses which may be incurred and found due under the appeal.

Fees to be taken.

XXXII. And be it enacted, That the following and no other or higher fees or dues of consignation shall be allowed to be taken for any matters done in any cause or prosecution raised under the authority of this Act —

Clerk's Fees in Causes under this Act.

Summons, including precept of arrestment, one shilling :
Each copy for service, sixpence .
Entering in procedure book, sixpence :
Renewed warrant to arrest on dependence, and entering in book, one shilling :
Certificate loosing arrestment, one shilling ·

Bond of caution, one shilling and sixpence:

Second diligence for compelling witnesses or havers to attend, one shilling

Decree, including extract, if demanded, one shilling:

Hearing after decree in absence, one shilling and sixpence

Indorsation of decree or warrant, and entering in book, one shilling

Receiving report of sequestration and appraisement, and entering in book, one shilling:

Receiving report of sale under sequestration, and entering, one shilling:

Receiving report of poinding and sale, and entering, one shilling and sixpence

Officer's Fees, including Assistants

Citation of a party or intimation of counter claim, and execution of citation given personally, one shilling ·

Ditto, ditto, if citation not given personally, sixpence:

Citation of a witness or haver, sixpence.

Charging on decree, and returning execution of charge, one shilling.

Arrestment, and returning execution thereof, sixpence ·

Intimation of loosing arrestment, and execution thereof, sixpence.

Poinding or sequestration and inventory, two shillings and sixpence ·

Sale and report, two shillings and sixpence

Officer's travelling expenses, for each complete mile from the cross or tron or other usual place of measurement in the town or place where the court is held, where there is any such, or if there be none such, then from the court house of such town or place to the place of execution or service, the distance travelled in returning after execution of the duty not to be reckoned, sixpence:

Assistants, each *per* mile, in the same manner, fourpence.

Crier's Fee.

For calling each cause, one penny, payable when summons is issued.

XXXIII. And be it enacted, That an exact copy of the immediately preceding section of this Act shall be printed on each summons or complaint, and on each service copy thereof, and shall also be at all times hung up in every sheriff clerk's office, and in every Sheriff Court place during the holding of any sheriff's Small Debt Court; and any sheriff clerk from whose office any summons or service copy thereof shall be issued not having such copy of the said section printed thereon, or at any time omitting to have such copy hung up in his office or in the Sheriff Court place as aforesaid, or not causing the roll of causes each Court day to be publicly exhibited, or not causing the number and names of the parties in such roll to be called in their order as aforesaid, except with leave of the sheriff upon cause shewn in open Court, shall be liable in a penalty not exceeding forty shillings, to be recovered at the instance of any person who shall prosecute for the same, and to be disposed of as the sheriff shall direct.

Table of fees to be printed and hung up.

XXXIV. And be it enacted, That in all or any of the cases above mentioned, where any decree or warrant shall have been indorsed as aforesaid, the sheriff's officer of the county where such decree or warrant has been originally issued, as well as of any county wherein the same is indorsed, are hereby authorized and required to obey and enforce such decree or warrant within such other county; and any sheriff's officer failing to report any sequestration or poinding and sale as above directed, or violating or neglecting any other duty intrusted to him under this Act, or wilfully acting contrary to any provision thereof, shall be liable in a penalty not exceeding forty shillings, to be recovered at the instance of any per-

Officers neglecting duty to be fined.

son aggrieved thereby, and to be disposed of as the sheriff shall direct, reserving always all further claim of damages otherwise competent against any such officer, and without prejudice to the sheriff's lawful authority to remove and punish all officers of his Court for misbehaviour or malversation in office.

Privileged persons not exempt.   XXXV. And be it enacted, That no person whatsoever shall be exempt from the jurisdiction of the sheriff in any cause or prosecution raised under the authority of this Act on account of privilege, as being a member of the College of Justice, or otherwise.

~~...~~ may ~~...~~ fees in ~~...~~ es not ~~...~~eding 6s. 8d.   XXXVI. And be it enacted, That in all causes and prosecutions wherein the debt, demand, or penalty shall not exceed the value of eight pounds six shillings and eightpence sterling, exclusive of expenses and fees of extract, which shall in future be brought or carried on before any Court not according to the summary form herein provided, it shall be lawful for the Judge in such Court notwithstanding to allow no other or higher fees or expenses to be taken or paid than those above mentioned.

Meaning of words in this Act.   XXXVII. And be it enacted, That in all cases in this Act, or in the schedules hereto annexed, the word " sheriff" shall be held to include sheriff depute and steward depute, and sheriff substitute and steward substitute ; the words " sheriff " substitute" to include steward substitute ; the words " Sheriff Court" to include and apply to the Court of the sheriff or steward or their substitutes ; the words " sheriff clerk" to include steward clerk and depute sheriff clerk and depute steward clerk ; the word " shire" or "county" to include stewartry, the word " sheriffdom" to include and be included in the words shire, county, or stewartry , the word " person" to extend to a partnership, body politic, corporate, or collegiate, as well as an individual ; the word " landlord" to include any person having a right to exact rent, whether as owner, liferenter, heritable creditor in possession, principal tenant, or otherwise , and every word importing the singular number only shall extend and be applied to several persons or things as well as one person or thing ; and every word importing the plural number shall extend and be applied to one person or thing as well as several persons or things , and every word importing the masculine gender shall extend and be applied to a female as well as a male : Provided always, that those words and expressions occurring in this clause to which more than one meaning is attached shall not have the different meanings given to them by this clause in those cases in which there is anything in the subject or context repugnant to such construction.

Act may be repealed, &c.   XXXVIII. And be it enacted, That this Act may be repealed, altered, or amended by any Act or Acts to be passed during the present session of Parliament.

SCHEDULES to which the foregoing Act refers.

SCHEDULE (A.)

No. 1.

Summons or Complaint in a Civil Cause.

A. B., sheriff of the shire of   to
officers of Court, jointly and severally.

Whereas it is humbly complained to me by *C. D.* [*design him*], that *E. F.* [*design him*], defender, is owing the complainer the sum of
[*here insert the origin of debt or ground of action, and whenever possible, the date of the cause of action or last date in the account*], which the said defender refuses or delays to pay; and therefore the said defender ought to be decerned and ordained to make payment to the complainer, with expenses: Herefore it is my will, that on sight hereof ye lawfully summon the said defender to compear before me or my substitute in the Court house at   upon the
day of   at   of the clock, to answer at the complainer's instance in the said matter, with certification, in case of failure, of being held as confessed; requiring you also to deliver to the defender a copy of any account pursued for, and that ye cite witnesses and havers for both parties to compear at the said place and date, to give evidence in the said matter; and in the meantime that ye arrest in security the goods, effects, debts, and sums of money belonging to the defender as accords of law. Given under the hand of the clerk of Court
at   the   day of

J. P., Sheriff-Clerk.

No. 2.

Citation for Defender.

E. F., defender, above designed, you are hereby summoned to appear and answer before the sheriff in the matter, and at the time and place, and under the certification set forth in the above copy of the summons or complaint against you.
   This notice,   served upon the
day of   by me,

J. T., Sheriff-Officer.

No. 3.

Execution of Citation of Defender.

   Upon the   day of   one thousand eight hundred
and   I duly summoned the above-designed *E. F.*, defender, to

appear and answer before the sheriff in the matter, and at the time and place, and under the certification above set forth.   This I did by leaving a full copy of the above summons or complaint, with a citation thereto annexed,*
for the said defender [in his hands personally, *or otherwise, as the case may be*]

J. T., Sheriff-Officer.

* If there is an account mentioned in the complaint, the officer must serve a copy of it along with a copy of the summons or complaint

---

No. 4.

Execution of Notice of Counter Claim by Defender against Pursuer.

Upon the   day of   I gave notice to C.D., pursuer, of the above counter account [*or* claim] intended to be pleaded against him by E. F., defender in the small debt action to which the said defender was summoned to appear before the sheriff at   upon the day of   at   of the clock.   This I did by leaving a copy of the above account [*or* notice of claim, *shortly explaining it*] for the said pursuer [in his hands personally, *or otherwise, as the case may be*]

J. T., Sheriff-Officer.

No. 5.

Citation for Witnesses.

M. N. [*design him*], you are hereby summoned to appear before the sheriff of the shire of   or his substitute, in the Court house at upon the   day of   one thousand eight hundred and   at   of the clock, to bear witness for the [pursuer *or* defender, *as the case may be*], in the summons or complaint at the instance of C. D. [*design him*] against E. F. [*design him*], and that under the penalty of forty shillings if you fail to attend.

This notice served on the   day of   by me,

J. T., Sheriff-Officer.

No. 6.

Execution of Citation of Witnesses.

Upon the   day of   one thousand eight hundred and   I duly summoned M. N. &c. [*design them*] to appear before the sheriff of the shire of   or his substitute, in the Court house at   upon the   day of one thousand eight hundred and   at   of the clock, to bear witness for the   in the summons or complaint at the instance of C. D. [*design him*], against E. F. [*design him.*]   This I did by delivering a just copy of citation, signed by me, to the said M. N. [personally, *or otherwise, as the case may be.*]

J. T., Sheriff-Officer.

No. 7.

Decree for Pursuer in a Civil Cause.

At   the   day of   One thousand eight hundred and   the sheriff of the shire of   finds the within-designed   defender, liable to the pursuer in the sum of with   of expenses, and decerns and ordains instant execution by arrestment, and also execution to pass hereon by poinding and sale and imprisonment, if the same be competent, after   free days.

        J. P, Sheriff-Clerk

No. 8.

Summons of Complaint for Statutory Penalty.

A. B., sheriff of the shire of   to   officers of Court, jointly and severally.

Whereas it is humbly complained to me by *C. D*, procurator fiscal of Court, [*or where a private party only,*] *G. H* [*designation,*] [*or where a private party prosecutes with the concurrence of the procurator fiscal,*] *G H*, with concurrence of *C. D*, procurator fiscal of Court, that *E. F.*, [*designation,*] defender, has incurred the penalty of   imposed by the Act of Parliament [*mention the Act,*]   the said defender having [*state the offence, specifying time and place,*] therefore the said defender ought to be decerned and ordained to make payment of the said penalty, with expenses [*state to whom and in what proportions payable, and the term of imprisonment where the same is the mode of recovery*] Herefore it is my will, that on sight hereof ye lawfully summon the said defender to compear before me or my substitute in the Court House at   upon the   day of   at   of the clock, to answer at the complainer's instance in the said matter, with certification, in case of failure, of being held as confessed; and that ye cite witnesses and havers for both parties to compear at the same place and date to give evidence in the said matter. Given under the hand of the clerk of Court at   the   day of

        J. P, Sheriff-Clerk.

Concurs *C D.*, Procurator Fiscal.

[*For citation for defender and execution thereof, and citation for witnesses and execution thereof, see Nos. 2, 3, 4, and 5, respectively.*]

No. 9.

Decree for Prosecutor in Prosecution for Penalty.

At   the   day of   One thousand eight hundred and   the sheriff of the shire of   finds that the within-designed *E. F.*, defender, has incurred the penalty of   as libelled, payable to   [*if there is a power to mitigate and mitigation, add,* " which is hereby mitigated to the sum of   ,"] and

, also finds the said defender liable in of expenses to the complainer, and decerns and ordains instant execution by arrestment, and also execution by poinding and sale and imprisonment, if the same be competent [*stating the term of imprisonment, where it is fixed,*] after free days

J. P., Sheriff-Clerk.

No. 10.

Decree of Absolvitor, with Expenses.

[*The following will answer either for Civil Causes or Prosecutions for Penalties*]

At the day of One thousand eight hundred and the sheriff of the shire of assoilzies the within-designed *E F*, defender, from the within complaint, and finds the within-designed *C. D*, pursuer, liable to him in the sum of of expenses, and decerns and ordains instant execution by arrestment, and also execution to pass hereon by poinding and sale after free days.*

J. P, Sheriff-Clerk.

* Where the pursuer does not return the original Summons, the above decree may be written on the copy served on the defender.

No. 11.

Charge on Decree.

E F, above designed, you are hereby charged to implement the decree, of which, and of the complaint whereon the same proceeded, the above is a copy, within days from this date, under pain of poinding and sale without further Notice. This charge given by me, on the day of before *O. P.* [*design him.*]

J. T, Sheriff-Officer.

No 12.

Execution of Charge.

[*To be on the same Paper with the Complaint and Decree*]

On the day of One thousand eight hundred and I duly charged *E. F.*, above designed, to implement the above decree, within the time and under the pains therein expressed. This I did by delivering a just copy of the foregoing complaint and decree, and a charge thereto annexed subscribed by me, to the said *E. F.* [personally, *or as the case may be,*] before *O. P.* [*design him,*] witness hereto, with me subscribing.

J. T., Sheriff-Officer.

O. P., Witness.

SCHEDULE (B)

Summons of Sequestration and Sale at the Instance of a Landlord.

A. B. sheriff of the shire of   to officers of Court, jointly and severally.

Whereas it is humbly complained to me by *C. D.*, pursuer [*design him,*] that *E F.*, defender, [*design him,*] is owing to the pursuer the sum of   , being the rent for [*describe the premises,*] possessed by him from   to   [*if any partial payments have been made let them be here stated,*] and which rent [or balance of rent, *as the case may be,*] the said defender refuses or delays to pay; therefore warrant ought forthwith to be granted to inventory, appraise, sequestrate, and, if need be, secure the goods and effects upon or within the said premises, and decree ought to be pronounced decerning the defender to make payment of the said rent [or balance of rent, *as the case may be,*] to the pursuer, with expenses, and warrant ought also to be granted to sell the goods and effects sequestrated in payment of the said rent [or balance of rent, *as the case may be,*] and expenses: Herefore it is my will, that on sight hereof ye lawfully summon the said defender to compear before me or my substitute, within the Court house of   upon the   day of   at   of the clock, to answer at the pursuer's instance in the said matter, with certification, in case of failure, of being held as confessed, and decree and warrant pronounced as craved · And my will further is, that ye forthwith inventory, sequestrate, and, if need be, secure the goods and effects upon or within the said premises until the further orders of Court, or until the said defender shall make payment to the pursuer of the amount of the rents pursued for, with the expenses, or shall consign in the hands of the clerk of Court the amount of the rents pursued for, with Two pounds sterling to cover expenses; and that ye cite witnesses and havers for both parties to compear at the said place and date, to give evidence in the said matter. Given under the hand of the clerk of Court at   the   day of

J. P., Sheriff Clerk.

[*After hearing the cause, the decree and procedure in the sequestration and sale will be similar to the forms in ordinary causes, the words* " sequestration" *and* " sequestrated" *being introduced when necessary, instead of* " poinding" *and* " poinded."]

SCHEDULE (C)

Arrestment on the dependence of an Action.

By virtue of a warrant of the sheriff of the shire of   , given under the hand of the clerk of Court at   on the   day of   for arrestment on the dependence of an action raised before the said sheriff at the instance of *C. D.* [*design him,*] complainer, against *E. F.* [*design him,*] defender, I hereby fence and arrest, in the hands of you *K. L.* [*design him,*] all sums of money owing by you to the said defender, or to any other person, for his use and behoof, and all goods and effects in your custody belonging to the said defender [*or, in the case of ships or maritime subjects, say,* I hereby fence and arrest the ship *M.* of *N.* presently lying in the harbour of *O.*, with her boats, furniture, and apparelling, or other maritime subjects,] and that to an amount or extent not exceeding the value of Eight pounds six shillings and eightpence sterling, all to remain under sure fence and arrestment, at the complainer's instance, until due consignation be made, or until sufficient caution be found as accords of law. This I do on the   day of   before O.P. [*design him,*] by delivery of a copy of this execution to you [personally, *or as the case may be*]

J T., Sheriff-Officer.

Execution of Arrestment on the Dependence of an Action.

[To be on the same Paper with the Summons or other Warrant of Arrestment.]

Upon the   day of   , One thousand eight hundred and   , betwixt the hours of   and   by virtue of the foregoing warrant of arrestment, I lawfully fenced and arrested in the hands of K. L [*design him,*] all sums of money owing by him to the foresaid E F., defender, or to any other person for his use and behoof, and all goods and effects in the custody of the said arrestee belonging to the said defender, [*or, in case of ships or maritime subjects, as before,*] and that to an amount or extent not exceeding the value of Eight pounds six shillings and eightpence sterling, all to remain under sure fence and arrestment, at the foresaid complainer's instance, until due consignation be made, or until sufficient caution be found as accords of law. This I did by delivering a just copy of arrestment, subscribed by me, to the said arrestee personally [*or as the case may be,*] before O. P. [*design him,*] hereto with me subscribing.

O. P., Witness.   J T. Sheriff-Officer.

Bond or Enactment of Caution for Loosing Arrestment

At   on   day of   One thousand eight hundred and   , compeared G. H. [*design him,*] who hereby judicially binds himself, his heirs, executors, and successors, as cautioners acted in the Sheriff Court books of the shire of   , for E. F. [*design him,*] common debtor, against whom arrestment was used at the instance of C. D. [*design him,*] in the hands of K. L. [*design him,*] on the   day of   in virtue of [*describe the warrant,*] dated the   day of   , that the sums of money, goods and effects owing or belonging to the said common debtor arrested as aforesaid, shall be made forthcoming as accords of law.

G H

Certificate for Loosing Arrestment used on the Dependence of an Action.

Whereas arrestment was used on the dependence of an action at the instance of C. D. [*design him,*] against E. F. [*design him,*] in the hands of K. L. [*design him, or as the case may be,*] on the   day of   , by virtue of a warrant of the sheriff of the shire of   given under the hand of the clerk of court at   the   day of   : And whereas the said E.F. has now made sufficient consignation in the hands of the sheriff clerk of   [*or, if caution has been found, say*] has found sufficient caution acted in the sheriff court books of   by G.H. [*design him,*] his cautioner, [*here state the nature of the caution,*] in order to the loosing of the said arrestment, warrant for loosing the said arrestment is hereby granted accordingly. Given under the hand of the clerk of court at   the   day of

J. P., Sheriff Clerk.

Intimation of Loosing Arrestment

[*To be on the same Paper with a Copy of the foregoing Warrant.*]

K. L. [*design him,*] take notice, That by virtue of the warrant whereof the above is a copy of the arrestment on the dependence of the action above mentioned, used in your hands at the instance of the foresaid *C. D.* against the foresaid *E. F.*, is loosed and taken off. This notice served on the   day of by me.

J. T., Sheriff-Officer.

Execution of Intimation of Loosing Arrestment.

[*To be on the same Paper with the original Warrant for loosing the Arrestment.*]

Upon the   day of   One thousand eight hundred and I duly intimated the above warrant to *K. L* [*design him,*] arrestee. This I did by leaving a full copy thereof and intimation thereon, subscribed by me, for him [in his hands personally, *or as the case may be.*]

J. T., Sheriff-Officer.

SCHEDULE (D)

Summons of Complaint in Cases of Forthcoming.

A. B. sheriff of the shire of   to   officers of court, jointly and severally.

Whereas it is humbly complained to me by *C. D.* [*designation,*] upon and against *K L.* [*designation,*] arrestee, and *E. F.* [*designation,*] common debtor, that the said common debtor is owing the complainer the sum of   contained in [*describe shortly the decreet or bill, or bond et cætera, by which the debt is constituted,*] and that the complainer on the   day of years, in virtue of a warrant by   dated the   day of , arrested in the hands of the arrestee [*here insert the terms of the arrestment used,*] which ought to be made forthcoming to the complainer Therefore the said arrestee, and the said common debtor for his interest, ought to be decerned and ordained to make forthcoming, pay, and deliver to the complainer the money, goods, and effects arrested as aforesaid, or so much thereof as will satisfy and pay the said sum of   owing to the complainer as aforesaid: Herefore it is my will, that on sight hereof ye lawfully summon the said arrestee, and the said common debtor for his interest, to compear before me or my substitute in the court house at   upon the   day of   years, at   of the clock, to answer at the complainer's instance in the said matter, with certification in case of failure of being held as confessed, and that ye cite witnesses and havers for both parties to compear at the said place and date to give evidence in the said matter. Given under the hand of the clerk of court at the   day of   years.

J. P., Sheriff-Clerk.

[*The Citations and Executions, and Decree for the defender, with Expenses, may be the same as in schedule* (A.)]

i

Decree for the Pursuer in Cases of Forthcoming.

At   the   day of   One thousand eight hundred
and   the sheriff for the shire of   decerns and ordains the
within-designed   arrestee, to make forthcoming, pay, and deliver to
the also within-designed   pursuer [*if the arrestee has money arrested
in his hands the rest of the judgment will be the same as in ordinary cases ; if
there are goods and effects to be made forthcoming the rest of the judgment will
be as follows :*] the arrested goods and effects following ; videlicet,   ,
and grants warrant to sell the same, or as much thereof as will satisfy the sum of
          and   of expenses of process and the expense of sale ; and
failing the said arrestee making forthcoming and delivering the said goods and
effects within   , then to make payment to the said pursuer of the said
sum of   , for recovery of which sums, the said period being elapsed
without forthcoming and delivery of the said goods and effects, ordains instant
execution by arrestment, and also execution to pass hereon by poinding and sale
and imprisonment, if the same be competent, after   free days

                                        J P., Sheriff-Clerk.

SCHEDULE (E.)

Summons of Multiplepoinding.

A. B. sheriff of the shire of   to   officers of
Court, jointly and severally.

WHEREAS it is humbly shown to me by *A. B.,* pursuer, [*design him,*] that he
is holder of [*here state the fund or subject in medio, and if necessary refer to the
account thereof produced,*] belonging to *E. F.,* common debtor, [*design him,*]
which fund the pursuer is ready to pay [*or deliver*] to the said common debtor,
or to whomsoever shall be found to have best right thereto, but he is distressed
by claims being made thereon by the persons following, videlicet, [*here state the
names and designations of all the claimants so far as known to the holder or raiser of
the action;*] wherefore the said pursuer ought to be found liable only in once and
single payment [*or delivery*] of the said fund or subject to whomsoever of the said
parties or others interested shall be found by me to have best right thereto [*or in
the meantime consignation ought to be ordered of the fund or subject or sale of the
subject in medio*] deducting the pursuer's expenses, and decree ought to be pronounced accordingly, and all other parties ought to be prohibited from molesting
the pursuer thereanent in all time coming · Herefore it is my will, that on sight
hereof ye lawfully summon the said common debtor and the said claimants [*and in
case of the action being raised by a claimant in name of the holder it will be necessary also to summon the nominal pursuer,* to compear before me or my substitute
in the Court House of   upon the   day of   at
of the clock, to attend to their several interests in the said matter, with certification in case of failure of being held as confessed ; requiring you also to deliver to
the said common debtor a copy of any account produced with the summons, and
that he cite witnesses and havers for all parties to compear at the said place and
date to give evidence in the said matter.   Given under the hand of the clerk of
the Court at   the   day of

                                        J. P. Sheriff-Clerk.

Form of Claim in Multiplepoinding.

I, *A. B.*, [*design him,*] hereby claim to be preferred on the fund in the multi-plepoinding raised in name of [*mention the raiser,*] against [*mention the defenders,*] for [*state the claim*] of principal due to me by [*here state generally the ground of debt, whether by bond, bill, account, &c., as the case may be,*] with interest from with expenses.

A. B.

Form of Interlocutor of Preference.

Prefers [*here design him,*] claimant for [*here specify the sum.*]

[*To be signed by the Sheriff.*]

[*The citations and procedure to be as nearly as may be in the forms in other causes, and warrant to sell the subjects forming the fund in medio to be granted and carried into effect in the ordinary form.*]

SCHEDULE (F.)

No.	Dates of Complaints	Pursuers	Defenders	Nature and Amount	How cited	By what Officer	Leave and Cause of Procurator's Appearance	Interlocutors and Decrees.

N. B.—After the name of each pursuer and defender let the letter P. or A. be added, in order to mark whether the party was present or absent when the cause was called; and should the party appear by or with any other person or a procurator, his or her name shall be marked as so appearing. Let expenses be also entered under the head of "Interlocutors."

SCHEDULE (G.)

Report of Sequestration or Poinding and Sale.

[*To be varied according to Circumstances*]

Report of the sequestration or poinding and sale at the instance of *C D.* [*design him,*] against *E.F.* [*design him.*]

Lots.	EFFECTS.	Appraised at			Sold at		
		£	s.	d.	£	s.	d.
1.	An eight-day clock, . .	4	0	0	4	10	0
2	Six chairs at 6s , .	1	16	0	1	18	0
3.	One table, . . .	0	8	0	0	8	0
4.	One chest of drawers, . .	1	12	0	1	12	0
		L.7	16	0	L 8	8	0

Upon the   day of   one thousand eight hundred and   between the hours of   and by virtue of a decree of the sheriff of given under the hand of the clerk of court at   on the   day of   at the instance of *C. D.* above designed, against *E.F.*, above designed, for payment of the sums of   I passed with the witnesses and appraisers after named and designed to   , and then and there, after demanding payment of the sums contained in the said decree past due, and payment not being made, I poinded the effects above enumerated belonging to the said debtor, and after making an inventory or list thereof, and getting the same duly appraised on oath at the several values respectively above specified in the first column, and amounting in all to [*here insert the Amount in Words,*] and leaving a copy of such inventory or list and appraisement with the said debtor personally [*or as the case may be,*] I carried the said effects to the   of [*or as the case may be,*] and there betwixt the hours of and   and after public notice of at least hours, I sold the said effects by public roup to the highest bidder, at the prices above specified in the second column for each lot respectively,* and amounting in all to [*here insert the amount in words*] ; these

* *If the effects are not sold, the tenor of the report must be altered according to the state of the fact; for instance,* ["I exposed the said goods and effects to public sale, but no " person having offered the appraised value, therefore I declared the same to belong to the " said *C.D* at the said respective appraised values in payment to that amount of the sums " in said decree"] *In case the goods poinded, or part of them, shall sell for more than the sums in the decree, and expenses of poinding and sale, say,* ["I sold part of the said effects, " viz. Lots 1, 2, and 3, by public roup to the highest bidder at the prices above specified in " the second column for each of said lots respectively, and amounting in all to [*here insert* " *the amount in words ,*] and I return to the said debtor the sum of " being the overplus of the price, after payment of the sum decerned for past due, and the " sum of   being the expenses of poinding and sale conform " to the Act of Parliament; and I also return to the said debtor the effects specified in the " other lots above enumerated."]

things were so done before and with *O. P.* and *Q R* [*design them,*] witnesses
and appraisers, in the premises hereto with me subscribing
J. T., Sheriff-Officer.

    O. P. witness and appraiser.
    Q. R. witness and appraiser.

   Reported to the sheriff clerk of the shire of
at   the   day of
by me,
J. T, Sheriff-Officer.

SCHEDULE (H.)

Counties.	Places at which Circuits are to be held.	Counties.	Places at which Circuits are to be held.
Aberdeen	Inverury ... . Four Times. Tarland...... ..... Four Times. Turriff .... Four Times. Peterhead . ... .Six Times Huntly. .... Four Times. Old Deer .. .. .Four Times.	Haddington ..	North Berwick .....Three Times. Dunbar .. .. Six Times. Tranent... . . .Four Times.
Argyle.... ...	Oban ....Four Times. Bowmore, Island } Four Times. of Islay. . . . Dunoon .. . . .. Four Times Lochgilphead . .....Four Times	Inverness ...	Kingussie .. .. ..Three Times. Fort Augustus Three Times. Grantown . ... . Three Times.
		Kincardine...	Laurence Kirk ..Three Times Bervie .... .. Four Times. Durris. ... ... Three Times.
Ayr...	Saltcoats. . ...Four Times. Largs . ....Three Times Kilmarnock. ..TwelveTimes. Beith .. . Three Times. Old Cumnock . .Three Times. Girvan . ...Three Times Maybole .... Four Times.	Kirkcudbright	New Galloway. Three Times. Maxwelltown ....Four Times. Castle Douglas..... Four Times. Creetown.... .Three Times
		Lanark ...	Biggar ....Four Times Airdie. .... Twelve Times. Douglas .. . Three Times.
Berwick	Lauder .... .Three Times Dunse ....Six Times. Coldstream .... Six Times Ayton . ..... Three Times	Linlithgow	Bathgate ....Four Times Queensferry. . Three Times.
		Orkney... ...	St Margaret's Hope Three Times Stromness.. . .....Three Times Sanday .. . .Three Times.
Banff..........	Cullen... .. ..Three Times. Keith . ... Six Times Dufftown .. ..Three Times	Shetland	Burravoe. ....Two Times.
Bute	Brodick in Arran. Four Times. Milport. . ...Four Times	Perth.	Crieff. .. ... . Four Times. Callander ...... Four Times. Kincardine } Four Times (Tullialan) } Dunkeld. . .. Four Times Aberfeldy. . ...Three Times. Blairgowrie . ....Four Times. Cupar-Angus... ... Four Times.
Caithness ..	Thurso... ..... Eight Times Lybster . ... Six Times.
Dumbarton ..	Kirkintulloch. .. . Four Times. Helensburgh ....Four Times.
		Renfrew	Lochwinnoch .... Six Times. Pollokshaws. ....Six Times]
Dumfries	Sanquhar ....Four Times. Annan . ...Four Times Langholm. .. ...Four Times Moffat.... . ...Four Times. Lockerbie........ . Three Times	Ross and Cromarty..	Kincardine..... Two Times Jeantown .... .Two Times. Fortrose.. . ...Four Times. Invergordon .. . . Four Times.
Edinburgh....	Mid-Calder...........Four Times. Dalkeith ....Six Times Musselburgh .. ..Six Times Stowe.. . ...Two Times.	Roxburgh	Melrose.... . .... Four Times. Hawick ... . Six Times. Kelso .. . ...Six Times. Newcastleton....... Three Times.
Elgin	Fochabers .. ... Three Times. Grantown ....Three Times Forres .... Six Times	Selkirk.... .	Galashiels .. . ..Four Times.
		Stirling	Drymen .... Four Times. Lennox Town of } Four Times. Campsie ......} Balfron . ... ..Four Times.
Fife...	Auchtermuchty.....Four Times. Newburgh....... ..Four Times. St Andrews. . .Four Times. Colinsburgh . .....Four Times. Kirkaldy.. .... Six Times.
		Sutherland .	Lairg. .... Two Times. Tongue. .. ... .Two Times. Port Gower. .....Two Times.
Forfar........ .	Brechin .. Six Times Montrose. ...,, . Six Times. Arbroath ... .Six Times. Kirriemuir....... . Four Times.	Wigton.	Stranraer .. ..Six Times Whithorn....... ...Four Times. Newton Stewart .Four Times.

Note—The number of Courts and places where held have been considerably changed, with authority of the Secretary of State, since the passing of the Act.

SCHEDULE (I)

Notice.

A B. [*add designation,*] residing   is the depute sheriff clerk to whom application for summonses and every thing else necessary for the sheriff circuit at this place for small debt causes must be made [*or, in case the depute shall not be resident, say A. B.* [*add designation and place of residence,*] is the depute sheriff clerk, who will officiate at in the Sheriff's Small Debt Circuit Court, and *C. D.* [*add designation,*] residing at   is the person who will issue summonses or complaints to be brought in such court.]

Date.
Place.

———

SCHEDULE (K)

Notice.

The sheriff will hold circuit courts for small debt causes at on the   day of   at   of the clock, and on every [*fix the time periodically, or if not new notice to be given*]

A. B. [*add designation and residence*] is the clerk for this place.

Date.
Place.

ANNO DECIMO SEXTO & DECIMO SEPTIMO

VICTORIÆ REGINÆ.

CAP. LXXX.

An Act to facilitate Procedure in the Sheriff Courts in Scotland.—
[15th August 1853]

7 W. 4. &
1 Vict. c.
41.

1 & 2 Vict.
c. 119.

WHEREAS an Act was passed in the First Year of the Reign of Her present Majesty, intituled *An Act for the more effectual Recovery of Small Debts in the Sheriff Courts, and for regulating the Establishment of Circuit Courts for the Trial of Small Debt Causes by the Sheriffs in* Scotland; and another Act was passed in the Session of Parliament held in the First and Second Years of the Reign of Her present Majesty, intituled *An Act to regulate the Constitution, Jurisdiction, and Forms of Process in Sheriff Courts in* Scotland · And whereas it is expedient to facilitate Procedure in the Sheriff Courts in *Scotland*, and to make further Provision for the cheap and speedy Administration of Justice in the said Courts · Be it therefore enacted by the Queen's most Excellent Majesty, by and with the Advice and Consent of the Lords Spiritual and Temporal, and Commons, in this Present Parliament assembled, and by the Authority of the same, as follows :—

*Proceedings
in Ordinary
Causes.*

*Short Form
of Sum-
mons*

I With respect to Cases in the Sheriff Court, other than those provided for by the first recited Act as extended by this Act, be it enacted as follows :

The Summons shall be in the Form, as nearly as may be, of the Schedule (A.) annexed to this Act, and such short Form shall be equally effectual to all Intents and Purposes, including Arrestment on the Dependence where the Summons contains a Warrant to arrest in Terms of such Schedule, as the Forms at present in use.

*Decree in
absence.*

*Provision
for re-
poning.*

II. Where no appearance shall be entered for the Defender, the Sheriff may, at any Court held *after* the Day of Compearance, give Decree in Terms of such Summons, in like manner as at present where no Appearance is made for the Defender, and such Decree shall be in all respects equivalent to a Decree in absence obtained under the Forms at present in use · Provided always, that the Defender may obtain himself reponed against such Decree, whether extracted or not, at any Time before Implement has followed thereon, or against such Part thereof as may not have been implemented, by lodging with the Sheriff Clerk a Reponing Note in the Form in Schedule (B.) annexed to this Act, and consigning therewith the Sum of Expenses decerned for, a Copy of which Note shall *at the same Time* be delivered or transmitted through the Post Office to the Pursuer or his Agent in the Action, and a Certificate by the Sheriff Clerk that such Note has been lodged shall operate as a Sist of Diligence; and where such Note shall have been lodged and Consignation made as aforesaid, the Sheriff shall pronounce a Judgment reponing the Defender, and shall also appoint the consigned Money to be paid over to the Pursuer, unless Special Cause be shown to the contrary, and the Cause shall thereafter proceed in all respects as if Appearance were made therein, in manner herein-after provided, of the Date of such Judgment : Provided always, that where a Charge has been given, or any Step of Diligence has been taken, on the Decree, prior to the Application to be reponed, it shall be competent to the Sheriff in the course of the Proceedings in the Cause to decern in favour of the Pursuer for the Expense of such Charge or Diligence, or such Part thereof as shall be just.

III. Where the Defender intends to state a Defence, he shall enter Appearance by lodging with the Sheriff Clerk, at latest on the day of Compearance, a Notice in the Form of Schedule (C) annexed to this Act, and on the First Court Day thereafter, or on any other Court Day to which the Diet may be adjourned, not being later than EIGHT Days thereafter, the Sheriff shall hear the Parties in Explanation of the Grounds of Action and the Nature of the Defence to be stated thereto, and if satisfied that no farther written Pleadings are necessary, he shall cause a Minute in the Form of the Schedule (D.) annexed to this Act to be written on the Summons, setting forth concisely the Ground of Defence, which Minute shall be subscribed by the Parties or their Procurators, and the Sheriff shall thereupon close the Record by Writing under the said Minute "Record closed," and signing and dating the same, but if the Sheriff shall be satisfied that the Record cannot properly be made up without Condescendence and Defences, he shall pronounce an Order for the same, and in such Event the Pursuer shall, within SIX DAYS thereafter, lodge with the Sheriff Clerk a Condescendence setting forth articulately, and as concisely as may be, without any Argument or unnecessary Matter, the Facts necessary to Found the Conclusions of the Summons which he avers and is ready to prove, together with a Note of Pleas in Law, and the Defender shall, within TEN DAYS after the lodging of such Condescendence, lodge his Defences, setting forth articulately his Answers to such Condescendence, and also, where necessary, setting forth articulately, under a separate Head, any counter Statements necessary for his Defence which he avers and is ready to prove, and there shall be appended to such Defences a Note of the Defender's Pleas in Law, and such Defences shall be framed as concisely as may be, without any Argument or unnecessary matter.

Procedure where Defender enters Appearance.

Condescendence and Defences to be lodged.

IV. The Sheriff Clerk shall, as soon as Defences are lodged, transmit the Process to the Sheriff, who shall consider the same, and shall as soon may be, and at latest within SIX DAYS after the date of lodging the Defences, appoint the Parties or their Procurators to meet him, and shall at such Meeting, if dilatory Defences have been stated, dispose at once, where possible, of such dilatory Defences, or may reserve Consideration of them till a future stage of the Cause ; and unless where the Pursuer is willing to close on Summons and Defences, the Sheriff may, if he thinks fit, order One Revisal of the Condescendence and Defences respectively, which revisal shall be made upon the original Papers, unless the Sheriff, for Special Cause assigned, shall direct to the contrary ; and as soon as Revised Defences are lodged, the Sheriff Clerk shall transmit the Process to the Sheriff, who shall thereupon appoint the Parties or their Procurators to meet him as soon as may be, and at latest within SIX DAYS after the Date of the lodging of the revised Defences ; and at such Meeting after the lodging of the Defences, or the revised Defences, as the Case may be, or at an adjourned Meeting, if the Sheriff has seen fit to adjourn (which he is hereby authorised to do, where necessary, but for no longer Period than EIGHT DAYS), the Sheriff shall allow the Pursuer or his Procurator to put upon Record, in concise and articulate Form, where this has not been already done, his Answers to the Defender's Statement of Facts, or a simple Minute of Denial where that shall be deemed by the Sheriff to be sufficient, and shall allow each Party to adjust his own part of the Record, and shall strike out of the Record any Matter which he may deem to be either irrelevant or unnecessary, and the Record shall then be closed by the Sheriff writing upon the

Record to be made up and closed.

Interlocutor Sheet the Words "Record closed," and signing and dating the same.

After Record is closed Sheriff to hear Parties, or to appoint Diet for Proof, and to dispose of Case.

V. After the Record is closed the Sheriff shall hear the Parties or their Procurators upon the Merits of the Cause, and upon their respective Pleas, or, where he deems Proof to be necessary, shall appoint a Diet for Proof on an early Day, and shall hear the Parties or their Procurators after such Proof is led, and after such Hearing, or such Proof and Hearing, as the Case may be, the Sheriff shall pronounce Judgment with the least possible Delay· Provided always, that it shall be competent to the Sheriff, on the written Consent of both parties, to dispose of the Cause upon the Papers without further Statement or Argument.

Periods for lodging Papers peremptory; but Prorogations may be granted of Consent, and once on Cause shewn.

VI. Where any Condescendence or Defences, or revised Condescendence or revised Defences, or other Paper, shall not be given in within the Periods prescribed or allowed by this Act, the Sheriff shall dismiss the action, or decern in Terms of the Summons, as the Case may be, by Default, unless it shall be made to appear to his Satisfaction that the Failure to lodge such Paper arose from unavoidable or reasonable Causes, in which Case the Sheriff may allow the same to be received, on Payment of such Sum in Name of Expenses as he shall think just : Provided always, that the Periods appointed for lodging any Paper, or for transmitting any Process to the Sheriff, or for closing a Record, may always be once prorogated by the Sheriff without Consent on special cause shown, and may always be prorogated by written Consent of the Parties, with the Approbation of the Court ; and in every Interlocutor prorogating on special Cause shown the Time for lodging any Paper, the Nature of such Cause shall be set forth, and a definite Time shall be therein fixed within which the Paper is to be lodged.

Provision for Causes commenced by Petition.

VII In all Applications before the Sheriff which are at present commenced by Petition, and are not otherwise regulated by this Act, the Petition shall be as nearly as may be in the Form of Schedule (E.) annexed to this Act , and thereafter the Procedure under such Petition shall, as nearly as may be, be the same as herein-before provided in regard to ordinary Actions

Procedure in Multiple poindings.

VIII. In actions of Multiplepoinding, the Party raising the Summons shall set forth in the Body thereof who is the real Raiser of the Action ; and the Sheriff shall, at the First Calling of the Cause, where no Defences are stated, or where Defences are stated and repelled at the First Calling thereafter, pronounce an Order for Claims within a short Space ; and it shall be competent for any Number of Parties whose Claims in such Action depend upon the same Ground to state such Claims in the same Paper ; and as soon as the Parties who shall appear and claim an Interest in the Fund shall have lodged their Claims, or had Opportunity allowed them for doing so, the Sheriff shall appoint the Parties or their Procurators 'o meet him , and at such Meeting he shall allow each Party to adjust his own Part of the Record, and to meet the Averments of any other Claimant or Claimants so far as necessary, and the Procedure at such Meeting, and in the after Progress of the Cause, shall be as nearly as may be the same as is hereinbefore provided with reference to ordinary Actions after Defences have been lodged.

Short Forms of Execution provided.

IX. Every Execution of a Summons, and every Execution of Service of a Petition, shall be written at the End of the Summons or Petition itself, and where necessary or continuous Sheets, but not on a separate Paper ; and such Execution shall be in the Form, or as nearly as may be in the Form, of Schedule (F) annexed to this Act, which Form shall be equally valid and effectual in all respects as the longer Form of Execution at present in use.

Written Proofs abolished , and Proofs how to be taken

X. Where Proof shall be allowed, a Diet of Proof shall be appointed, at which the Evidence shall be led before the Sheriff, who shall with his own Hand take a Note of the Evidence, setting forth the Witnesses examined, and the Testimony given by each, not by Question and Answer, but in the Form of a Narrative, and the Documents adduced, and any Evidence, whether oral or written, tendered and rejected, with the Ground of such Rejection, and a Note of any Objections taken to the Admission of Evidence, whether oral or written, allowed to be received; which Note of the Evidence shall be forthwith lodged in Process, and the Sheriff Clerk shall mark the Documents admitted in Evidence, and also, separately, any Documents tendered and rejected; and the Diet of Proof shall not be adjourned, unless on special Cause shown, which shall be set forth in the Interlocutor making the Adjournment; and the Proof shall be taken as far as may be continuously, and with as little Interval as the Circumstances or the Justice of the Case will admit of, and the Note of the Evidence given by each witness shall be read over to him by the Sheriff, and signed by the Witness (if he can write) on the last Page in open Court before the Witness is dismissed: Provided always, that in the event of the Sheriff being unavoidably prevented from taking such Notes with his own hand, he shall dictate the same to any competent Person he may select. Provided always, that it shall be competent to the Sheriff, where any Witness or Haver is resident beyond the Jurisdiction of the Court, or by reason of Age, Infirmity, or Sickness is unable to attend the Diet of Proof, to grant Commission to any person competent to take and report in Writing the Evidence of such Witness or Haver; provided also, that it shall be competent to the Sheriff to remit to Persons of Skill or other Persons to report on any Matter of Fact, and where such Remit shall be made of Consent of both Parties the Sheriff shall hold the Report to be final and conclusive with respect to the Matter of such Remit.

[margin: Absent or aged or infirm Witness may be examined on Commission Remits may be made to Person of Skill, and if of Consent his Report shall be final.]

XI When a Diet of Proof shall be appointed by the Sheriff, a Copy, certified by the Sheriff Clerk, of the Interlocutor fixing such Diet, or of that portion of such Interlocutor which relates to that Matter, shall be a sufficient Warrant to any Sheriff Officer in *Scotland* (acting within his own County) to cite Witnesses and Havers, at the Instance either of the Pursuer or Defender, to attend such Proof; and such Warrant shall have the same Force and Operation in any other County as in the County in which it was issued, the same being, in every Case in which it is executed in another County from that in which it is issued, indorsed by the Sheriff Clerk of such other County, who is hereby required to make and date such Indorsation; and the Citation and Execution thereof shall be in the Form of Schedule (G) annexed to this Act; and if any Witness or Haver duly cited on a Citation of at least FORTY-EIGHT HOURS shall fail to appear, he shall forfeit and pay a Penalty not exceeding *Forty Shillings*, unless a reasonable Excuse be offered and sustained by the Sheriff, for which Penalty Decree shall be given by the Sheriff in favour of the Party on whose Behalf he was cited, and it shall be further competent to the Sheriff to grant Second Diligence for compelling the Attendance of such Witness or Haver, the Expense whereof shall in like Manner be decerned for against the Witness or Haver against whom the same has been issued, unless a special Reason to the contrary be stated, and sustained by the Sheriff.

[margin: Certified Copy Interlocutor of Proof to be Warrant for citing Witnesses and Havers, and to be operative, by simple Indorsation, in other Counties.]

XII. The Parties or their Procurators shall be entitled to be heard orally when the Cause shall be ripe for Judgment, and on the Import of any concluded Proof, and at any other Stage of the Cause when Argument may be necessary and shall be appointed by the Sheriff; and it shall not be competent, at any Stage of the Cause, to receive any written argumentative Pleading, excepting as herein-after provided, but the Sheriff shall, if required by either of the Parties, take a Note of the Authorities cited in the course of the oral Argument, and also where he shall see fit of the Argument, and such Note shall form Part of the Process

[margin: Written argument abolished, and oral Pleadings substituted.]

XIII In all Cases where a Sheriff Substitute or Sheriff pronounces an Interlocutor disposing of a dilatory Defence or sisting Process, or deciding on the Admissibility of Evidence or any Plea of Confidentiality, or giving any Interim Decree, or disposing in whole or in part of the Merits of the Cause, it shall be the Duty of such Sheriff Substitute or Sheriff, as the Case may be, to set forth in such

[margin: Sheriff in deciding to state the Grounds of his Judgment.]

Interlocutor, or in a Note appended to and issued along with it, the Grounds on which he has proceeded.

Decree for Expenses to include Expense of Extract. XIV. Every Decree for Expenses pronounced after the passing of this Act shall be held to include a Decree for the Expense of extracting the same.

Action not prosecuted dismissed. XV. Where in any Cause neither of the Parties thereto shall during the Period of THREE consecutive Months have taken any Proceeding therein, the Action shall at the Expiration of that Period (eo ipso), stand dismissed, without Prejudice nevertheless to either of the Parties within Three Months after the Expiration of such First Period of THREE Months, t　　thereafter, to revive the said Action on showing good Cause to the Satisf　　of the Sheriff why no Procedure had taken place therein, or upon Payment to the other Party of the Preceding Expenses incurred in the Cause, whereupon such Action shall be revived and proceeded with in ordinary Form, with Power to the Sheriff, if he shall see fit, to disallow such Expenses or any Part thereof in the Accounts of the Agent of either Party against his Client. Provided always, that nothing herein contained shall apply to Cases in which the Right under such Action has been acquired by a Third Party, by Death or otherwise, within such Period of SIX Months.

Judgment of the Sheriff Substitute may be appealed against by Petition or Hearing. XVI. Where any Judgment shall be pronounced by the Sheriff Substitute, which under this Act may be brought under the Review of the Sheriff, the Party who proposes to appeal against the same shall, within SEVEN DAYS from the Date thereof, engross and sign by himself or his Agent under the Interlocutor appealed against the Words "I appeal against this Interlocutor," and thereafter it shall be competent for such Party to lodge with the Sheriff Clerk WITHIN EIGHT DAYS a Reclaiming Petition against the said Judgment and any prior Judgment which may under this Act be then appealed, which Reclaiming Petition the Sheriff Clerk shall forthwith transmit to the Sheriff, who may order Answers thereto, and shall thereafter dispose of such Appeal, or otherwise the Party appealing may intimate by Notice lodged with the Sheriff Clerk within the Period aforesaid his Desire to be heard orally before the Sheriff on such Judgment or Judgments, in which case the Sheriff shall hear the Parties or their Procurators on such Appeal, and shall dispose of the same ; and the Sheriff shall have Power in Cases requiring extraordinary Despatch to order a Reclaiming Petition and Answers instead of hearing the Parties orally, but it shall not be competent in any Case in reviewing such Judgment both to receive a Reclaiming Petition and to hear the Parties orally.

Review by Sheriff to be obtained by simple Appeal. Provided always, that if no Reclaiming Petition shall have been lodged, and if neither Party shall within the Period above mentioned require to be heard before the Sheriff, he may proceed to dispose of such Appeal without farther Argument, and it shall be competent for the Sheriff, where the Cause is before him on Appeal on any Point, to open up the Record ex proprio motu, if it shall appear to him not to have been properly made up

No Appeal allowed during the leading of the Proof; XVII. It shall not be competent, prior to the closing of the Proof, to appeal to the Sheriff against any Interlocutor of the Sheriff Substitute, on the Admissibility of Evidence pronounced during the leading of the Proof, but it shall be competent, on the Proof being declared closed, or within SEVEN DAYS thereafter, to appeal against all or any of such Interlocutors ; and the Sheriff shall pronounce such Judgment on the Appeal as shall be just, and shall appoint any Evidence which he may think ought not to have been rejected, to be taken before the Case shall be advised on its Merits.

Except by Persons pleading Confidentiality, or objecting to Production of Writings XVIII Provided always, That nothing in this Act contained shall preclude any Person, whether Party to the Cause or not, who may plead Confidentiality, whether with reference to documentary or oral Evidence, or any Person, not being a Party to the Cause, who may object to produce Writings, whether on Pleas of alleged Hypothec or otherwise, from taking to review any Judgment of the Sheriff Substitute or Sheriff disposing of such Pleas, in whole or in part, but the Judgment of the Sheriff Substitute disposing of such Pleas shall only be reviewable by such Person taking an appeal at the Time in open Court, which Appeal shall be minuted by the Sheriff Substitute, and thereupon such Part of the Proceedings as may be necessary for the Disposal of such Appeal, or as the Sheriff may require, shall be transmitted by the Sheriff Clerk to the Sheriff, who shall dispose of the same summarily, but may appoint a Hearing before giving Judgment Provided also, that no such Appeals by any such Person pleading Confidentiality as aforesaid, or by any such Person objecting to produce Writings as aforesaid, shall be held to remove the Cause from before the Sheriff Substitute as regards any Point or Points not necessarily dependent on the Interlocutor or Judgment appealed from ; but, as to all such Points, the Cause may be proceeded with before the Sheriff Substitute as if no such Appeal had been taken

XIX. Until an Interlocutor shall have been pronounced disposing in whole or in part of the Merits of the Cause, it shall not be competent to appeal to the Sheriff against any Interlocutor of the Sheriff Substitute, not being an Interlocutor — *No Appeal allowed (except in certain Cases) till Judgment on the Merits.*

    Disposing of a dilatory Defence, or
    An Interlocutor sisting Process ; or
    An Interlocutor allowing a Proof; or

To appeal to the Sheriff against any Interlocutor of the Sheriff Substitute, on the Admissibility of Evidence pronounced during the leading of the Proof, except as herein-before provided for ; but it shall be competent in every Case in which an Appeal against any Interlocutor is taken also to appeal against all or any of the Interlocutors previously pronounced, whether before or after the Date of closing the Record, or whether the Record has been closed or not, and the Sheriff shall pronounce such Judgment on the Appeal as shall be just.

XX It shall be competent to any Sheriff Substitute or Sheriff to correct any merely clerical Error in his Judgment at any Time before the Proceedings have been transmitted to the Judge or Court of Review, not being later than SEVEN DAYS from the Date of such Judgment. *Where Mistakes in a Judgment may be corrected without Review.*

XXI The Procedure in Consistorial and Maritime Causes shall be as nearly as may be the same as is herein-before provided with reference to ordinary Actions. *Procedure in Consistorial and Maritime Causes.*

XXII. It shall not be competent, except as herein-after specially provided for, to remove from a Sheriff Court, or to bring under Review of the Court of Session, of Sheriff or of the Circuit Court of Justiciary, or of any other Court or Tribunal whatever, by Advocation, Appeal, Suspension or Reduction, or in any other Manner of Way, any Cause not exceeding the Value of Twenty five Pounds Sterling, or any Interlocutor, Judgment, or Decree pronounced or which shall be pronounced in such Cause by the Sheriff *Judgment of Sheriff in Causes not exceeding L 25 to be final.*

XXIII. It shall be competent in all Civil Causes above the Value of Twelve Pounds, competent before the Sheriff, for the Parties to lodge in Process a Minute, signed by themselves or by their Procurators, setting forth their Agreement that the Cause should be tried in the summary Way provided in the said first-recited Act, and the Sheriff shall thereupon hear, try, and determine such Action in such summary Way, and in such Case the whole Powers and Provisions of the said first-recited Act shall be held applicable to the said Action Provided always, that the Parties, or any of them, shall be entitled to appear and plead by a Procurator of Court. *Causes of any Value may be tried in a summary Way by Consent of all the Parties.*

XXIV It shall be competent, in any Cause exceeding the Value of Twenty- *In Cases exceeding L 25, Re-*

viewlimited five Pounds, to take to review of the Court of Session any Interlocutor of a
to final Sheriff.—
Judgments,
&c.   Sisting Process; and

Any Interlocutor giving Interim Decree for Payment of Money, and

Any Interlocutor disposing of the whole Merits of the Cause, although no Decision has been given as to Expenses, or although the expenses, if such have been found due, have not been modified or decerned for; but it shall not be competent to take to review any Interlocutor, Judgment, or Decree of a Sheriff, not being an Interlocutor sisting Process, or giving Interim Decree for Payment of Money, or disposing of the whole Merits of the Cause as aforesaid; and the Provisions of an Act passed in the Fiftieth Year of the Reign of His Majesty King

50 G. 8. c. George the Third, intituled *An Act for abridging the Form of extracting Decrees of*
112. *the Court of Session in Scotland, and for the Regulation of certain Parts of the Proceedings of that Court*, and also the Provisions of an Act passed in the Sixth

6 G. 4 c. Year of the Reign of His Majesty King George the Fourth, intituled, *An Act for*
120 *the better regulating of the Forms of Process in the Courts of Law in Scotland*, are, in so far as inconsistent with this enactment, hereby repealed. Provided always, that when any Interlocutor shall be brought under review of the Court of Session, it shall be competent for that Court also to review all the previous Interlocutors pronounced in the Cause.

Where   **XXV.** All Cases of Advocation which shall come to depend before the Court
either Party of Session may be brought in the first instance before One or other of the Divi-
desires it, sions of the Court of Session, or by Consent of both Parties before any Lord Or-
Case to go dinary in the Outer House, in which last Case the Judgment to be pronounced by
at once to such Lord Ordinary, shall be final, and shall not be subject to Review by the Inner
the Inner House, or by Appeal to the House of Lords.
House.

Small Debt **XXVI.** And with respect to Small Debt Cases not exceeding Twelve Pounds ·
Jurisdic- The Provisions of the said first-recited Act shall be extended to all Causes,
tion extend- Prosecutions, Applications for Sequestration and Sale, and other Actions and
ed to Causes Proceedings of the Nature set forth in the said first-recited Act, wherein the Debt,
not exceed- Demand, or Penalty in question, or the Fund *in medio*, shall not exceed the Value
ing L 12. of Twelve Pounds, exclusive of Expenses and Fees of Extract; and the said first-
recited Act shall be read and construed as if the Words "Twelve Pounds" were substituted for the Words "Eight Pounds Six Shillings and Eightpence," wherever these latter Words occur in the said first recited Act. Provided always, that in any Case in which a Decree pronounced by the Sheriff in the Small Debt Court for any Sum exceeding Eight Pounds Six Shillings and Eightpence shall have been put to execution by Imprisonment, the Party so imprisoned shall be entitled to bring such Decree under Review of the Sheriff by way of Suspension and Liberation, and such Suspension and Liberation shall proceed in the Form provided for summary Petitions by this Act.

Proceedings **XXVII** And with respect to Proceedings before the Sheriff Court for Seques-
in Seques- tration and Sale for Recovery or in Security of Rents, be it enacted as follows
trations for Every Petition for Sequestration and Sale for Recovery or in Security of Rents,
Rent. whether such Petition be presented after the Term of Payment or *currente termino*,
———— may contain a Prayer for a Decree for Payment of the Rent with reference to
Petition for which the Petition is presented, and it shall be competent to the Sheriff to pro-
Sequestra- nounce, under such Petition, Decree for Payment of such Rent or any Part
tion may thereof, and every such Decree shall be extractable in ordinary Form, and shall
also con- otherwise have the same Force and Effect in every respect as any Decree for Pay-
clude for ment pronounced in any Petition for Sequestration and Sale in which Decree for a
Payment Payment of Rent might be competently inserted before the passing of this Act.

Operation **XXVIII.** The Provisions of the said first-recited Act for the summary Trial
of Provi- and Determination of Sequestrations for Rent where the Rent or Balance of Rent
sions in

does not exceed the Sum of Eight Pounds Six Shillings and Eightpence (and ^{first-recited} which Provisions are made applicable by this Act to Sequestrations for Rent where ^{Act ex-} the Rent or Balance of Rent does not exceed the Sum of Twelve Pounds), are ^{tended.} declared to extend, and the same are hereby extended to all Sequestrations applied for *currente termino* or in Security.

XXIX. And with respect to Actions of Removing before the Sheriff Court, be *Proceedings* it enacted as follows : *in Actions*
It shall be competent to raise a Summons of Removing at any Time, provided *of Remov-* there be an Interval of at least *Forty* Days between the Date of the Execution of *ing.* the Summons and the Term of Removal, or where there is a separate Ish as re- Time with- gards Land and Houses or otherwise, between the Date of the Execution of the *in which* Summons and the Ish which is first in Date. Summons may be raised.

XXX. Where any Lands or Heritages are held under a Probative Lease, spe Lease, con- cifying a Term of Endurance, such Lease, or an Extract thereof from the Books taining Ob- of any Court of Record, shall have the same Force and Effect in every respect as ligation to any Extract Decree of Removing obtained in any ordinary Action of Removing at remove, the Instance of the Party, Granter of such Lease, or in the Right of the Granter equivalent of such Lease, against the Party in possession under such Lease, whether such to Decree Party in Possession be the Lessee named in such Lease or not, decerning such ing, pro- Party in possession, his Family, Sub-tenants, Cottars, and Dependants, with their vided Forty Goods and Gear, to be removed and ejected from the said Lands or Heritages at Days' No- the Term or Terms corresponding to the Expiration of the Term or Terms of En- given durance specified in such Lease ; and such Lease or Extract thereof shall, along with a written Authority signed by the Landlord or his Factor or Agent, be a sufficient Warrant to any Sheriff Officer or Messenger at Arms of the County within which such Lands or Heritages are situate to remove and eject such Party in possession, and his foresaids, from such Lands or Heritages on the Elapse of such specified Term or Terms respectively, and to return an Execution thereof in common Form . Provided always, that previous Notice to remove shall be given to such Party in possession, at least *Forty* Days before the Expiration of the Term of Endurance specified in such Lease, or where the Lease has a separate Ish as regards Land and Houses or otherwise, at least *Forty* Days before that Ish which is first in Date, by causing to be delivered to such Party in possession, or to be left at his ordinary Dwelling House, or to be transmitted to his known Address through the Post Office, previous to the Commencement of such Period of Forty Days, a Notice by a Sheriff Officer of the County in which such Lands or Heri- tages are situate, or Messenger at Arms, in the Form in Schedule (I) annexed to this Act , and a Certificate endorsed on such Lease or Extract that such Notice has been duly given, signed by a Sheriff Officer of such County, or Messenger at Arms, and attested by One Witness, in the Form in Schedule (J.) annexed to this Act, or an acknowledgment to that Effect endorsed thereon by such Party in possession himself or by his known Agent on his Behalf, shall be sufficient Evidence that such Notice has been given Provided also, that no such Removal or Eject- ment by virtue of this Enactment shall be competent after *Six Weeks* have elapsed from the Expiration of the Term of Endurance specified in such Lease, or where the Lease has a separate Ish as regards Land and Houses or otherwise, after Six Weeks have elapsed from that Ish which is last in Date ; and provided further, that nothing herein contained shall be construed to prevent any Proceedings under this Enactment from being brought under Suspension in common Form

XXXI. Where any Tenant in possession of any Lands or Heritages shall, Letter of whether at the Date of entering upon his Lease or at any other Time, grant a Removal Letter of Removal, either holograph or attested by One Witness, in the Form in granted by Schedule (K.) annexed to this Act, such Letter of Removal shall have the same equivalent Force and Effect in every respect as any Extract Decree of Removing obtained in to Decree any ordinary Action of Removing at the instance of the Party to whom such of Remov- ing, provided Forty Days' Notice be given.

Letter of Removal is granted, or of the Party in his Right, against the Party Granter of such Letter of Removal, or the Party in his Right as Tenant, decerning such Party Granter of such Letter, or such Party in his Right, as the Case may be, his Family, Sub-tenants, Cottars, and Dependants, with their Goods and Gear, to be removed and ejected from the said Lands and Heritages at the Term or Terms of Removal respectively specified in such Letter of Removal, and such Letter of Removal shall be a sufficient Warrant to any Sheriff Officer of the County within which such Lands or Heritages are situate, to remove and eject such Party Granter of such Letter of Removal, or such Party in his Right, and his foresaids, from such Lands and Heritages, on the Elapse of such specified Term or Terms respectively, and to return an Execution thereof in common Form: Provided always, that where such Letter of Removal shall bear Date more than *Six Weeks* before the Term of Removal, or the Ish first in Date, specified in such Letter of Removal, previous Notice to remove shall be given to the Party Granter of such Letter of Removal, or to such Party in his Right, at least *Forty* Days before such Term of Removal, or where such Letter of Removal specifies a separate Ish as regards Lands and Houses or otherwise, at least Forty Days before that Ish which is *first* in Date, by causing to be delivered to such Party Granter of such Letter of Removal, or to such Party in his Right, or to be left at his ordinary Dwelling House, or to be transmitted to his known Address through the Post Office, previous to the Commencement of such Period of Forty Days, a Notice by a Sheriff Officer of the County in which such Lands or Heritages are situate, in the Form of Schedule (I) annexed to this Act, and a Certificate endorsed upon such Letter of Removal that such Notice has been duly given, signed by a Sheriff Officer of such County, and attested by One Witness, in the Form of Schedule (J.) annexed to this Act· or an Acknowledgment to that Effect endorsed thereon by the Granter of such Letter of Removal, or other Party in his Right, or by the known Agent of the Granter of such Letter of Removal, or other Party on his Behalf, shall be sufficient Evidence that such Notice has been given: Provided also, that no such Removal or Ejectment by virtue of this Enactment shall be competent after *Six* Weeks have elapsed from the Expiration of the Term of Endurance specified in such Letter of Removal, or where such Letter of Removal has a separate Ish as regards Lands and Houses or otherwise, after *Six* Weeks have elapsed from that Ish which is *last* in Date; and provided further, that nothing herein contained shall be construed to prevent any Proceedings under this Enactment from being brought under Suspension in common Form

Arrears of Feu Duties for Subjects of Small Amount may be sued for in Sheriff Court.

XXXII. And whereas it is desirable that the Jurisdiction of the Sheriff should be extended to Questions relating to Non-payment of Feu Duties for real Subjects of small Amount, wherever, in Subjects not exceeding in yearly Value the Sum of *Twenty-five Pounds*, the Vassal shall have run in arrear of his Feu Duty for *Two Years*: It shall be competent for the Superior to raise an Action before the Sheriff, in ordinary Form, setting forth that the Subject is of the Value, and that the Feu Duty has run in arrear as aforesaid, and concluding that the Vassal should be removed from his Possession, and that Warrant to that Effect should be granted, and thereafter the Cause shall proceed in the Manner herein provided in ordinary Actions, and if the Defendant shall fail to appear, or if it shall be proved to the Sheriff by such Evidence as he may require that the Subject is of the Value, and that the Feu Duty is in arrear as aforesaid, he shall grant Warrant in Terms of the Conclusions of the Summons, which Warrant shall be executed at the First Term of *Whitsunday* or *Martinmas*, which shall first occur, *Four Months* after the same is issued by the Sheriff, and such Warrant, so executed, shall have the Effect, in relation to the said Possession, of a Decree of Irritancy *ob non solutum Canonem*. Provided always, that it shall be competent to the Vassal, at any Time within *One Year* from the Date of such Removal, to raise an Action of Declarator in the Court of Session for Vindication of such Subject on any Ground proceeding on Challenge of the Title of the Superior, which shall not be called in question before the Sheriff, except on Grounds instantly verified by the Titles of the Superior, and that it shall be competent to the Vassals, at any Time before such Warrant is executed, to purge the Irritancy incurred by Payment of the Arrears pursued for, with the Expenses incurred by the Superior in such Proceedings; provided also, that in Leases for a longer Endurance than Twenty-one Years, the Landlord shall have the like Remedies against his Tenant, in case of the Non-payment of Rent, *mutatis mutandis*, that are hereby given to the Superior against his Vassal.

Proceedings in Criminal Prosecutions.

XXXIII And in respect of Criminal Prosecutions before the Sheriff, be it enacted as follows :—

Libels may be written or printed, or partly both, but authenticated as Libels now are.

The Principal or Record Copies of all Criminal Libels before the Sheriff Courts may be either written or printed, or partly written and partly printed, provided that the same shall be authenticated in the same Manner as the written Criminal Libels now in use are authenticated.

Libel printed or partly printed to be inserted in Record Book.

XXXIV. When a Criminal Libel in any Sheriff Court is either wholly or partly printed, a Copy of it, either wholly or partly printed, shall, instead of being copied in Writing into the Record Book of Court, as at present, be inserted in such Book, either in its proper Place in the Body thereof or at the End of the Volume wherein the relative Procedure is recorded, in which last Case it shall be distinctly referred to as so appended.

The Will of Criminal Libels to contain Two Diets of Compearance as in Schedule, and Accused to be called upon at First Diet to plead Guilty or Not Guilty.

XXXV. In the Prosecution of all Criminal Offences which shall not be tried summarily the Will of the Criminal Libel shall contain Two Diets of Compearance in the Form of the Schedule (L.) hereunto annexed; and at the *First* of such Diets, which shall not be sooner than *Five Days* from the Service of the Libel, the Court Sitting in Judgment shall call upon the accused Party to plead Guilty or Not Guilty to the Crime of which such Party may be therein accused; and if such Party shall plead Guilty the Court shall forthwith pronounce Sentence upon such Party according to the Form now in use; and if the Party accused shall plead Not Guilty the Trial of such Party shall take place on the *Second Diet* of Compearance set forth in the Will of the Libel, which Second Diet shall not be sooner than *Nine* clear Days after the First Diet, and at such *Second Diet* the Party accused shall again be called upon to plead as aforesaid; and if such Party shall then plead Guilty the Sentence of the Law shall be forthwith pronounced according to the Form now in use, and if such Party shall plead Not Guilty a Jury shall then be empannelled, and the Trial shall proceed and be followed out according to Law, unless the Diet shall be further adjourned or deserted according to the existing Law and Practice.

Sheriff not to ask Party more than once to plead.

XXXVI. It shall not be necessary for the Sheriff at each such Diet to ask the Party accused more than once whether such Party pleads Guilty or Not Guilty.

Salaries of Sheriffs and Sheriff Substitutes.

XXXVII. And with respect to the Salaries and Remuneration of Sheriffs and Sheriff Substitutes, be it enacted as follows :—

Salaries of Sheriffs and Sheriff Substitutes may be increased and additional Sheriff Substitutes may be appointed

It shall be lawful to grant to any Sheriff such Salary as to the Commissioners of Her Majesty's Treasury may seem meet, not being less than Five hundred Pounds by the year, and to any salaried Sheriff Substitute now in Office, or to his Successor, or to any Sheriff Substitute who may be hereafter appointed by virtue of this Act, such Salary as to the Commissioners of Her Majesty's Treasury may seem meet, the same not in any Case exceeding One thousand Pounds by the Year, and not less than Five hundred Pounds by the Year; and every Salary payable to such Sheriff or Sheriff Substitute shall be paid by Four equal quarterly Instalments out of the Funds from which the Salaries of Sheriffs are payable, and it shall be lawful for Her Majesty and Her Heirs and Successors, upon the joint Recommendation of the Lord President of the Court of Session, Her Majesty's Advocate, and the Lord Justice Clerk, all for the Time being, to grant Authority

l

to any Sheriff to appoint One or more additional Sheriff Substitutes. Provided always, that such joint Recommendation shall expressly bear that the Appointment of such additional Officer or Officers is essentially necessary for the Public Service; and provided also, that no more than Two additional Sheriff Substitutes in each County shall be appointed under the Powers hereby conferred.

Provision for Retiring Allowance to Sheriffs and Sheriff Substitutes disabled after long Service.

XXXVIII. It shall be lawful for the Commissioners of her Majesty's Treasury to grant to any Person who has held, now holds, or may hereafter hold the Office of Sheriff Substitute such Annuity as is by the said second-recited Act authorized to be granted in respect of long Service for One or other of the Periods specified in the said second-recited Act, notwithstanding such Service may not have been continuous, and may have been in different Counties, and the said Commissioners shall have the same Powers of granting Annuities to Sheriffs in respect of long Service as are conferred by the said second-recited Act and by this Act with reference to Sheriff Substitutes, and such Annuities shall be payable out of the Funds from which the Salaries of Sheriffs are payable: Provided always, that no such Annuity shall be granted to any Sheriff or Sheriff Substitute, unless the Periods of his actual Service as Sheriff or Sheriff Substitute, as the Case may be, shall, when taken together, extend to One or other of the Periods of Service specified in the said second-recited Act, and that in computing the Amount of Retiring Allowance of such Sheriffs the Emoluments drawn by them on Average of the Five preceding Years shall be held to constitute their Salary.

Sheriffs' Salaries to be in lieu of all Fees, &c.

XXXIX. The Salaries henceforth to be paid to the Sheriffs and Sheriffs Substitute shall be in full of all Fees and Emoluments whatever.

Commissions to Sheriffs Substitute to extend over the whole County.

XL. The Commissions already granted or to be granted by all Sheriffs to the Sheriffs Substitutes shall extend over the whole County.

Compensation to Sheriff Clerks

Provision for the sittings of Sheriff Courts

XLI. In case the Operation of this Act shall affect the Emoluments of any Sheriff Clerk not now paid by Salary, it shall be competent to such Sheriff Clerks to apply to the Commissioners of Her Majesty's Treasury of *Great Britain* and *Ireland*, who shall have Power, upon Proof to their Satisfaction of the Diminution of the Emoluments of such Sheriff Clerks through the Operation of this Act, to award such Compensation to such Sheriff Clerks respectively as to the said Commissioners shall seem just; and it shall be in the Power of any such Sheriff Clerk to require that he should be paid by Salary, in Terms of the said recited Act First and Second *Victoria*, Chapter One hundred and nineteen; and it shall be lawful to the Commissioners of Her Majesty's Treasury to adjust the Salary of every Sheriff Clerk now in Office, and who is paid by Salary, regard being had to the Expenses of such Office, as may seem to them just.

Sheriff Courts to sit such Days during Session for Despatch of Civil Business as may be fixed by Sheriff and approved of.

XLII. And with respect to the Sittings of the Sheriff Courts, and the more efficient Operation of this Act, be it enacted as follows:—

Each Sheriff Court, except those held at a Place where an ordinary Sheriff Substitute does not reside, shall sit for the Despatch of ordinary Civil Business for such Number of Days weekly during the Session as shall be fixed by each Sheriff by a Regulation of Court, to be approved of by the said Lord President and Lord Justice Clerk, and to be advertised at least once a Year in a Newspaper published in the County, or where there is no such Newspaper, in a Newspaper published in some County immediately adjoining.

Sheriffs to hold Three Sessions in each Year

XLIII. Each Sheriff shall hold *Three* Sessions in each Year.

The first of which shall commence on the *Fifteenth Day of January*, or the First ordinary Court Day thereafter, and shall continue until the *Fifteenth Day of March following*.

And the Second shall commence on the *Third Day* or the *Fourth Day of April*, and shall continue until the *Thirty-first Day of July following*.

And the Third shall commence on the *First Day of October*, or the First ordinary Court Day thereafter, and shall continue until the *Fifteenth Day of December following*; and in case at any time there shall be any Arrear of Business undisposed of, it shall be the Duty of the Sheriff from Time to Time to appoint additional Court Days, whether in time of Session or Vacation, for the Purpose of disposing of such Arrear

XLIV. All summary Causes may proceed equally during Vacation as during Session, and it shall be competent to the Sheriff, if he thinks fit, to pronounce Interlocutors in Time of Vacation, in all Causes, whether summary or not. Sheriff may act in Time of Vacation.

XLV. The Sheriff shall, before the Termination of each Session, appoint at least *One* Court Day during each Vacation for the Despatch of all ordinary Civil Business, including the calling of new Causes, and the Receipt of Condescendences, Defences, and other Papers, which, if the Court had not been in Vacation, would have required to be previously lodged. Sheriff to fix One Court Day in each Vacation for Despatch of ordinary Court Business

XLVI. Every Sheriff shall, unless prevented by Indisposition or other unavoidable Cause, hold annually in his County Sittings for the Discharge of the Judicial Business of the County, that is to say, the Sheriffs of *Sutherland*, *Caithness*, and *Inverness*, *Ross* and *Cromarty*, *Argyle*, *Banff*, and *Elgin* and *Nairn*, shall hold *Three* such sittings, and the Sheriffs of the *other* Counties shall hold *Four* such Sittings, in the course of the Year, and such Sittings shall continue until the Causes ready for Trial or Hearing when such Sittings commence be disposed of; and such Sittings shall, except as regards the Counties of *Ross*, *Inverness* and *Argyle*, be held at each of the Places within his County at which the ordinary Courts of the Sheriff Substitutes are held, and such other Places as the Sheriff with approval of the Secretary of State for the Home Department, may appoint, and as regards the Counties of *Ross*, *Inverness* and *Argyle* at such Places as the Sheriff with approval of the Secretary of State may appoint: Provided always, that the Sheriffs of the said *Three* Counties shall at least *twice* a Year hold *One* such Sitting at *each* of the Places at which the ordinary Courts of the Sheriff Substitutes are held; and each Sheriff shall give due Notice to the County of the Times and Places of such Sittings, and such Sittings shall take place at Intervals of not less than *Six Weeks*, and each Sheriff shall, *once* in the Year, go on the Small Debt Circuit in use to be held by the Sheriff Substitute, and shall on such Occasions, in addition to holding the Small Debt Court, despatch as much of the ordinary Business as may be ready for Adjudication, or as Time may permit, and each Sheriff shall annually, within *Ten Days* after the *Twelfth Day of November*, make a Return to Her Majesty's Principal Secretary of State for the Home Department of the Number of Sittings held by him, and of the Periods of holding each such Sitting, in the immediately preceding Year, stating the Cause of Absence in case the Sittings herein-before directed shall not have been held by him in Terms of this Act; provided that none of the said Provisions shall extend to the Counties of *Orkney* and *Shetland*, and *Midlothian* and *Lanark*; and so much of an Act passed in the First and Second Year of the Reign of Her present Majesty, intituled *An Act to regulate the Constitution and Jurisdiction and Forms of Process of the Sheriff Courts in* Scotland, as relates to the Courts to be held by each Sheriff Depute in his County, excepting the said Counties of *Orkney* and *Shetland*, is hereby repealed. Sittings to be held by Sheriffs in their Counties. 1 & 2 Vict. c. 119.

XLVII. It shall be lawful for any Sheriff to pronounce and sign any Interlocutor, Judgment, or Decree when furth of his Sheriffdom; and such Interlocutor, Judgment, or Decree shall have all the like Force and Effect as if pronounced and signed by the Sheriff while within the Limits of his Sheriffdom. Sheriff may sign Interlocutors when furth of his County.

XLVIII. No person whatsoever shall be exempt from the Jurisdiction of the Privilege of Members of

College of Justice abolished.   Sheriff Court, in any Cause, on account of Privilege by reason of being a Member of the College of Justice.

Court of Session to frame Tables of Fees.   XLIX. The Court of Session shall be and is hereby authorised and required to frame from Time to Time a Table or Tables of Fees for Business in the Sheriff Courts of *Scotland*, and such Table or Tables of Fees so framed shall be submitted to the Secretary of State for the Home Department, and if approved of shall form the Rule of professional Charge for Business performed in such Courts.

Interpretation Clause   L. In construing this Act, unless where the Context is repugnant to such Construction, the Word " Sheriff " shall be held to include " Sheriff Substitute ," the Word " Tenant ' shall include Sub-tenant , and the Word " Lease " shall include Sub-lease.

Recited Acts, &c. repealed   LI The said recited Acts, and all Laws, Statutes, Acts of Sederunt, and Usages now in force, shall be and the same are hereby repealed, but that in so far only as may be necessary to give effect to the Provisions of this Act, and no further or otherwise.

Act to take effect from 1st Nov. 1853.   LII. This Act shall take effect from and after the first day of *November* One thousand eight hundred and fifty-three.

SCHEDULES referred to in the foregoing Act.

___

SCHEDULE (A.)

Petitory Summons.

A.B., Sheriff of the County of   to Officers of Court, jointly and severally ; Whereas it is shown to me by *C.D.* [*design him*], Pursuer, against *E F.*, [*design him*], Defender, in terms of the Conclusions under-written : Therefore the Defender ought to be decerned to pay to the Pursuer the Sum of   contained in a Bill drawn by the Pursuer upon and accepted by the Defender, dated   and payable   after Date, with the legal interest thereof, till Payment [*or to make Delivery to the Pursuer of*   sold by the Defender to him ; *or to pay to the Pursuer the Sum of*   for Goods sold by the Pursuer to the Defender, per Account commencing the   Day of   and ending the   Day of   annexed hereto ; *or to pay to the Pursuer the Sum of*   being Damages sustained by the Pursuer, in consequence of the Defender having slandered the Pursuer by stating   *or otherwise, according to the Nature and Circumstances of the Action*], with Expenses And my Will is that ye summon the Defender to compear in my Court House, at   upon the Sixth Day next after the Date of your Citation, in the Hour of Cause, with Continuation of Days, to answer in the Premises ; with Certification, in case of Failure, of being held as confessed ; [*and if Arrestment on the dependence is required, add*] and that ye arrest in security the Defender's Goods, Monies, Debts, and Effects. Given at   the   Day of

           G.H., Sheriff Clerk.

Summons of Count and Reckoning and Payment.

A.B. &c. [*as before*] : Whereas, &c. [*as before*]. Therefore the defender ought to be decerned to produce before me a full account of his Intromissions as Cash-keeper to the Pursuer, [*or otherwise, as the Case may be*], that the true Balance due to the Pursuer thereon may be ascertained ; and the Defender should be decerned to pay to the Pursuer such Sum as may be found to be the true Balance on said Account with the Interest which may be due thereon ; and if he fail to produce such Account the Defender should be decerned to pay to the Pursuer the Sum of   which should in that case be held to be the Balance due, with Interest thereon from the   Day of   with Expenses : And my Will is, &c. [*as before*].

Summons of Multiplepoinding.

A.B &c. [*as before*] : Whereas it is shown to me by *A.B.* [*design him*], Pursuer, against *C.D.* [*design him*], common Debtor, and *K L.* [*insert Names and Designations of the other Defenders, and state who is the real Raiser*], alleged Creditors of, the said *C.D.*, in Terms of the Conclusions under-written : Therefore it should be declared that the Pursuer is Holder of a Fund in medio, [*specify the Amount or Nature of it*], and is only liable in single Payment of the said Fund to those having right thereto ; and the Defenders should produce their Claims, and the Pursuer should be decerned to pay the said Fund, deducting his Expenses of Process, in such way as may be just ; and such of the Defenders as shall be found to have no Right should be prohibited from troubling him in Time coming · And my Will is, &c. [*as before*].

SCHEDULE (B.)

[*Date.*]   *Reponing Note.*

In the Action *A.* against *B.*

The Defender craves to be reponed against the Decree in absence, dated [*add, where necessary* so far as unimplemented.] The Expenses decerned for are consigned with the Sheriff Clerk.

>   *A.*, Defender.
> [*Or*]   *C.*, Agent for Defender.

SCHEDULE (C.)

Notice of Appearance.

In the Action *A.* against *B.*

B [*design him*], Defender, enters Appearance to defend said Action.

>   *B* , Defender.
> [*Or*]   *D.*, Agent for Defender.

SCHEDULE (D.)

Minute at the first calling of Cause and where Defender makes Compearance.

Edinburgh,   1853   Act.   Alt.

The Defender's Procurator stated that the Defence was [*here state succinctly the Ground of Defence, dilatory, or peremptory, as*] no Title to pursue, *or* Prescription, *or* the Goods specified in Account libelled were not ordered or not received by Defender, *or* Compensation, conform to Account due by Pursuer, amounting to L.   herewith produced, *or* the Defender, who was Drawer of the Bill sued on, received no Notice of Dishonour, *or otherwise, in like Manner, as the Case may be.*

SCHEDULE (E.)

Petition.

Unto the Sheriff

>   A. B.
>   v.
>   C. D.

Or, In the Action presently before your Lordship.

>   A. D.
>   v.
>   C. D.

The Petitioner   humbly showeth,

That [*here state briefly the Circumstances, as*] of this Date   the Effects of   were duly sequestrated, and it is now necessary to sell, *or* Whereas an Action between   for the Price of a Horse is now depending before your Lordship, and it is expedient or necessary to sell the said Horse, *or* In consequence of   wrongously and unwarrantably using, or disposing of and making away with, *or* encroaching on, *or* withholding and refusing Delivery of, the Property, Effects, *or* Documents of, *as the Case may be.*

May it therefore please your Lordship to grant Warrant of Sale, *or* for Delivery, *or* for Interdict, *&c. &c. &c.*

SCHEDULE (F.)

Form of Execution of Summons or Petition.

This Summons [*or* Petition] executed [*or* served] by me [*insert Name*] Sheriff Officer, against [*or* upon] [*insert Name or Names*] Defender, [*or* Defenders *or* Respondent *or* Respondents*], [*state whether personally or otherwise*], in Presence of [*insert Name and Designation of Witness*, this Day of Eighteen hundred and Years.

E.F., Sheriff Officer.

L M , Witness.

SCHEDULE (G.)

Citation of Witnesses and Havers

C. D. [*design him*]. You are hereby cited to attend in the Sheriff Court of the County of on the Day of at o'Clock, within to give Evidence for the Pursuer, [*or* Defender] in the Action at the Instance of *A.* [*design him*], Pursuer, against *B* [*design him*], Defender, and that under the Penalty of Forty Shillings Sterling if you fail to attend. [*If a Haver, say,*] And you are required to bring with you [*specify documents required*]. Dated this Day of

E. F., Sheriff Officer.

SCHEDULE (H.)

Execution against Witnesses and Havers.

Upon the Day of I duly cited *C.D.* [*design him*] to attend in the Sheriff Court of the County of on the Day of at o'Clock, within to give Evidence for the Pursuer [*or* Defender], in the Action at the instance of *A.* [*design him*], Pursuer, against *B.* [*design him*], Defender. [*If a Haver, say,*] And I also required him to bring with him [*specify Documents*]. This I did by delivering a just Copy of Citation to the above Effect, signed by me, to the said *C.D.* personally [*or otherwise, as the Case may be*].

E. F. Sheriff Officer.

SCHEDULE (I.)

Notice to Remove.

[*Place and Date.*]

You are required to remove from the Farm of [*insert name by which usually known*], at the Term of next, as to the Houses and Grass, and at the Separation of the Crop from the Ground as to the Arable Land [*or as the Case may be*], in terms of the Lease thereof [*or in Terms of Your Letter of Removal*], dated

E F., Sheriff Officer.

[*Address*] G H
[*design him.*]

SCHEDULE (J.)

Certificate of Notice to Remove.

[*Place and Date.*]

I, *E. F.* Sheriff Officer of the County of　　　certify, that on the　　　Day of　　　Notice to remove, in terms of this Lease [*or* Letter of Removal] at　　　next [*according to the Terms of the Notice*], was in Presence of *L. M.* [*design him*], subscribing Witness, given by me to *G. H,* the Tenant, by delivering such Notice to him personally [*or* by leaving such Notice at his ordinary Dwelling House at　　　, *or* by transmitting such Notice to him through the Post Office to his known Address, as follows : (*insert Address to which Notice sent.*)]

E. F. Sheriff Officer.

L. M. Witness.

SCHEDULE (K.)

Letter of Removal.

[*Place and Date.*]

Sir—I am to remove from the Farm of [*insert Name by which usually known*], at the Term of　　　Eighteen hundred and　　　, as to the Houses and Grass, and at the Separation of the Crop from the Ground as to the Arable Land [*or as the Case may be*].

I am,

Your obedient servant,

[*Signed by the Tenant.*]

[*Address.*]

Note.—If this Letter is not Holograph of the Granter of it, it must be attested by One Witness, thus,—

I. M. Witness.

SCHEDULE (L.)

Herefore it is my Will, and I command you, that on Sight hereof ye pass, and in Her Majesty's Name and Authority and mine lawfully summon, warn, and charge the said [*accused Party*] to compear personally before me, or any of my Substitutes, in a Court to be holden by us, or any of us, at　　　upon the　　　Day of　　　in the Hour of Cause, at　　　o'Clock, Forenoon, for the First Diet, there to plead Guilty or not Guilty, and to underlye the Law for the Crimes above mentioned ; and also, if required, upon the　　　Day of　　　for the Second Diet, at　　　o'Clock, Forenoon, again to plead Guilty or not Guilty, and to underlye the Law as aforesaid ; as also, if required for the said Second Diet alternately, that ye summons an Assize hereto, being not fewer than the Number of Forty-five Persons, together with such Witnesses as best know the Verity of the Premises, whose Names are hereto subjoined in a List subscribed by the Complainer personally, or at their Dwelling Places, all to compear before me or any of my Substitutes, Time and Place of said Second Diet of Compearance.

[*And so on to the End of the Will now in common Use.*]

ANNO DECIMO SEXTO & DECIMO SEPTIMO

VICTORIÆ REGINÆ.

CAP. XCII.

An Act to diminish the number of Sheriffs in Scotland. and to unite certain Counties in Scotland, in so far as regards the Jurisdiction of the Sheriff.—[20th August 1853.]

WHEREAS it is expedient that the number of sheriffs in _Scotland_ should be diminished, and that provision should be made for uniting certain counties in so far as regards the jurisdiction of the sheriff Be it therefore enacted by the Queen's most Excellent Majesty, by and with the advice and consent of the Lords Spiritual and Temporal, and Commons, in this present Parliament assembled, and by the authority of the same, as follows :

I. Whenever a vacancy shall occur in the office of sheriff of any counties or county specified in the schedule hereunto annexed, such counties or county and the other counties or county named and included therewith in the said schedule shall be united into one sheriffdom, under the title specified in the said schedule, and the functions of the sheriff of the counties or county in which the vacancy shall occur shall thereupon devolve on and be discharged by the sheriff of such other counties or county so included therewith ; and such sheriff shall thereafter be and be denominated the sheriff of the said united counties and sheriffdom, without the necessity of any new commission being issued in his favour, and shall have and exercise all the jurisdiction, powers, privileges, and authority competent to the sheriffs of the said counties respectively.

Counties specified in schedule to be united, and Provision for discharge of the functions of Sheriff of the united counties

II. Whenever a vacancy shall occur in the office of sheriff of the county of _Peebles_ the said county shall be united with the county of _Mid-Lothian_ into one sheriffdom, to be called the sheriffdom of _Mid-Lothian_ and _Peebles_, and the functions of the sheriff of the said county of _Peebles_ shall thereupon devolve on and be discharged by the sheriff of _Mid-Lothian_, who shall be and shall be denominated the sheriff of _Mid-Lothian_ and _Peebles_, without the necessity of any new commission being issued in his favour, in like manner and to the like effect as is herein-before provided.

County of Peebles to be united with county of Midlothian.

III. No separate appointment shall hereafter be made to the office of sheriff of the said county of _Peebles_, or of any of the counties specified in the said schedule, but appointment shall only be made to the office of sheriff of such united counties or sheriffdoms as vacancies shall occur after such union as aforesaid.

No separate appointments to be made to the office of sheriff of counties to be united.

IV. Provided always, That, excepting as regards the person by whom the office of sheriff shall be held and discharged, nothing herein contained shall affect

be united.

Saving
rights,
privileges,
and liabi-
lities of
counties.

Sheriffs of
united
counties
not to be
entitled to
additional
salary.

or alter in any way the rights, privileges, or liabilities of the said counties respectively.

V. Provided also, That nothing herein contained shall give any right to the sheriff of any such united counties to any additional salary beyond that enjoyed by him as sheriff of any counties or county prior to any vacancy occurring as aforesaid.

SCHEDULE referred to in the foregoing Act.

Counties to be united.	Title of Sheriffdom.	Title of Sheriff
The County of Sutherland and the county of Caithness.	Sutherland and Caithness.	The Sheriff of Sutherland and Caithness.
The County of Banff and the Counties of Elgin and Nairn.	Banff, Elgin, and Nairn.	The Sheriff of Banff, Elgin, and Nairn.
The County of Linlithgow and the Counties of Clackmannan and Kinross.	Linlithgow, Clackmannan, and Kinross.	The Sheriff of Linlithgow, Clackmannan, and Kinross
The County of Dumbarton and the County of Bute	Dumbarton and Bute.	The Sheriff of Dumbarton and Bute.
The County of Haddington and the County of Berwick.	Haddington and Berwick.	The Sheriff of Haddington and Berwick.
The County of Roxburgh and the County of Selkirk.	Roxburgh and Selkirk.	The Sheriff of Roxburgh and Selkirk.
The County of Wigton and the Stewartry of Kirkcudbright.	Wigton and Kirkcudbright.	The Sheriff of Wigton and Kirkcudbright.

Lightning Source UK Ltd.
Milton Keynes UK
UKHW030630161122
412291UK00008B/368